D1265614

# Faith & Knowledge

G. W. F. Hegel

# Faith & Knowledge

Translated by Walter Cerf

and H. S. Harris

State University of New York Press

Albany 1977

Originally Published in 1802 as *Glauben und Wissen*

Published by State University of New York Press
99 Washington Avenue, Albany, New York 12246

Translation © 1977 State University of New York

Printed in the U.S.A.

Library of Congress Cataloging in Publication Data

Hegel, Georg Wilhelm Friedrich, 1770–1831.
Faith and Knowledge.

Translation of *Glauben und Wissen* published in
the Critical Journal of Philosophy, v. 2, pt. 1,
1802.
Bibliography: pp. 193–7
Includes index.
1. Kant, Immanuel, 1724–1804.   2. Jacobi,
Friedrich Heinrich, 1743–1819.   3. Fichte, Johann
Gottlieb, 1762–1814.   4. Faith and Reason
I. Title.
B2921.E5   1976   121   76–10250
ISBN 0–87395–338–X
ISBN 0–87395–339–8 microfiche.

# Contents

# Translators' Preface

The occasion for the initial attempt to translate Hegel's essay on *Faith and Knowledge* (1802-3)[1] into English, was the giving of graduate courses on "The Young Hegel" and on "Post-Kantian Philosophy" by Walter Cerf at the University of the City of New York and the University of Wisconsin during the 1960s. Our first thanks must go to the students in those courses, who never tired of suggesting improvements, and to the City University of New York, which contributed $100 to help cover the expense of typing and mimeographing that first draft.

The mimeographed translation was duly registered with the Translation Center of the University of Southern Illinois. We owe a great debt of gratitude to Professor Fritz Marti whose brainchild this Center is. He never wavered in his interest in, and encouragement of, our translation and he put at Walter Cerf's disposal certain pages of his own translation. Had it not been for Marti's Translation Center, it is very doubtful that H. S. Harris (at Glendon College of York University in Toronto) would ever have learned of the existence of the Cerf translation, and Cerf is certain that without the cooperation of Harris the translation would not have reached the stage of publication.

Harris became involved during a sabbatical leave from York University in 1971-72. Thanks are due both to York University and to the Canada Council for providing the leisure that made his participation possible. The research grant that went with his Canada Council Leave Fellowship also paid for the typing of the final draft of the translation.

Our cooperative effort was from beginning to end under a lucky star of complementarity. Translating *Faith and Knowledge* fitted in nicely with Harris' research for the second volume of his *Hegel's Development*.[2] Cerf's interest in Hegel, on the other hand, has been motivated more by his studies of Kant. The reader will find therefore, that Harris' introduction to the essay seeks both to connect it with the earlier and later thought of Hegel, and to offer explanatory com-

1. As likewise *Difference between Fichte's and Schelling's Systems of Philosophy* (1801), Albany: State University of New York Press, 1977.
2. The first volume—*Toward the Sunlight, 1770-1801*—was published by the Clarendon Press, Oxford, in 1972.

ments on the detail of the rather difficult text. Cerf's introduction, on the other hand, is directed to readers who may not be too familiar either with Kant's Critical Idealism or with Schelling's Philosophy of Identity. He deals in the main with the difference between reflective and speculative philosophy and with the concept of intellectual intuition.[1] We have each studied and criticized the other's contribution, and both of us have profited greatly (though of course we have not always agreed perfectly).

Harris is a native speaker of English, but his knowledge of German is by no means perfect. Cerf is a native German whose forty years of sojourn in the United States have not prevented German from remaining in the full sense his mother tongue. Cerf must therefore bear the main responsibility for mistakes in the rendering of Hegel's text. But Harris assumes a full share of the responsibility for any errors of interpretation, since he will not allow the fault to rest with Hegel (though Cerf maintains, and Hegel's own first audience agreed, that Hegel's German offers difficulties frequently insurmountable even to a native German).

We were agreed on making a translation that would be as faithful to Hegel's German as could be reconciled with its readability in English. Harris was more inclined to sacrifice readability to faithfulness, Cerf faithfulness to readability. Moreover, while Harris believed he could detect in the language of the *Essays* a consistency and precision commensurate to their content, Cerf tended to detect in it speculative insouciance and even simple carelessness, the latter no doubt due to the extraordinary speed with which Hegel wrote the *Essays*. The translators hope that they have hit an acceptable balance in trying to reconcile their divergent tendencies. Our paragraphing generally follows that of Lasson rather than Hegel. The frequently monstrous sentences of the original, some of which cover more than a full page of small print, were ruthlessly cut into manageable pieces. But Hegel's actual language has been rendered with a sort of flexible rigidity. That is to say that although there are many cases where the same German expression is rendered by two different English expressions, there are

---

1. Cerf wrote two introductions: one inquiring into ways of making the Hegel of the *Essays* interesting to contemporary analytic philosophy, the other putting the accent on existentialism's relation to Hegel. The first one—of which there was only one copy—was lost in transit between Toronto and Brandon. But as the second introduction was also meant to be useful to readers having little acquaintance with either critical or speculative philosophy it was decided to print it with each of the two *Essays*.

almost no cases where the same English word is used for two different words in German. Our desire to maintain this much consistency
has led us to adopt the artificial expedient of marking three breaches
in it with daggers. The English words "formal," "ideal," "real" are,
in most contexts, the only possible representatives of the three *pairs*
of terms *formal/formell†*, *ideal†/ideel* and *real†/reell*. For the most
part Hegel appears to use these pairs as synonyms; but there are oc-
casions where we suspect that he intends some distinction of meaning
between them. We have therefore marked the occurrence of the *less
frequent* member of each part with a dagger (i.e., the daggers in our
translation indicate the German words here marked). We must draw
the reader's attention to our using "Reason" for the peculiarly Hegelian conception of what Kant called *Vernunft*, and "intellect" for
his conception of what Kant called *Verstand*.

For both of us, the labor of translation was far greater than we had
expected at the outset. The work had to be relegated to hours that we
could spare from other assignments; and our lucky star was often hidden behind the clouds of a postal service that ranged from dead slow
at the best to dead stop during the Canadian postal strikes. We are all
the more grateful therefore to Caroline Gray, who helped with the
Bibliography, and to Lawrence Lyons, who did much of the dullest
work for the analytical Index. Nor should the labor of several willing
and able typists be forgotten, though their names are not here re-
corded. Above all, we wish to thank our respective spouses whose love
and patience sustained us over the years.

Finally, acknowledgment is due to Professor Marvin Farber, editor
of the series Modern Concepts of Philosophy, and Warren H. Green,
the publisher of the series. After years of patiently waiting for our
translation they very graciously permitted us to transfer the publication to the State University of New York Press whose director, Nor-
man Mangouni, and editor, W. Bruce Johnson, have been most cooperative and helpful.

Walter Cerf
H. S. Harris

Brandon and Toronto, Lady Day, 1976

# Speculative Philosophy and Intellectual Intuition: An Introduction to Hegel's *Essays*.

I. SPECULATIVE PHILOSOPHY: A FIRST SKETCH

"Speculation" is a bad word nowadays. On the stock market speculators are people who, wanting to get rich fast and without work, invest their money in untested stocks or on the basis of information that gives the prediction of success only a hazardously low degree of probability. And so, when we believe that a scientific hypothesis or a presumed psychological insight or indeed even a statement claiming to be "factual" has no evidence or hardly any evidence that could serve as foundation of its truth claims, we say: "This is mere speculation."

Yet when the congressional committee investigating the wild girations of the stock market asked Bernard Baruch what he did for a living he is supposed to have answered proudly, "I am a speculator." Rather surprisingly, old Bernard Baruch and the young Hegel of these *Essays* have one thing in common: they were proud of being engaged in speculation. Of course they meant two different things by "speculation"—even though the latter-day use of the word is connected in some bizarre way with the earlier meaning.

The term "speculation" comes from "speculare," which is taken to be synonymous with "intuire" (from which comes "intuition"). In a very preliminary way we can describe what the author of the *Essays* meant by speculation as the intuition or vision of the true nature of the relations among God, nature, and self-consciousness or reason. "Self-consciousness" and "reason" are interchangeable on the basis of the Kantian "I think"—"I think the categories"—rather than on the basis of the Cartesian "cogito," which comprises acts other than those of thinking, let alone "pure" thinking. It was Schelling who tried to articulate this vision of the true nature of the relation of God, nature and self-consciousness in his Philosophy of Identity—so called because the relation was to be one of identity, a basically simple design trying to hold together a complex composition. The vision was of course not a sensuous intuition, but an intellectual intuition.[1] When Hegel speaks of speculative philosophy he has the Philosophy of Identity in mind and its intellectual intuition of the all-comprising and ultimate whole of God, nature, and self-consciousness.

The Philosophy of Identity had to have the form of a system whose organic wholeness, reflecting the wholeness of the vision, was to be the test of the truth of the vision. The system consisted of two parts: the Philosophy of Nature and the Transcendental Philosophy, a division obviously at odds with the Kantian as well as the pre-Kantian divisions of philosophy. At the time when Hegel wrote the *Essays* Schelling had published several drafts of the Philosophy of Nature[2] and one of the Transcendental Philosophy.[3] Although Schelling was forever revising his system, the holistic vision behind it is clear. It was a singularly beautiful vision. If ever the time should come when philosophy is judged in terms of æsthetic criteria, the general scheme of the Philosophy of Identity (rather than the detailed execution) would surely be among the crowned victors. Its vision of the whole is the vision of an unconscious God (Spinoza's *natura naturans*) revealing Himself in the ever ascending levels of nature (*natura naturata*) until self-consciousness emerges in rational man. This is the story the Philosophy of Nature tells. The Transcendental Philosophy, on the other hand, claims to trace God's coming to know Himself in a sequence of stages that culminate in art, according to Schelling; in religion or rather, a re-union of art and religion, according to the young Hegel; and in philosophy, according to the mature Hegel. For although Hegel's mature thought and system became more complex and subtle, they never completely lost their connection with the basic vision and division of the Philosophy of Identity. His Philosophy of Nature, like Schelling's though critical of it, was still meant, if not to replace the natural sciences altogether, at least to provide them with the basic framework without which they lose themselves in the infinite chaos of experience and remain atomistic and mechanistic instead of becoming holistic and dynamic. And Hegel's *Logic*, his *Philosophy of History*, and perhaps even his *Phenomenology*, may be said to explicate themes that Schelling's Transcendental Philosophy was unable to shelter and develop in its relatively simplistic frame. Further, Hegel could integrate these themes into the total vision.

In any case, the Hegel of the *Essays*, following Schelling though not without reservations, is convinced that philosophy has finally come into its own as speculative philosophy envisioning the inner unity of God, nature, and self-consciousness, and it has gained its systematic presentation in the Philosophy of Identity with its two organic parts, the Philosophy of Nature tracing the emergence of self-consciousness, and the Transcendental Philosophy tracing the emergence of God's knowledge of Himself.

None of this is likely to sound convincing to a reader with an analytically trained intellect. I shall try in Section III of this Introduction to make the conception of speculative philosophy appear less strange by pointing out how speculative philosophy takes care of objections which non-speculative philosophy raises against it. Nor will speculative philosophy make sense to any historian of philosophy who knows that "speculation" is just another term for "intellectual intuition" and is aware of what Kant did to that concept. In Section IV I hope to show where in Kant's work the speculative philosophers believed to find justification for reintroducing intellectual intuition into the cognitive enterprise of philosophy. In Section II, however, I shall try my hand at an entirely different approach to the Philosophy of Identity, an approach by way of the human or, to use a fashionable term, existential motivations that drove Hegel into the arms of Schelling's Philosophy of Identity.

But first we must return for a moment to the term "speculation." It was of course precisely its Philosophy of Nature that brought speculative philosophy into disrepute. The triumphant march of the natural sciences throughout the nineteenth century turned speculation *qua* intellectual intuition into speculation *qua* unwarranted by any acceptable evidences. In their Philosophy of Nature Schelling and Hegel were like two brave medieval knights fighting a division of tanks. The battle was lost before it began. Yet the thought is perhaps not without some twilight charm that someday the sciences themselves will feel a hankering after a unity that could not be satisfied by the logical reconstruction of the language of science and to which the holistic passion that shaped these now forgotten Philosophies of Nature may be congenial. To be sure, the fuzzy-heads that make up the small but noisy army of today's anti-science and anti-technology prophets may joyfully return to the speculative Philosophy of Nature and claim it as an ally. But its sound re-appropriation, if there is to be another one after the débacle of Bergson's *élan vital*, will have to arise from a need within the sciences themselves.

## II. HEGEL AND THE PHILOSOPHY OF IDENTITY

In his introduction to the *Difference* essay Hegel writes that philosophy becomes a need in times when the simple and beautiful harmony of existence is sundered by the awareness of basic dichotomies and antinomies, when the believers become alienated from the gods, man from nature, the individual from his community. In historical situations of this sort philosophy is born and re-born in order to prepare through its systematic thought the revolution through which civilization's many-dimensional alienation will be overcome in a higher cultural synthesis.

We can see by inference from his early theological writings[4] and by what we know of the circumstances of his first thirty years that these views reflect Hegel's own existential situation. On the level of values he was torn apart by clashing loyalties, loyalties to Greek Apollo, Christian Jesus, and Judeo-Prussian Kant. Liberated in mind by the French Revolution like every young German worth his salt, he yet remained in political bondage to the absolutist Duke of Württemberg. He was tied down to the study of dogmatic theology, although there was probably little that interested him less at the time. He who later drew the wide panorama of human history and civilizations into his philosophy lived as a young man in exceedingly narrow conditions of financial, social, and sexual deprivation as stipendiate in Tübingen and as tutor in private homes of the moderately wealthy in Bern and Frankfurt. Only an iron self-discipline can have kept him from exploding and going mad as his friend Hölderlin did. His was a thoroughly alienated existence in which the clash between the life he led and his aspirations, between what was the case and what should and could be the case drove him, as it drove so many of his generation, to dream the idealizing dream of the Hellenic age and of the Christian Middle Ages and to trust in philosophy to prepare the revolution of the German situation. It is important to be aware of the personal urgency in Hegel's commitment to philosophy. What motivated and energized his philosophical beginnings were not at all intellectual puzzles, but the deeply felt disturbances of the situation in which he found himself and his generation, with the clash between Apollo, Jesus, and Kant the most articulate of these personal aspects of the general malaise. At least that much the young Hegel and our own existentialists have in common: matters of personal urgency rather than an interest in intellectual puzzles motivated their philosophizing. And when Kierkegaard compared the later Hegel's Logic with a dance of skeletons he was not aware—and in fact could not have been aware—of how similar the personal problems behind his *Either-Or* were with the clash of value constellations that split the young Hegel. Although their motivational situation was similar they took off in very different directions indeed, doing so on the basis of the sort of decision which is not exactly made by men, but which rather makes men: Kierkegaard to explore, and lead his public into what, in this time and place of his, it should mean to be a Christian in Christianity, and Hegel to explore and finally present what, in this time and place of his, the system of *philosophia perennis* is.

How did the existential situation of the young Hegel lead him in the *Essays* to embrace Schelling's Philosophy of Identity?

To be sure, Hegel might never have become a Schellingian if the accidents of life had not brought him together with Schelling in Tübingen and made them good enough friends to remain in contact even after they went their different ways from Tübingen, Schelling to fame and professorship in Jena, Hegel to the obscurity of a private tutorship in Bern and Frankfurt. Nor must it be forgotten that Schelling, in making Hegel his neighbor and his colleague at the University of Jena, freed Hegel from the social and financial—if not sexual—frustrations of the preceeding decades. It is not cynical to ascribe importance to biographical data of this sort. On the other hand, there must have been something in Schelling's Philosophy of Identity that made it look attractive to Hegel as philosophy from the perspective of his own existential travail.

Kant's Critical Idealism lay before the public in its whole extension and depth. There was Fichte's philosophy as *Wissenschaftslehre*. Hegel was familiar with both. In the rich firmament of Goethe's Germany there was a multitude of other philosophers, now known only to specialist scholars but then quite visible stars, a few of them generally believed at the time to be stars of the first magnitude. What Hegel could see in Schelling's philosophy and in none of the others was the construction—or at least the sketch for it—of a harmonious whole in which Hegel's own basic conflicts, though expressed in the most abstract terms, found their solution. He was able to project the longing after harmony that was energized by his personal turmoil into Schelling's philosophy, a philosophy which aimed at overcoming and bringing into systematic unity the basic conceptual dichotomies and antinomies that had evolved in modern metaphysics from Descartes to Kant around the relation between the infinite and the finite (God and His creation) and between the subject and object (man and nature, the knower and the known). It was not at all impossible to project one's own alienations into these and connected dichotomies and to consider the Philosophy of Identity, with the interdependence of its two parts and their intrinsic relation to the Absolute, as the vehicle of one's own reconciliation with God, nature, and society. Thus Hegel, quite unlike Kierkegaard, took the first and decisive step away from his existential motivations and moved toward the grand tradition of modern philosophy—whose Plotinus he was destined to become. His *Essays* are the documents marking the beginning of his career. Without this first step Hegel rather than Kierkegaard might have become the father of existentialism. His gifts—among which ordinary logical thinking was conspicuously absent—might have well prepared him for this; and the influence which parts of the *Phenomenology* had, for example on Sartre, corroborate it.

III. SPECULATIVE VERSUS REFLECTIVE PHILOSOPHY

Our excursion in the preceding section was intended to aid in an understanding of how the general scheme of Schelling's system—with its view of the Absolute revealing itself in nature and rational self-consciousness and revealing itself to itself in the two parts of the Philosophy of Identity—found a ready response in Hegel. The schisms characteristic of his situation and that of his generation, when expressed in philosophical dichotomies such as those of the infinite and finite and of subject and object, could find their harmonious solution in the Philosophy of Identity, which seemed to offer on the academic level a view of the whole uniting in harmony all sorts of opposites. As such, it could serve as a philosophical basis for the revolution that would turn modern civilization, sick from and of its schisms, into a truly integrated culture to be described in metaphors taken from the romantic conception of nature: a living whole of which the individuals were organs rather than atoms. As each part was sustained and enriched by the whole, so each part functioned to sustain the whole.

But here a problem arises. If speculative philosophy, having its sight on that final whole of God, nature, and self-consciousness, is philosophy as it has finally come into its own truth, then what about all those philosophical efforts that cannot be said even by the most tolerant historian to anticipate speculative philosophy at least germinally? That is, what about all non-speculative philosophy? And what about the interrelations, if any, between speculative and non-speculative philosophy? These questions are among the questions which Hegel himself takes up in his Introduction to the *Essays*.

The *Essays* have a name for non-speculative philosophy: reflective philosophy. The term has here only an indirect connection with the various uses Kant assigned to 'reflection' and 'reflective' in *The Critique of Pure Reason* and *The Critique of Judgment*. Basically, Hegel uses it as Schelling had done in his *System of Transcendental Idealism* (1800), where reflection was what the second of the three "epochs" in the "history of self-consciousness" led to, reflection going hand in hand with analysis, both being opposed to the "productive intuition" and "synthesis" that characterize the first epoch. And Kant's philosophy was taken to be the typical culmination of the epoch of reflection. (The third epoch was that of "the absolute act of will.") But as no concept remained quite the same when Hegel took it up in his own thought, we can understand what Hegel meant by 'reflective philosophy' without discussing Schelling's view.

The distinction between reflective and speculative philosophy is not meant to be a distinction between different schools of philosophy. To Hegel, English empiricism from Locke on as well as continental rationalism (with the exception of Spinoza) were reflective philosophies. The whole philosophy of the Enlightenment was reflective. And so was most of Kant's transcendental idealism. Reflective philosophy is philosophy that has not come to the true conception of philosophy, philosophy that is not really philosophy—inauthentic philosophy over against authentic philosophy which is, and cannot but be speculative. In terms of the Kantian faculties, reflective philosophy is philosophy of the intellect (*der Verstand*), speculative philosophy is philosophy of Reason (*die Vernunft*), but of a Reason which has been allowed to trespass on territory Kant believed to be inaccessible to finite man. It is typical of reflective philosophy, though it does not exhaust its nature, that it relies on arguments, proofs, and the whole apparatus of logic, that it insists on clear-cut dichotomies in terms of abstract universals, dichotomies such as those of the infinite and the finite, subject and object, universal and particular, freedom and necessity, causality and teleology, etc., etc.; that it tries to solve intellectual puzzles rather than give the true conceptual vision of the whole; that it sticks to the natural sciences as the source of the only reliable knowledge of nature, thus committing itself, in the first place, to a concept of experience reduced to sense perception and to a concept of sense perception reduced to some causal chain, and in the second place, to a pervasive atomism that reduces the whole to the sum of its parts, and to a mechanism that excludes teleology from a positive role in cognition. No reflective philosophy need have all of these characteristics although any one of them would be the indication of a philosophy that has not reached the one authentic conception of philosophy.

Hence, any assault that reflective philosophy directs against speculative philosophy can be taken care of simply by pointing out that it is a reflective assault. Answering it by counterarguments would turn the speculative philosopher into a reflective one. What is wrong with the attack is that it is reflective; it is made in a style of doing philosophy that is not truly philosophical. Whatever the argument may be which a reflective philosopher uses against speculative philosophy, his very arguing shows that he is not really a philosopher. Contempt is the only answer to all reflective assaults. No dialogue is possible.

We shall soon observe that this is only one side of Hegel's attitude toward reflective philosophy. But before we come to the other side we may want to illustrate this conception of the relation between reflective and speculative philosophy by way of a contemporary parallel. I mean the relation between existentialism and analytic philosophy.

There can be no doubt at all that our own contemporary analytic philosophy, in its narrowest as well as in its widest meaning (which excludes only the existentialists, the Whiteheadians, and the Thomists), would be judged by Hegel to be a very typical reflective philosophy. There must be considerable doubt, however, whether or not Hegel would acknowledge existentialism to be speculative philosophy. From the viewpoint of the Philosophy of Identity, existentialism spoiled its chance of being authentic philosophy by concentrating not just on man but on man as condemned to finitude. And from the viewpoint of existentialism Hegel spoiled his chance of being the first modern existentialist when he permitted the urge that drove him into philosophy to find satisfaction in the more or less traditional apparatus of the Philosophy of Identity. Yet there are several aspects of existentialism in which the Hegel of the *Essays* could recognize himself. Besides the already mentioned motivational factor (one does not do philosophy to solve intellectual puzzles, though a positive version would have to have recourse to some colorless formula such as searching for meaning in a world become meaningless, which fits neither Hegel nor existentialism), Hegel would recognize his contempt for the philosophy of the intellect in existentialism's contempt for a civilization in which the empirical sciences and technology have become predominant and where philosophy has very largely become the handmaiden of science. He would recognize, as we already did, his distinction between reflective and speculative philosophy in the distinction so dear to existentialists, the distinction between what is authentic and what is inauthentic, between *eigentlich* and *uneigentlich*. And speculation itself, intellectual intuition as vision of the whole, has its analogue or rather, its subjective caricature in the cognitive function existentialists ascribe to moods, the mood of boredom, for example, being said to reveal the Whole of Being or Being as a Whole. In any case, whether or not existentialism is what speculative philosophy would have come to be in our own day, it is quite certain that the reaction existentialism has shown towards even the most devastating attacks launched against it by analytic philosophers is very much the same as the reaction of speculative philosophy towards reflective attacks. These attacks are attacks that need not be answered except by classifying them as analytic, that is, as basically unphilosophic, as philosophically inauthentic. From the side of existentialism no dialogue is possible between it and analytic philosophy, just as from the side of speculative philosophy no dialogue is possible between it and reflective philosophy. (From the side of analytic philosophy as from the side of reflective philosophy in general, the situation is of course quite different as they are committed to the idea of rational discourse. It seems to them incomprehensible that there are philosophies which in principle refuse to argue or, if they condescend to argue, know that they are lowering themselves to a pseudophilosophical level.)

We had mentioned that the contempt for reflective philosophy will turn out to be only one side of Hegel's attitude toward reflective philosophy. To the reader of the *Essays* it may appear to be the most prominent part, as they abound with ferocious sarcasms directed at reflective philosophy in general and at this or that reflective philosopher in particular. Yet there is something authentically inauthentic, so to speak, about the very dichotomy of reflective and speculative philosophy. For like all the other dichotomies mentioned before, the dichotomy of reflective and speculative philosophy is itself typical of the style of reflective philosophy, and not at all typical of speculative philosophy, in which the reflective dichotomies are overcome in a vision of the organic whole that builds up its richness of harmony out of the tensions between its constituents. To be sure, unlike the reflective dichotomies separating the infinite from the finite, subject from object, freedom from necessity, etc., the dichotomy separating reflective from speculative philosophy is not a dichotomy *in* philosophy, but a dichotomy *about* philosophy, a second-level dichotomy. But this should make no difference at all; for meta-philosophy is itself an essential part of philosophy and the meta-philosophical dichotomy is philosophical—although Hegel should have called it a reflective philosophical dichotomy, a dichotomy which sets speculative philosophy the task of overcoming it as it is to overcome the first-level dichotomies that reflective philosophy prides itself of.

Here we reach the positive side of Hegel's attitude toward reflective philosophy. It is historical or at least, it is historical in a way. Only after reflective philosophy has gone through all its paces and realized its major possibilities can philosophy come into its own as speculative philosophy. The analytic gifts of the intellect must have bloomed and so made all the dichotomies of the time explicit before the bud (ever present?) of speculation can open up in its full glory. In particular, reflective philosophy must have reached the stage where it sees itself split into unsolvable antinomies and is forced into scepticism concerning the very problems that form its traditional core. It is at this historical point when philosophy despairs of metaphysics —as it does in Kant's Dialectic of Pure Reason—and forbids pure Reason to have any but a methodological ("regulative") role in cognition, that philosophy can and must come into its own as speculation. In Hegel's style of speculative philosophy this necessity is at once historical and conceptual—without much awareness of this reflective distinction. Rather it is taken for granted that the logical dependence of the concept of speculative philosophy—the overcoming of the dichotomies—on the concept of reflective philosophy is *eo ipso* a temporal sequence or, to express it in a somewhat different way, as if the teleological unfolding of philosophy is identical with the causal chain of historical events. (It needs no stressing that this sort of identification as it occurs in the *Essays*, is at the very heart of the later Hegel's elaborate and subtle historical dialectic.)

(In the *Essays* Hegel's view of the history of philosophy is rather ambivalent. At times he does seem to view the history of philosophy as leading "necessarily" in its last stages from reflective philosophy to speculative philosophy. At other times he seems to think that any philosophy which deserves the name is germinally speculative, but kept from knowing itself as such by the cultural situation in which it makes its appearance. Yet there is Spinoza, the great inspirator of the Philosophy of Identity. It seems difficult for either of these views to account for Spinoza's system appearing at the time when it did appear.)

There are two images that the *Essays* occasionally use for the relation between reflective and speculative philosophy, and they show how ambiguous Hegel's concept of this relation is. In one image, what philosophy is about is compared with a grove. To speculative philosophy the grove is where the god dwells. To reflective philosophy, the grove is a number of trees. In the other image, philosophy is compared with a temple. Speculative philosophy dwells in it, but reflective philosophy remains in the forecourt.

The first image appears to make the difference between reflective and speculative philosophy so radical as to exclude all relation, let alone dialogue, between them. Yet in his earlier theological writings Hegel also uses the image of the hallowed grove for the youthful organic and holistic culture of Hellas, in which nature and the divine were not yet split one from the other nor the individual from his community. If we remember this, then we may also interpret the hallowed grove image with respect to speculative philosophy in a dialectical way: reflective philosophy had to separate the sacred grove into its component trees so that in speculative philosophy the divine, the natural, and the rational could achieve consciousness of their unity.

Exactly the opposite holds for the other image, that of the temple and its forecourt. Obviously, if there is a forecourt one cannot enter the temple of speculative philosophy without passing through the forecourt of reflective philosophy. On the surface, then, the second image seems to be that of a necessary connection between reflective and speculative philosophy. But why does there have to be a forecourt at all? And in fact, Hegel stresses that there is no approach to speculative philosophy but a *salto mortale, à corps perdu*, by a jump that must be lethal to reflective philosophy if it is to be resurrected as speculation.

Besides the rather hedged-in admission that reflective philosophy had to run its full course before the true conception of authentic philosophy could arise, the *Essays* contain a second positive appraisal of reflective philosophy. For it would seem that Hegel concedes that the very language of speculative philosophy must for purposes of communication be to a large extent the language of reflective philosophy and even the language of ordinary discourse. There are certain indications that the writer of the *Essays* had already given considerable thought to the problem of how to communicate speculative philosophy. He is convinced that it should not be done *more geometrico,* not even in the very attenuated form in which it occurs in Fichte's *Science of Knowledge* and Schelling's publications up to 1801. This logical apparatus is hopelessly reflective. Nor would Hegel's own inclinations and logical gifts be appropriate to it. But then, how can speculation, extra-ordinary and extra-reflective as it is, be communicated at all? How can ordinary language and reflective philosophical discourse be made to do an extra-ordinary and non-reflective job? There is quite a similarity here between the speculative philosopher and Kierkegaard. Kierkegaard focused in on this sort of problem very early and his whole literary style is a deliberate answer to it, an answer full of astonishing deviousness. Even the most prejudiced Hegelian will have to admit, I think, that in this respect Kierkegaard was much the greater craftsman of the two. Hegel found the full measure of his style only in the *Phenomenology* (1807) when he was 37 years old, and it consisted mainly in various singular ways of adapting the grammar and terms of ordinary and reflective discourses to the presentation of an ever ongoing movement of concepts fed by dialectical tensions. Kierkegaard was an artful spider weaving intricate nets to catch his readers, Hegel a busy bird bravely bending and stretching the available material to build a fine nest for his dialectical eggs, and the reader be damned. Some of this bending and stretching can already be observed in the *Essays.* Hegel's style in the *Essays* was unlike that of anybody else then writing in German philosophy. This is not necessarily a praise, least of all in Hegel's own judgment, which condemns the idiosyncratic in philosophy. I am somewhat inclined to agree with those critics who say that the main stylistic rule of the *Essays* is this: the more complex the grammatical construction of a sentence and the less clear its meaning, the more speculative it will be. In any case, the uniqueness of his style in the *Essays* seems due less to any clear insight into how speculative philosophy should and could be communicated than to a rather tentative groping in many divergent directions of adapting the linguistic medium to speculative purposes. The reflective dichotomy, for example, of subject and object is overcome linguistically with Schelling's aid by way of the awkward formulas at the heart of the Philosophy of Identity: "the subjective Subject-Object" and "the objective Subject-Object." The latter is dealt with in the Philosophy of Nature, the former in the Transcendental Philosophy. The same procedure might have been used for the reflective dichotomy of the Infinite and the Finite, but neither Schelling nor Hegel does so, though they use "the finitely Infinite" and "the infinitely Finite," neither of which would indicate what it should: the overcoming of the dichotomy in the "identity" of the Infinite and the Finite. To speak of God in epistemological terms as Subject-Object must have seemed less iconoclastic and objectionable than to speak of Him as the Finite-Infinite. One shudders to think of Schelling and Hegel extending the symbolization of the identity of subject and object to other dichotomies such as those of freedom and necessity or causality and teleology.

Parenthetically we may note here that Hegel is rather flexible in relating these two basic dichotomies of subject and object and of the infinite and the finite to one another. Sometimes it is the subject that is infinite and the object finite, sometimes the other way around, a flexibility that only a philosophy contemptuous of reflective philosophy could allow itself.

In any event one has to keep in mind the whole glorious scheme of the Philosophy of Identity to give to the 'objective and subjective Subject-Object' the flesh and blood it seems to lack in the *Essays.* One must keep in mind, moreover, that these abstract identity formulas were alive with the existential agony felt by Hegel and his contemporaries and that the holistic passion at the living core of the Philosophy of Identity was fed by the alienation of the individual from nature, community (*das Volk*), and God.

Speculative philosophy, in sum, defends itself against the attacks of reflective philosophy by labelling the attacks reflective, and not by arguing with them—because it would then abandon itself as speculation and surrender to reflection. On the other hand, reflective philosophers, *cupidi rerum novarum*, see in the speculators an interesting new sort of monkey they would like to get better acquainted with. In fact, if the monkey could convince them that his system is not just another cage but what he claims it to be, the ultimate whole as known in the only sort of knowledge that deserves the name, the reflectors might in the end want to share the cage with him. But instead of trying to convince them in the style they expect from a philosopher, the monkey develops his *salto mortale* rhetoric which is as convincing as telling a healthy man that he must go through cancer of the brain in order to enjoy true health. So what can speculative philosophy actually do to convince reflective philosophy (as well as common sense and the general public) that it is what it claims to be?

Perhaps this is one of the problems, taken in its most catholic scope, that the *Phenomenology,* as the prolegomena to Hegel's system, was later intended to answer. In the *Essays* the answer is an inaudible sigh of regret joined with an affirmation of hope. The sigh of regret: if only THE speculative system existed, not in fragments and sketches as in Schelling, but as an organic whole detailed in its totality! The affirmation of hope: once this system exists, the spirit of the time will reach out toward it, its time will have come, *es wird sein Glueck machen.*[5] For civilization is longing to be cured of the dichotomies that rend it and that reflective philosophy had the task of bringing into the open.

And the spirit did reach out toward it. However, it was not in the Philosophy of Identity that the spirit recognized itself, not in Schelling and not in the Hegel of the *Essays*. It recognized itself in the Hegel of the *Phenomenology*, the *Logic* and the *Philosophy of History*. In them, speculative philosophy, though greatly changed, fulfilled its promises, and died (except in England, where religion found a strong ally in it, and in Italy, where liberalism was the ally and where national pride could claim Vico to be St. John the Baptist to Hegel, the savior).

After all is said and done it must yet be admitted that the *Essays*, notwithstanding Hegel's unwillingness to let speculative philosophy descend to the level of reflective philosophy, give not only a speculative judgment on reflective philosophy, but also a reflective approach of sorts to speculative philosophy. Contemptuous of the forecourt of the temple, the *Essays* manage just the same to spend much time and effort in it—just as Michelangelo did in *la bella rusticana*, the little Quattrocento church on the hills of Florence whose simple static harmonies he was in need of as a foil for the complex dynamic tensions of his own revolutionary style.

IV· INTELLECTUAL INTUITION

We might begin in a cavalier fashion by saying that intellectual intuition furnishes the evidences on which the Philosophy of Identity is built. In saying this we are, however, already victims of reflective philosophy. For the concept of "being based upon . . ." involves some logical relation pertaining to induction or deduction, as if intellectual intuition either furnished the evidences that could verify or falsify the truth claims of statements, or were some set of self-evident axioms at the basis of a body of theorems. In the former case the Philosphy of Identity would be an empirical science with an exceedingly strange sort of evidence as its experiential ground. In the latter case it would be like geometry as traditionally conceived, and hence subject to the threat of the Kantian question whether the apriority of the axioms is analytic or synthetic; and if synthetic a priori, the possibility of their objective reference would have to be made intelligible. But this whole apparatus remains of course in the forecourt of the temple of philosophy and is, or should be, foreign to speculative philosophy—which dwells in the temple itself.

We have already suggested that intellectual intuition became, in Schelling and Hegel, the vision of the whole, a vision in which God, nature, and self-consciousness (or reason) come into their truth. Spinoza's *scientia sub specie æternitatis* becomes *scientia sub specie totalitatis atque harmoniæ*. (In the following generations this vision of the whole will be degraded to *Weltanschauung*, leading to the relativization not only of moral and æsthetic standards but also of the basic theoretical categories, emerging as sociology of sorts in France, and in Germany as Dilthey's typology of *Weltanschaungen*.) Kant, however, had surely meant by intellectual intuition something quite different from this vision of the whole. And he had clearly and decisively disallowed intellectual intuition to have any positive role in human cognition. How was it then that intellectual intuition turned into this holistic vision and organized itself into something that claimed to be THE system of knowledge under the name of the Philosophy of Identity?

I shall let Schelling and Hegel speak for themselves, letting them talk *univoce* without drawing a line between what Schelling said and what Hegel said. Nor shall I draw a line between what they did say and what they might have said. It must of course not be assumed that the way they understand Kant is my own way.

What the speculators said and might have said to Kant is this:

"You admit that the concept of an intuitive intellect or intellectual intuition harbors no logical contradictions and that therefore there could be such a thing as intellectual intuition; but you also assert that as a matter of fact human beings do not possess it. For the basic way in which anything can be knowable to us as an object of experience is by its being given to us, and the only way in which it can be given to us is by its becoming a datum to our senses: it must cause a sensation in us. Having sensations, however, is very different from having knowledge. So you bridge the gap between having sensations and having knowledge by an impressive analysis of the apparatus which our sensibility and the reason (*der Verstand*) contribute on their own account to the objectivity of possible objects of experience. We say '*our* sensibility' and '*the* reason' because you do play with the idea of non-human subjects whose sensibility might have forms different from those human sensibility has. And you do *not* play with the idea of rational beings whose forms of judgment and therewith categories might be different from those of man. This is part of your Stoic background, about which more later. Sensibility contributes (the forms of) space and time; reason contributes twelve basic concepts in accordance with the twelve forms of judgment and, dependent on the categories and their schematization, your twelve 'principles of the pure understanding.' In consequence, what you allow us to have knowledge of in our experience are not the things as they are in themselves but only as they affect us, that is, as they appear to us. You revel in the dichotomy of things in themselves—which are unknowable to us—and their appearances—which are all we are ever permitted to know. Even what you call our synthetic a priori knowledge such as mathematics does not reach beyond the possible objects of experience.

"If we examine the nature of your prejudice against intellectual intuition more closely we find it to be rooted in dubious psychology, theological dogma, and the procedures of the natural sciences. To begin with the last, you state that the knowledge claims of the natural sciences are well founded to the extent that their judgments, from statements of observation to the most general theories, can be tested empirically, that is, by perception; and perception, according to the causal theory of perception which you unquestionably accept, has as its basic stratum visual, acoustic, and similar sensations. So the triumphant course of the natural sciences since Galileo and Newton over against the debacle of the metaphysical knowledge claims of the rationalists leads you to assert that we must claim no knowlege of any object, ourselves included, that cannot be related in certain prescribed ways to something that is given to us either in externally or in internally perceptual experience. (The prescribed ways in which any object we claim to know must be related to what is sensuously given to us are spatial, temporal and those formulated in your principles of the pure understanding.)

"The lesson which the natural sciences taught you goes beautifully hand in hand with your theological bias. This is your conviction of the inescapable finitude of rational man. You find the index of this finitude in the fact that objects can be known to us if and only if they (a) affect our sensibility and (b) conform to the spontaneously imposed conditions of our intellect. Our sensibility is merely passive and our spontaneity is limited to the mere forms of objectivity. Over against this doubly finite relation of the human subject to the objects of his cognitive experiences you conceive of a kind of knowledge which is spontaneity all through. There would be no receptivity in it at all and spontaneity would not be limited to the mere forms. This is what you call intellectual intuition. It is divine creativity seen in the perspective of your epistemological and psychological presuppositions.

"Your psychological presuppositions have already come to the fore. Man has the capacity to receive sensations, and you call this receptivity sensibility. This is one psychological stem from which knowledge grows. The other is the faculty of freely forming concepts, combining them in judgments, and combining judgments in syllogisms. This is reason. What sort of psychology is this? If it were rational psychology à la Wolff and Baumgarten, you yourself would have destroyed it in the Paralogism section of your Dialectic of Pure Reason. If it were empirical psychology you would seem to have founded, at least in part, your explanation of the possibility of empirical knowledge on empirical knowledge and this is hardly a convincing foundation.

"Besides, there is the basic contradiction that you got yourself into. Jacobi summed it up when he said that without the thing-in-itself one cannot get into *The Critique of Pure Reason* and with the thing-in-itself one cannot stay in it. What is it that causes the sensations in us? This cause of our sensations cannot be found in the objects of our experiences, whether we mean by the objects of our experiences ordinary objects like trees and houses or scientific objects like gravity and atoms.[6] The objects of our experiences cannot be the causes of our sensations, for according to your own theory the possibility of any object is rooted in the forms of our sensibility and the forms of the intellect having shaped the sensuous material. So the X that causes the sensation must be the thing-in-itself unknowably hidden behind the veil of appearances. But in making the thing-in-itself the cause of our sensations you have done what is *verboten* by your own *Critique*. You have applied one of the categories, the category of causality, to the thing-in-itself. It is inconceivable in terms of your theory that the thing-in-itself causes sensations. One could more easily receive a letter from outer space, even one written in English.

"Now what would you say if we show you that you yourself unknowingly make intellectual intuition the ultimate basis of all knowledge claims that you consider soundly grounded? We are of course referring to your transcendental apperception, the 'I think,' of which you say that it is the highest point to which must be fastened the applicability of the categories to time (and space), therewith the possibility of experiencing objects and therewith the possibility of objects of experience. For according to your first *Critique* the unity of nature as the totality of all possible objects of experience depends in the last analysis on the unity of the I in its synthetizing categorial acts of thinking. But precisely in making the thinking I the highest point you give it the characteristic that is definitory of intellectual intuition. To think oneself as thinking—pure self-consciousness—is to *give* oneself existence as pure I. Your transcendental apperception lives up to your own concept of intellectual intuition. You have overcome your dichotomy of receptivity—in which objects are given —and spontaneity—in which they are thought. The pure Ego gives itself to itself in the pure act of thinking itself as thinking. This is how it exists. Naturally, 'existence' does not have the meaning it ordinarily has. It does not have anything to do with being localizable in time and space, which is the reason why the I must not be said to create itself. Fichte prefers to speak of the Ego 'positing' itself. We use 'constructing,' others 'constituting.'

"Your transcendental apperception, however, does not only overcome your dichotomy of receptivity and spontaneity. It also is the beginning of a synthesis of your two most radical and basic opposites, that of the subject and object and that of the infinite and the finite.

"As to the dichotomy of subject and object, it is seen at once that the 'I think' of the pure apperception—the I that thinks itself as thinking—is at the same time both subject and object, or as we prefer to say, the identity of subject and object. *Nous noei heauton*. This, though, is Aristotle. The Greek roots of your philosophy are Stoic rather than Platonic or Aristotelian. So were those of Rousseau, whom you so admired. The light that gave the Enlightenment its name was the *lumen naturale*, the Stoic spark of reason, the representative part of divine reason in all rational beings making them all free, equal, and brothers, as the French Revolution concluded.

"The metaphysical rationalism of Stoicism also forms the hidden background of your transcendental apperception. For the 'I' of your 'I think' is not at all that of any I-saying individual, who is no less appearance than the objects he experiences. One might rather say that the I of the pure apperception is that of the Leibnizian monad which, as the I-in-itself, is hidden behind the subject as it appears to itself. This monadological background of the pure apperception would seem to be undeniable. Yet it must not ever be forgotten that the monadic subject-in-itself is given, in the spirit of the age, the features of the Stoic spark of reason, the same divine reason in each rational individual. So there is occasion for a secret tug-of-war between the Leibnizian and the Stoic background. In any event, at the bottom of your *Critique* there is the Stoic philosophy of identity. It is a very limited one in comparison with ours. It excludes all of nature. For though divine reason is said by Stoic metaphysic to rule over nature, the laws of nature being decrees issued by it, Stoicism does not allow divine reason to be present inside nature as the unconscious urge driving it toward the emergence of self-consciousness. Thus your Stoic identity is limited to the divine reason ruling the universe and its representative sparks residing in human individuals, and through that very residence standing in constant danger of being infringed and becoming polluted. To this extent, then, and only to this extent, your transcendental apperception is also the overcoming of the finite-infinite dichotomy. Without this Stoic identity between infinite and finite reason, each monadic subject would have its own world and you would have to appeal to the hypothesis of a pre-established harmony to explain the illusion of a world shared by all. You would not be able to explain that our experience, instead of being a flux of private sensations, gives us knowledge of a common world. On the other hand, your monadological background might have permitted you a more subtle way of accounting for the pre-personal individuation of the sparks of reason—of the indexing function of the I of the transcendental apperception—than Stoicism itself would have been able to do. In either case, though, for either monad or spark of reason the use of language, in any of the customary senses of 'language,' is a disquieting problem, though not within the Philosophy of Identity as it knows God's becoming man.

"Here we must return for a moment to what we have said about your overcoming of the subject-object dichotomy. For the 'I think' of your transcendental apperception is not just the Ego's thinking itself as thinking—and thus in this very narrow sense the identity of subject and object. Your 'I think' is an incomplete expression. You yourself stress that what the I thinks are the categories and through them the twelve principles of the pure understanding to which the objectivity of the objects of our experience is due. 'I think the categories' is, in terms of our Philosophy of Identity, a formula for the identity of that part of the subject which you call *Verstand* and the form of objectivity. In claiming that the twelve principles are the conditions furnished by reason which allow our experience to be of objects you may also claim, as we would express it, the identity of the rational self with the form of objectivity.

"In sum, then, your transcendental apperception is indeed intellectual intuition unilaterally defined from the perspective of the dichotomy of receptivity and spontaneity as the overcoming of this dichotomy. At the same time, however, and again without your recognizing the fact, the transcendental apperception is the very limited overcoming of the dichotomies of the subject and object and of the infinite and the finite that your philosophy allows. And intellectual intuition does all this right at the most crucial point of your philosophy, where you deny the possibility of intellectual intuition to the finite beings men are. From all this we conclude that your concept of intellectual intuition is much too narrow. Intellectual intuition must be conceived as the construction of the identity underlying all the dichotomies you reflectors have been proud of establishing, and particularly the subject-object and infinite-finite dichotomies. It is this enlarged concept of intellectual intuition which we call speculation and which thus becomes the holistic vision of the complex identity of subject and object and of the infinite and the finite or—in terms that join these basic dichotomies—of God, nature and self-consciousness.

"Transcendental apperception as intellectual intuition, however, is not the only motive in your Critical Idealism that leads directly into the speculation of our Philosophy of Identity. We have always been fascinated by an aside of yours that you let slip in an unguarded moment. This is your remark that perhaps the two stems of our cognitive faculties, sensibility and reason, have the same root.[7] You must have had in mind something like an unconscious intellectual intuition, an identity of receptivity and spontaneity prior to their reflective separation. We think we are justified in seeing this as an anticipation of the unconscious God revealing Himself in nature. For one inspired moment you came close to our philosophy of nature.

"We also like to connect this aside of yours with your equally inspired conception of the role of productive imagination in your Transcendental Deduction of the Categories. The role productive imagination is given in your Deduction is that of synthetizing the pure manifold of time in accordance with the rules as which the categories function in the objectification of experience. Pure imagination, as the great synthetizer, is the mediator between time and the categories. It does not seem to us far-fetched to see in the role you ascribe to imagination an anticipation of the speculative construction of the identity of these opposites. Productive imagination, instead of merely putting two different pieces in an external unity, is their inner unity, their 'common root' raised from its unconscious pre-reflective status to post-reflective awareness.

"The role you ascribe to productive imagination in your Deduction anticipates our speculative philosophy, or is at least a step in the right direction, also with respect to the finite-infinite dichotomy. For in overcoming through productive imagination your own rigorous confrontation of receptivity and spontaneity, you are also undoing, however cautiously and limitedly, your stubborn insistence on the finitude of man. And at the same time you are advancing beyond the Stoic philosophy of identity with its restriction to the sparks of reason as the only divine element in man. To be sure, you still exclude the sense data from the Ego's productivity. It was Fichte to whom we owe this giant step. But in making productive imagination the great synthetizer you have given to the pure Ego, at least within the cognitive sphere, a spontaneity that goes far beyond the mere thinking of the categories. The Ego is now coming close to being a 'finitely infinite.' By the same token you have transcended the limitations of your Stoic background. To the Stoic reason which is pure thought you have added productive imagination to do the work which reason cannot do, the work of synthetizing the pure manifold of time. Though there is no labor involved in this sort of work, it is at least doing something while the pure manifold of time, on the left of productive imagination, and the pure thinking of the categories, on its right, are in one sense and another not doing anything at all. You have gone beyond the contemplative god of Stoicism; yet you have not come closer to the active God of Christianity.

"In your theoretical philosophy God functions as a merely methodological rule in the ongoing business of exploring the world: do not ever stop exploring. In your practical philosophy God is a postulate, though a necessary one, to guarantee justice in distributing blessings according to deserts. Your Stoicism turns Judaic in the moral sphere. You totally separate reason and the universal moral law grounded in it from the beautiful sphere of human passions. Moreover you are unable to explain how the universal moral law can

actually function as such in human life and you admit that even if
it does no one can ever be sure that it is doing so. This is what the
Father, the Son and the Holy Spirit have come to in your philosophy.
Your hidden metaphysical Stoicism is Hellas' revenge on Christianity.

"We regret to have to say this. Our Philosophy of Identity has as
much of the Christian God as any metaphysic can possibly have
that claims to be knowledge. You must not suspect us of being friv-
olous when we see the total relationship of God, nature and self-
consciousness in analogy with the Father, the Son and the Holy
Spirit.[8]

"But quite apart from this somewhat esoteric analogy taken from
the tradition of Christian theology—not for nothing did we spend
years in the *Stift* in Tübingen—speculation achieves its overcoming
of all the basic reflective dichotomies in the organistically conceived
vista of THE WHOLE as presented in the Philosophy of Identity. Its
Philosophy of Nature deals with the objective Subject-Object, whose
unconscious self-revelatory dynamics replaces your dichotomy of the
thing-in-itself and its appearances. The Transcendental Philosophy
deals with the subjective Subject-Object and solves the problems,
unsolvable within your Critical Idealism, of the relation of the pure
apperception to God on the one hand, and to the (logico-historical)
development of rationality in man on the other. The God who reveals
Himself in nature is not, as such, the God who comes to know Himself as having revealed himself in nature. That God He becomes only
in the evolution of human rationality. Man's re-construction of God's
creativity in nature is thus itself a chapter—the last one?—of God's
creation of Himself.

"It surely cannot be said against our system with its superb balance of idealism and realism that there is still a vestige of an idealistic imbalance in it because the Philosophy of Nature was not written
by nature itself but had to wait for the birth and development of
rationality in man. One could just as well talk about an imbalance
in favor of realism in that the whole ascending chain of God's unconscious revelations in nature was needed to bring forth that rationality in man which becomes the instrument of God's knowledge of
Himself.

"To use an analogy which is not at all congenial to us but may
become fashionable someday, your *Critique* sets new rules for the
game of METAPHYSICS. Yours is a game somewhat like tennis. The ball
must always pass above the net of empirical statements. The game
begins with a rally in which the ball must hit the ground in the nar-

row part of the area that you call the synthetic a priori, namely, that part of the synthetic a priori that gives 'the conditions of the possibility of objects of experience.' This is the rally of meta-metaphysics. Once this rally is over and the properly metaphysical part of the game begins, the ball must hit the ground in the area of analytic judgments and logical inferences and, strangely enough, also in an area adjacent to the synthetic a priori but having certain empirical ingredients—as in your *Metaphysische Anfangsgründe der Naturwissenschaft* (1786) and *Die Metaphysik der Sitten* (1797). We say, 'strangely enough,' for after you had drawn a line of absolute opposition between the empirical and the a priori you yet proceed as if there were a gradual transition from one to the other. This may very well serve as another example of your overcoming your own dichotomies; but it is not of the same interest to us as the examples of the transcendental apperception and productive imagination.

"Our game is quite different: it is rather like doing a jigsaw puzzle. Directed perhaps by what we retain from the picture when we first saw it before it was taken apart, we reconstruct it by finding the proper place for each part within the whole, the only rule being that we have to follow faithfully the outline of each part so that they fit together as their maker meant them to. There is only one solution to the jigsaw puzzle, and it is ours.

"From the viewpoint of our system as a whole your *Critique of Judgment* with its discussion of the role of teleology in cognition is almost as important to us as your first *Critique*. For the process as which we see the whole cannot but be teleological, and so we had to undo your typically reflective position with respect to teleology in your *Critique of Judgment*. However, as we aim in this speech of ours to show the germs of true speculation in your philosophy, we have no reason to go into your treatment of teleology where you stubbornly insist on the finitude of human cognition. (Just the same, we wish to advise anyone who wants to understand our Philosophy of Identity from the inside out to study carefully the Critique of the Teleological Judgment—Part II of the *Critique of Judgment*—and particularly §§ 74–78.)

"However, there is one famous remark of yours that we wish to comment on. You are convinced that there never will be a Newton able to explain as little as the origin of a blade of grass according to laws of nature that were not arranged by design (*Absicht*)[9]. In other words, you believe the biological realm to be ultimately impervious to that atomistic-mechanistic approach that is celebrating triumph after triumph in physics and chemistry. And yet at the same time you seem to resign yourself to the fact that biology as science has no choice but to use the methods of physics and chemistry as far as they can go, and beyond that point there is no knowledge that is scientific. This is absurd. To us biology in its largest sense is truly theogony and instead of reducing it as much as possible to physics and chemistry we extend to the subjects of physics and chemistry the holistic and dynamic vision of theogonic biology.

"May we now talk to you about Fichte, your erstwhile disciple and our erstwhile mentor and friend. Knowing how he annoyed you with his interpretation of your first *Critique*, we shall talk about him only for a moment, though we have much to say about him in the *Essays*.

"We have already mentioned the importance of his translating your 'I think' into 'The Ego posits himself.' This translation made it clear to us that your transcendental apperception is intellectual intuition. Prompted by us, Fichte accepted this. The ultimate basis of your *Critique* and his *Science of Knowledge* is intellectual intuition. His second important merit was his radical elimination of the thing-in-itself, although others had seen its paradoxical role in your idealism before him. He eliminated it, in the first place, through the Ego's second *Tathandlung*: the Ego posits the non-Ego. However, this would not take him any further than your own grounding of the form of objectivity in the subject. The step that leads him radically beyond your 'formal' idealism is his showing that the sensations themselves, far from being caused by the thing-in-itself, as well as their spatial and temporal relations, are doings, though unconscious ones, of the Ego. The historical merit of this doctrine is that it is so paradoxical. Thinking our way through the paradox greatly assisted us in bringing to birth the true system of philosophy. The paradox as presented from the side of the object of knowledge, that is, from the side of nature, consists in the fact that Fichte's doctrine totally de-naturalizes nature so that nature becomes even less than it is in your philosophy. In the *Critique* nature is mere appearance, but it is the appearance of something that is, the thing-in-itself, even though it is unknowable to us and not even definable as to the sense in which it can be said to be. The paradox from the side of the subject is that the Ego has lost your index of its finitude, for it is all spontaneity. Yet it is not allowed to be God nor is *The Science of Knowledge* allowed to be a text about God's acquiring knowledge of Himself. Fichte's third *Tathandlung* posits the definite finalization of the Ego: the Ego's aspirations to become one with God will be fulfilled only in the infinitely distant future, that is to say, they will never be fulfilled.

"Over and against the Fichtean idealism, completely one-sided and perhaps rightly denounced as atheistic, we plead with you to see the profound balance and harmony, based on the speculative viewing of the relations among God, nature and self-consciousness, of our Philosophy of Identity, in which nature is as truly existent in God as God is subsistent in self-consciousness."

Kant had received his guests in his bedroom, seated in a chair by a closed window. When Schelling and Hegel finished with their plea Kant appeared to be asleep. The year is 1803 and he is sick and a little senile. He will die the following year, two years after the publication of the second of Hegel's *Essays*. (*Post hoc*, but not *propter hoc*—although if Kant had read the *Essays*, they might have shortened his life.) The silence continues. Hegel turns rather brusquely toward the door. He finds the stale air in the room oppressive. (Kant did not allow windows to be opened as he believed that bed bugs, which had been torturing him for years, fly in through the window.[10]) Schelling bows elegantly in the direction of Kant. It is then that Kant gets up from his chair with great effort, holding himself by the table next to his chair and, slowly returning the bow, mutters, "I honor humanity in you."[11] Schelling, quite touched, answers with a charming smile, "Sir, we honor divinity in you." He rushes to help the faltering Kant into his chair. But the old man does not want help. And Schelling, bowing once more, follows Hegel into the hall, leaving the great reflector to his bugs.

*Walter Cerf*

1. Cf. below, pp. XXIV ff.

2. *Ideen zu einer Philosophie der Natur als Einleitung in das Studium dieser Wissenschaft* (1797). *Von der Weltseele* (1798). *Erster Entwurf eines Systems der Naturphilosophie* (1799). *Einleitung zu dem Entwurf eines Systems der Naturphilosophie* (1799).

3. *System des Transcendentalen Idealismus* (1800).

4. First published by H. Nohl in 1907 and in large part translated by T. M. Knox and R. Kroner in 1948 (see Bibliographical Index).

5. See below, p. 55. Also *Difference*, p. 82.

6. These two sorts of objects, the ordinary and the scientific, were at that time not yet so different from one another as to cause much of a problem concerning their relation.

*xxxvi*
*Walter Cerf*

7. *Critique of Pure Reason*, A15, B29.

8. See H. S. Harris' Introduction to the *Difference* essay, p. 22.

9. *Critique of Judgment*, § 75.

10. Hermann Schwarz, *Immanuel Kant, Ein Lebensbild* (Halle a.S., 1907), p. 269.

11. Ibid., p. 378. In the spirit of this imaginary scene I have taken some liberties with the passages in Prof. Schwarz' book.

# Introduction to *Faith and Knowledge*.

## 1. HEGEL AND THE *Critical Journal*

Hegel's essay *Faith and Knowledge* was published in July 1802 as Volume II number 1 of the *Critical Journal of Philosophy*. Hegel was co-editor of the *Critical Journal* with Schelling. Both editors' names appeared on the title page of the *Journal*, and nothing in the *Journal* itself was signed. The first issue of the second volume was the largest of the six that appeared.[1] Because it contained only this one essay it was furnished with a distinctive second title page. No one was ever in doubt about its authorship.[2]

The essay was written under great pressure during the spring and early summer of 1802. Schelling was away from Jena for an extended period during these months, and he left his struggling coadjutor, already desperately overburdened with his own work, to edit the *Critical Journal* unaided. As a result, the manuscript of *Faith and Knowledge* was ready for the printer *before* the final copy of Volume I number 3 (all of which was written by Schelling). *Faith and Knowledge* was too big to be substituted for that issue, because the size of each volume (three issues) was fixed in the contract with Cotta. So Volume II number 1 appeared before Volume I number 3.

*Faith and Knowledge* was Hegel's most important contribution to the proclaimed agenda of the *Critical Journal*. His own short title for it was "The Kant-Jacobi-Fichtean Philosophy."[3] But according to its own title page it purported to deal with "the reflective philosophy of subjectivity in the complete range of its forms as Kantian, Jacobian and Fichtean Philosophy." Before we consider the meaning of this subtitle, however, we must briefly characterize the programme of the *Critical Journal* itself.

It was quite probably the publisher Cotta who gave the first impetus (at Easter 1798) to the many plans for a new literary-philosophical journal which were bandied about among an ever-increasing circle of potential contributors from that time onwards. Schelling had become involved even before he arrived at Jena in October 1798. Fichte was still at Jena then, though his days there were numbered because the controversy about his supposed "atheism" had already begun. There is no doubt that Fichte and Schelling influenced each other's ideas about the proposed journal, and for this reason there is just one incident in that wider story that is of special interest to us here. In describing *his* plans for a new journal to Schiller in December 1800, Fichte wrote:

> Science must be subjected to a vigorous examination as soon as possible, if the few good seeds that have been sown are not shortly to be brought to nothing by the abundantly flourishing weeds. In the realm of the first science, philosophy, which must help all the others out of confusion, folk are prosing on in the same old way as if no objections had ever been made to it . . . I consider it to be quite possible to reduce the philosophical chatterers to silence by a rigorous critique maintained over two or three years, and so make room for something better.[4]

This anticipates exactly the campaign upon which the *Critical Journal* of Schelling and Hegel embarked a year later. In June 1800 Schelling had proposed to Cotta that the new journal should be a purely philosophical one,[5] rather than a general review, and in August 1800 he proposed to Fichte that they should edit it together. He promised Fichte that he would do a "survey of the present state of philosophy as a whole" for the first volume—claiming that he already had this "partly worked out"—and he suggested that Reinhold and Bardili ("perhaps also Jacobi") should be analysed in an appendix.[6] But Fichte hung back from the proposed collaboration—probably because he already felt that a break with Schelling was inevitable—and Schelling finally turned to the unknown newcomer Hegel for assistance.[7] Hegel was by that time engaged with his own "examination" of Fichte, in the *Difference* essay, and the "taking to pieces" (*Zerlegung*) of Reinhold and Bardili formed an appendix to that.[8]

The first thing that the collaborators wrote for their new journal was a programmatic introduction. This was drafted by Hegel in August and revised—no doubt, quite extensively—by Schelling.[9] The philosophy of criticism set forth in it rests on the claim that there must be a basis for mutual recognition between author and critic. In spite of Schelling's assertion that the *Hauptgedanken* of the "Introduction" are his, this is unmistakeably a Hegelian position. It is the "Idea" (of philosophy or of Reason) that provides the required objective foundation, and any conception of philosophical discussion which does not acknowledge this, but regards philosophical differences as matters of personal opinion and attitude—as Reinhold did—is "unphilosophy." The attitude of a genuinely philosophical critic towards "unphilosophy" can *only* be negative. Where a position lacks an objective point of reference in the Idea, all that can be done is to show up its unphilosophical character. The "Introduction" claims that the principal result of Kant's critique of our mental capacities in its sceptical aspect, was to raise this "unphilosophy" to the dignity of philosophical form, by making it appear that a merely subjective, and hence quite unresolvable conflict of opposed views is the inevitable lot of human Reason. But in spite of its "subjective" aspect, Kant's philosophy offers much more than this justification of scepticism—indeed even Reinhold offers more than that.[10] "Consciousness has not developed beyond subjectivity" in the Critical Philosophy—for if it had, then the existence of a way out of the dialectic of pure Reason would be perceived and acknowledged. But

> though criticism cannot allow what has been achieved and done to be valid as shape of the Idea, still it cannot mistake the striving. The properly scientific concern here is to strip off the shell that still prevents the inner effort from seeing the daylight; it is important to be aware of the manifold reflections of the spirit, of which each must have its sphere in philosophy, and also of the subordinate and imperfect forms.[11]

In the first two issues of the *Journal* Hegel did not find much opportunity for this sort of critical development and appreciation. He wrote at some length about the work of W. T. Krug, but that was "unphilosophy" pure and simple; and although his long review of G. E. Schulze's *Critique of Theoretical Philosophy* contained an important positive revaluation of scepticism, it was mainly the ancient sceptics who were thus revalued—the scepticism of Schulze himself came off rather badly.

In *Faith and Knowledge* the program was put into effect, over its whole range. The candidates for critical evaluation here were among the best minds that the age had produced, and in the case of Kant, at least, there was and is no dispute about his being in the front rank among the philosophers of all time. By placing Kant in a veritable gallery of younger contemporaries Hegel contrived both to set off the magnitude of his achievement, and to show what was lacking in it. In this way he managed to illustrate "the manifold relations of the spirit" and to exhibit the connection between several "subordinate and imperfect forms" in the process of "stripping off the shell that still prevents the inner effort from seeing daylight." The technique, which he here uses for the first time, of making a series of partial visions criticize and supplement one another, is a still immature but nonetheless recognizable form of the method that is so impressively deployed in the *Phenomenology*.

And it is not only the method but the matter which makes *Faith and Knowledge* a first sketch for that still unthought of major work. *Faith and Knowledge* is Hegel's first attempt to survey the culture of the time, and to place all the signs of the advent of "absolute knowledge" in an ideal context which would cause them to reveal their meaning. The introductory pages even offer us a foretaste of the frustration that besets every serious student of the *Phenomenology* because he cannot always be certain just what "signs" of just what "time" Hegel is talking about. Also the unbalance, the unevenness of treatment, the seemingly distorted perspective that characterizes so much of the *Phenomenology* is illustrated in *Faith and Knowledge*. But in *Faith and Knowledge* it is perhaps a bit easier to decide how much to ascribe to the haste of the writing.

We can see how far Hegel's ideas of critical method have developed in a single year, if we compare his comments in the introductory pages of the *Difference* essay with his procedure in *Faith and Knowledge*. In the *Difference* essay the sheep of the true speculative tradition, the story of the "one eternal Reason," are separated sharply from the goats of finite reflection, and just as Virgil is excluded from the company of the true poets (D 89), so Kant is sadly but firmly banished from among the speculative saints: "even the Kantian philosophy had proved unable to awaken Reason to the lost concept of genuine speculation" (D 118).

In practice, of course, Hegel did not rest content even then, with this "Last Judgment" view of the history of philosophy. He could see the folly of it quickly enough, when someone like Reinhold indulged in it. Thus, when he defends the *Système de la Nature* as an expression of genuine speculation (D 177), Hegel makes it quite clear that he does not mean to ascribe greater speculative insight to D'Holbach than to Kant. His real position is that the work of every major thinker has two aspects, and the goatskin may very well be uppermost, so that we cannot recognize the lost sheep. His own analysis of Fichte's weaknesses by comparison with Schelling would have forced him to admit this:

> Notwithstanding the sharp difference between transcendental philosophy and dogmatism, the former is apt to pass over into the latter, when it constructs itself into a system . . . . Thus in

Fichte's system Ego = Ego is the Absolute . . . . The speculation
at the basis of the system demands the suspension of the opposites [Ego and non-Ego], but the system itself does not suspend
them (D 116–7).

But the explicit assumption that is basic to Hegel's position in the
*Difference* essay is that only the "speculative" aspect of a given philosophy really matters. In spite of the way that he was himself using
Fichte's weaknesses to demonstrate the superiority of a "system"
which had not yet really been worked out, the idea that the nonspec-
ulative, abstractly reflective, aspect of a theory may contain something
valuable is not explicitly recognized in the *Difference* essay.[12] When
we turn to Hegel's treatment of Fichte in *Faith and Knowledge* we
can see at once how different the situation is. For whereas in the *Difference* essay Fichte's philosophy is sharply contrasted with Kant's
as "the most thorough and profound speculation" (D 118; cf. D 173),
it is treated in *Faith and Knowledge* as the logical culmination of
Kant's "critical" labours, and as the "reflective" solution of the problems left by Kant.

One might think, indeed for a long time I did think, that this contrast is just an accidental result of the changed relations between
Fichte and the Identity theorists. The publication of the *Difference* essay itself caused an open breach between Schelling and Fichte. Once
the finality of the breach was accepted there was no point in emphasizing Fichte's speculative achievement, and every reason to concentrate attention on the failings of his "system." It is clear, anyway, that
Hegel does not mean to withdraw any of the speculative claims made
on Fichte's behalf in the *Difference* essay. According to Hegel it is
Fichte himself who wants to escape from his "speculative" achievement (p. 167 below). The apparent conflict between Hegel's two estimates of Fichte's achievement is quite done away with in his lectures
on the history of philosophy.[13] Of course, those lectures were prepared several years later (assuming that this part of Michelet's text,
at least, dates from 1805/6). But when we see how the estimates of
*both* the *Difference* essay *and Faith and Knowledge* are reasserted
side by side, in the lectures, we can hardly doubt that both estimates
were formulated in a perfectly consistent way in Hegel's mind from
the first.

But if we take the view that in *Faith and Knowledge* Hegel simply
moved from the role of guardian angel to the role of devil's advocate
*vis-à-vis* Fichte for reasons of academic policy, so to speak, we shall

lose sight of the main critical purpose of the essay, and so of one of the principal reasons for its enduring signficance. For if we view it in this way *Faith and Knowledge* becomes simply a polemic; and the contrast between the properly appreciative criticism of Fichte in the *Difference* essay and the treatment of Fichte here is just what gives the game away completely.

It is easy enough to fall into this mistake. The highly polemical tenor of the *Critical Journal* as a whole invites this misunderstanding, and even the most perceptive readers in Hegel's contemporary audience fell into it. It is not to be wondered at, that a lesser man such as Koeppen should report to Jacobi that a "mighty scorn" would prevail in the new journal.[14] Koeppen had not then received the rough handling that Hegel bestows on him in *Faith and Knowledge*; but polemic was something that he understood, and about all that he could appreciate in the work of the Identity Philosophers.[15] But even A. W. Schlegel complained to Schelling that Hegel ought not to have dealt with Fichte's *Vocation of Man* as if it had been written for philosophers.[16]

But no matter how natural and attractive it may be, the view that *Faith and Knowledge* is destructive polemic rather than constructive criticism *is* a mistake. What we have to recognize is that the attack on Fichte here is part of Hegel's constructive evaluation of *Kant*. He feels able to use Fichte in this way precisely because he has already done a *constructive* evaluation of Fichte's achievement in the *Difference* essay. It is as a balance sheet of what speculative philosophy owes to the founder of the *Critical* philosophy that *Faith and Knowledge* is *critically* important.

The overriding character of Hegel's concern with Kant shows itself most plainly in the fact that Hegel spends so much time overthrowing Jacobi's critique of Kant, and contrasting Jacobi's own efforts unfavorably with Kant's work. The Jacobi section is the longest in the essay, yet Jacobi's positive contribution to "reflective" philosophy is in Hegel's view rather slight, and his discussion of Jacobi's own philosophy is correspondingly brief. Schleiermacher's work is fairly explicitly declared to be of greater philosophical significance than Jacobi's.[17] Yet Schleiermacher is dealt with in an appendix, and Herder is dismissed in an interlude!

Of course the fact that Herder appears at all, constitutes something of a puzzle. He seems to have got in only because of his contribution to the Spinoza controversy. And one reason for the prominent role and the lengthy treatment accorded to Jacobi is that Jacobi was the great commentator on Spinoza. Antipathy to Spinoza forms a bond between Jacobi and Fichte. But Spinoza is only a looming presence in the background of *Faith and Knowledge,* just as he was in the *Difference* essay. There it was Fichte who was in the foreground, here it is Kant throughout. If we read the whole of *Faith and Knowledge* as a commentary on Kant we shall see how the highest aims of the *Critical Journal's* announced programme are fulfilled in it.

## 2. THE ''REFLECTIVE PHILOSOPHY OF SUBJECTIVITY''

Just as he does not change the estimate of Fichte already given in the *Difference* essay, so Hegel does not depart from the verdict there given on Kant either. The Critical Philosophy is *not* treated as a speculative philosophy, but as a systematic exposition of the highest "reflective" position that is achievable. In the Critical Philosophy it is assumed as axiomatic that there is a gulf between "what is," and all thought about it, or awareness of it. Consciousness, even at its furthest reach, its most "objective" and rational limit, can only *reflect on* a reality that is independent of, and indifferent to, its presence or absence. Knowledge, so far as it occurs, is an accident in the scheme of things. But it follows from this assumption that the understanding *of* the scheme of things claimed by the philosopher is itself not really a matter of knowledge but of *faith.* If our knowing is an accident in the scheme of things, then we cannot *absolutely know* that there *is* a scheme of things. What is *called* the "theory of knowledge" is actually a matter of articulating and explicating rational *faith.*

This was not quickly or easily recognized by those who first developed the critical "theory of knowledge." They saw themselves as defenders of knowledge *against* the tyrannical claim of faith. It required the genius of Kant to systematize their position so that the real relation of their finite knowledge to faith could become visible. Against Kant's sceptical and "problematic" conclusions, Jacobi reasserted the immediate certainty of the religious principle of faith; and finally Fichte systematized and completed the reconciliation of finite reason with religious faith already suggested in principle by Kant himself.

This is, in the briefest possible compass, the thesis of Hegel's essay. He is concerned to interpret, and to show the relation between, the history of "Protestant" thought and the history of "Protestant" religion. The critical theory of "knowledge" begins with Locke, and the "faith" of Kant, Jacobi and Fichte goes back to Luther. Hegel makes one or two explicit references to the medieval "age of faith," and more numerous though more covert allusions to the classical "age of Reason" before that. But it is the world-view of Protestantism that is the focus of his interest.

In this "modern" world, philosophy is no longer the "handmaid of faith." That is to say that—except in the backwaters of the Theological Faculty at Tübingen[18]—no one now thinks of the explication of a set of authoritatively "revealed" truths as the proper task of human Reason. But this revolution has come to pass partly because faith has changed its appearance and its dwelling place, and partly because both Reason and Faith have perished. This is another of Hegel's main themes: that the *reconciliation* of faith and reason in the rational religion of Protestant philosophy has involved a "transvaluation of values." The knowledge that reflective philosophizing can justify is the finite knowledge of our mundane experience. So when we seek to develop a "rational faith" we are inevitably bound to project the values and standards of that experience into the "beyond" of our faith.

This "bringing of Heaven to earth" in the sense of corrupting all sacred values into profane ones, exchanging all divine promises for a mess of worldly pottage, is the direct outcome of "the Enlightenment."[19] "The Enlightenment" was essentially the determination to make the knowledge of this world, and the life of this world sufficient for man. It was a conscious renunciation of any attempt to share in God's life or God's knowledge. This renunciation is the "death" of speculative philosophy, and since the Enlightenment made this renunciation, it could have no proper philosophy at all. It could produce *only* "imperfect" philosophies, for which a sociological explanation can be given, but not a rational justification. Only when we put all the finite pieces of the puzzle together does the movement of the empirical tradition from Locke to Kant become an intelligible whole, something that can be rationally comprehended in spite of its strictly "negative relation to the Absolute" (i.e., the renunciation of all claims to absolute knowledge).

It was probably through the teaching of "logic" according to his initial conception if it, that Hegel arrived at this view that even empirical, and hence fragmentary and unsystematic, philosophies could be ordered into a systematic relation with one another, so that they would reveal a totality of which their authors remained unconscious. Just after *Faith and Knowledge* appeared, the *Catalogus* of the University of Jena was sent to press with all the courses offered for the winter semester of 1802. Hegel undertook to lecture on "Logic and Metaphysic according to the book that will appear within a few weeks (*nundinis instantibus proditurum*)."[20] The book never did appear, and the manuscript on "Logic and Metaphysic" that survives was written two years later. But Rosenkranz has preserved for us a fairly lengthy excerpt from the opening lecture of a winter course which cannot be later than October 1802 and was probably delivered then. Here Hegel gave the following account of his intended syllabus:

"I shall . . . begin from the *finite* in order to proceed from it to the *infinite* when and so far as the finite has been nullified. Lecturing on philosophy has traditionally been in the form of Logic and Metaphysics. I too shall follow this form in my lectures, not because it has long authority behind it but on account of its utility.

To be precise, philosophy as the science of truth has infinite cognition, or the cognition of the Absolute, as its objective concern. Finite cognition, or *reflection*, stands opposed to this [infinite] cognition, or *speculation*. But not as if they were each the absolute opposite of the other; finite cognition abstracts only from the absolute identity of that which in rational cognition is connected to another or posited as equal to another—and only because of this abstraction is it finite cognition. So in rational cognition or philosophy, the *forms* of finite cognition are posited as well, but at the same time their finitude is nullified in virtue of the way they are *connected* with each other.— Thus the objective concern of a true logic is this: to set up the *forms of finitude* not just bundled together empirically, but just as they come forth from Reason, but being robbed of Reason by the intellect, they appear only in their finitude— Hence the efforts of the intellect to *imitate* Reason in the production of an identity must be set forth, showing how its copying can bring forth only a *formal identity*. And to recognize the imitative character of the intellect, we must always keep the original (*Urbild*) that it copies, the expression of Reason itself, before our eyes.—*In fine*, we must suspend the forms of understanding themselves by *Reason*, we must show what meaning and content these finite forms of cognition have for Reason. The cognition of Reason, so far as it appertains to logic, will therefore be a *negative* cognition of Reason.

I believe that, inasmuch as it fixes the finite forms as such, logic can serve as an introduction to philosophy only from this speculative side, where it cognizes reflection completely and gets it out of the way, so that it puts no hindrances in the way of speculation, and at the same time keeps the *pattern [Bild] of the Absolute* before us as it were a *mirror image* so that we become familiar with it. In accord with this general conception of *logic* I shall proceed in the following order (the necessity of the order will show up in the science itself):

I.   The *universal* forms, or laws, or *Categories of finitude,* in their objective aspect as well as their subjective one (i.e., in abstraction from this difference): to set forth these forms as a reflection of the Absolute, whether they be subjective or objective on their finite side.

II:   The *subjective* forms of finitude, or finite thought, the *intellect*: to treat this similarly and in its series of stages, concepts, judgments and syllogisms. With respect to the last it must be remarked that although the rational form expresses itself more clearly in syllogisms, so that they are commonly ascribed to Reason as being rational thought, we deal with them here only as formal syllogism, as pertaining to the intellect.

III:   Lastly, the *suspension* of this finite cognition through *Reason* must be demonstrated. This is the place to give the *speculative meaning of the syllogism,* the foundations of a scientific cognition in general.—It is the usual thing for an *applied* logic to be appended to this *pure* logic. But on the one hand what is usually dealt with under this head is too general and trivial to deserve any notice at all; and on the other hand the genuinely scientific content of applied logic is brought out in the third part under rational cognition.

From this third part of logic, namely the negative or nullifying side of Reason, we shall make the transition to genuine philosophy or *metaphysics.* Here we have, above all else, to construct for ourselves completely the *principle* of all philosophy. From the true cognition of this principle, there will arise the conviction that there has only been one identical philosophy *at all times.* So not only am I promising nothing new here, but rather I am concentrating my philosophical efforts precisely on the restoration of the oldest of old things, and on freeing it from the misunderstanding in which these recent times of unphiloso-phy have buried it. It is not long now since the very concept of philosophy was discovered in Germany, but it is only for our times that the discovery is a new one."[21]

The business of logic, as we see, is to "cognize reflection complete-ly and get it out of the way"; and to this end the forms of finitude must be set up in their rational order; "not just bundled together empirically."[22] It was a favorite complaint of the idealists from Fichte onwards, that Kant had "bundled the categories together empirical-ly" because he gave no justification for using the table of the forms of judgment just as he found it in traditional logic. But Kant was the philosopher who has made the most sustained effort to "imitate Reason" at the level of the intellect, so any proper survey of such efforts must necessarily deal with him. In *Faith and Knowledge* as we shall see, Hegel tries to present Kant's theory of the mind in a more organic, less "empirical" order than that adopted by Kant him-self. I take what Hegel does in his structural presentation of the Critical Philosophy to be an example of how one should use the *Ur-bild* of Reason to recognize the "copy."

But the "efforts of the intellect to imitate Reason in the production of an identity" were mentioned in the *Differenzschrift*[23] and the demonstration that "its copying can bring forth only a *formal iden-tity*" is *there* given for the particular case of Reinhold and Bardili's "reduction of philosophy to logic" (D 179–83, D 186–8). One can see how Hegel may have used the Reinhold/Bardili "reduction of phi-losophy to logic" as a jump-off point for his first course in Logic. But if he did so, he could not help being intensely aware of the arbi-trary, *ad hoc* character of his procedure; for Reinhold with his se-quence of philosophical "conversions" and his final arrival at a posi-tion which he had expounded himself years earlier, but now greeted as a revelation from the mouth of someone else, is the paradigm case of an "imperfect" philosophy that "pertains to an empirical necessi-ty." The desirability of a finite starting point for "logic" that was it-self capable of rational justification would inevitably present itself to Hegel's mind very forcefully.

The obvious starting point was the Critical Philosophy, since it was the historic point of origin for the Identity Philosophy, and marked

the moment of rebirth for speculation. *Faith and Knowledge* is Hegel's attempt to provide the rational justification that is needed. In his
initial approach to the problem Hegel gives two grounds for believing that a "rational" justification is possible. First, the "subjective
principle" of Kant, Jacobi and Fichte "is by no means a limited expression of the spirit of a brief epoch or of a small group" (57). And
secondly "the mighty spiritual form that is their principle achieved
in them perfect self-awareness, perfect philosophical formation and
definite self-expression as cognition." The main body of the essay is
devoted to the establishment of this second contention; but how the
first contention, which needs no establishing can constitute a valid
ground for Hegel's position is not easy to understand. Hegel seems to
have undermined its evidential value already by declaring that the
whole of the Enlightenment "was a hubbub of vanity without a firm
core" (56). The Enlightenment, after all, is neither a "brief epoch" nor
a "small group"; and if it can be thus summarily dismissed, the
weight of any argument for the rational importance of its principle
based on its prevalence in the "spirit of the age" would seem to be
slight.

But if we look more carefully, we see that it is the "positive aspect"
of the Enlightenment (i.e., its consciousness of the Absolute) that
Hegel has thus dismissed. Now the "subjective principle" of the "philosophy of reflection" is not the "positive aspect" either of the Enlightenment or of the Reformation. It is the principle both of Protestantism in religion, *and* of the Enlightenment in philosophy, but with
respect to the Absolute it is strictly *negative* because it is essentially
finite. In his religious feelings the true Protestant is aware of God,
but no intuition of God as an objective presence is possible for him,
precisely because his "flight from the world" makes the reverent
worshipper ever conscious that all finite experience is evil. This world
is delivered over to mortality and damnation. The "principle of
subjectivity" is expressed as the axiom that all human knowledge is
finite. God is *felt* as "beauty" (the *ideal* quality of sense-intuition);
but the beauty must not be expressed, for to give it any natural expression would be to fall into the "idolatry" of the old "pagans."
Hence the religious reformers were iconoclasts. They would not tol-
erate either prayers for the intervention of the saints, or "idolatrous"
statues and pictures in the churches. Protestantism, at its farthest
reach, is itself a cult of inward or subjective "beauty"—as Hegel will
argue in the crucial few pages on Schleiermacher. But the divine

beauty is never *objectively* intuited. Thus the age remains "without a core" on its positive side.

Because of its subjectivity, Protestant religious consciousness was a "yearning" for the Absolute that is *not* present, and a flight from the finite, the present reality of now and here. The Protestant principle of subjectivity is a *negative* one both for-itself because the subject *knows* that it is *not* the Absolute, and in-itself, because its whole being is a "yearning" for what is not present, and a continual denial and negating of the things and concerns of the present world. But "when the time had come'" the Protestant Reformation gave birth to the Enlightenment. Then the reconciliation of the finite subject with its finite world, the renunciation of its yearning for the Absolute, began. The old "yearning" *now* took the form of what we call "the Protestant ethic." The enlightened man turned his back on God, but he was still anxious to walk righteously in God's sight. His determination to preserve a "good conscience" was the only redeeming aspect of his resolute "pursuit of happiness." Unfortunately (as we shall see when we reach the analysis of Fichte's ethics) this sort of good conscience is the one thing that one cannot preserve when one becomes systematically concerned about the doing of one's duty. Conscience is still the voice of the absent God, and it remains true that "in God's sight shall no man living be justified."[24]

Any achievement of moral happiness would require a "speculative" breakthrough, with a consequent escape from a "purely negative relation to the Absolute" whether in the form of religious yearning or enlightened renunciation. But to begin with, the hopelessness of the situation is not apparent. The "pursuit of happiness" is a right of every individual, and the "law of nature" is that we should maximize the enjoyment of this right, and take care only that our pursuit of happiness does not interfere with the equal rights of others. *Utility* is the absolute value and "the empirical happiness of the individual" is the one and only goal of Reason. "The infinite, the concept . . . receives its content from . . . its opposite" (60). Heaven is just this world made happy, and if men cannot achieve it, they have no one to blame but themselves. In the world itself there are no sacred things—how could any finite thing be "sacred" once we have understood it properly?—only the "law of nature" must not be broken.

Above the actual order of nature, and the ideal or moral order of Nature's law, there is, of course, the "Author of Nature." But He is only the supreme Being of Deism—"an unknowable God beyond the boundary stakes of Reason."[25]

I have outlined "eudaemonism" with catchwords borrowed from Locke, even though Hegel means his audience (then and now) to think rather of Wolff. There is a better reason for this than the fact that most of my readers (like myself) will be more familiar and more comfortable with Locke. The reason is that, as Hegel himself admits, Locke was the authentic voice of this "enlightened view." Hegel may say scornfully that the Enlightenment is a "hubbub of vanity without a firm core." But as we have seen, *this* only refers to the hollowness of all religious consciousness in the period. The "enlightened principle of subjectivity" had a definite philosopher to speak for it. Hegel mentions "Locke and eudaemonism" as the *two* "earlier philosophical manifestations of this realism of finitude" (63). But that only reflects the fact that, while he was familiar with Locke's *Essay*, he had perhaps *not* read Locke's political treatises. The very apt quotation (68) from the Introduction to the *Essay* with which Hegel begins his analysis of Kant shows that he knew very well where the fountainhead of the "reflective philosophy of subjectivity" was.

But what has this utilitarian eudaemonism to do with Kant, Jacobi, and Fichte? They are at the opposite pole from it. However, just by being at the opposite pole from it, they show us the other side of it. They show us the meaning of that quest for "good conscience" which is its last link with the Protestant yearning that it has turned its back on. They set forth the *infinity*, the ideal aspect of the perfect reconciliation with the finite in eudæmonism. Every extreme in the eudæmonist account is complemented by its opposite so as to make an infinite whole. Pessimism takes the place of optimism, striving takes the place of satisfaction, duty takes the place of pleasure, law the place of inclination, domination the place of freedom. But it is always just a matter of the other side of the coin, the endlessness of all finite ends.

In the eudaemonist phase no philosopher looked hard at the "infinite" aspect of existence: "the concept is not posited in purity" (61). The exceptional case here was Hobbes; and Hegel may have Hobbes in mind when he remarks that "when the concept is posited negatively, the subjectivity of the individual is present in empirical form, and the domination is not that of the intellect, but is a matter of the natural strength and weakness of the subjectivities opposed to one another" (61). For his point here seems to be that, in the Kantian perspective the only alternative to the tyranny of the categorical imperative is the terror of the war of all against all. But except in Hobbes, the eudæmonists never "abstracted the concept."[26] Their "infinity" was just an indefinite projection of the synthesis of concept and intuition in finite satisfaction. They did not contrast a present state of being (i.e., satisfied existence) with the infinite concept as a particular intuition. Separated from its empirical content the infinite concept was for them simply the unthinkable, incomprehensible "Supreme Being." In the eudæmonist ideal of perfect bliss "the empirical is . . . an absolute something . . . for the concept" (62) because one could not *think* the concept (of "happiness") at all without relying on it.

This is the limitation that is overcome in the German thinkers. In their work, the phenomenal character of finite existence is explicitly recognized, and hence the *opposition* between finite and infinite becomes "objective." There are two *realms*, the phenomenal and the noumenal, the sensuous and the supersensuous: "the empirical is . . . an absolute nothing for the concept." This "perfect abstraction" is achieved at the cost of admitting that our "phenomenal" experience is not a knowledge of *what is* at all. Locke naively assumed that although his knowledge was limited it was real knowledge as far as it went. But Kant insists that we have *no* knowledge of "things-in-themselves"; Jacobi adds that we must therefore conclude that all our so-called knowledge is nothing but the organization of our ignorance.[27] As Hegel puts it "in theoretical philosophy knowledge of the empirical is nothing" (62). But all this is lost to us on the theoretical side is restored to us in the practical philosophy of Fichte.[28] There we shall see, in due course, how "the empirical has absolute reality for the concept."

Each of the three thinkers contributes something vital to the *complete* philosophy of subjective reflection. Kant completed the critique of our finite cognition which Locke was the first to attempt, and thus established the phenomenal/noumenal distinction. But his great advance was the establishment of the autonomy of practical Reason, as against the instrumental use of Reason in the older eudaemonism. Jacobi expressed the subjective meaning of this successful "abstraction of the infinite." The longing of Protestant faith and the "infinite grief" of God's death become, in Jacobi, the focal experience of Reason. Fichte overcame the antithesis between the objective autonomy of Reason and the subjective experience of despair, by postulating an "infinite progress" of feeling objectified as striving in accordance with duty. Thus the infinite *antithesis* to the finite thesis of eudæmonism finally achieved perfect expression.

But the infinity that the three philosophies express is only the "bad infinite" that was present, though implicit, in the thesis. The endlessness of striving was always there, but it was not previously perceived as the endless treadmill of moral obligation. The yearning and grief of Jacobi, since it is *not* the reflective development of a conceptual ideal, is simply the finite life of the enlightened utilitarian, looked at from the point of view of its hopelessness and futility. And the content of the moral striving, by which Fichte escapes from this despair, all comes from finite experience. The service of the moral law is "finite ideality" because, although the infinite ideal is proclaimed, we can never reach it. The infinite kingdom of ends is declared to be what is truly real but it is the striving of the finite self against its finitude that remains the one absolute certainty. Kant and Fichte "rise to the concept, but not to the Idea" (63). Jacobi does not even get that far.

The Idea is the *true* infinity of life, an infinity that is not, like the concept (the moral law, or the "law of Nature" in the earlier tradition), essentially *opposed* to the finite. It does not exist simply as a thought or concept to be *reflected* on by the finite consciousness. It is an infinity that contains the finite, a concept that involves existence, an ideal that is the life of the real. This is the *"Bild* of the Absolute" that we must see in the mirror of reflection, if all of our logical efforts are to prepare us for real speculation. All of us do have the *intuition* of the divine life, which is what we need if we are to overcome the opposition of concept and existence in reflection. This intuition is the element that Jacobi contributes to the intellectual "copy." But in its immediacy Jacobi's intuition is absolutely alien to reflection, so he can only be *hostile* to the conceptual efforts of Kant and Fichte. The intuition is also present in both Kant and Fichte, but only as the faith in a "beyond" which their conceptual structures can never comprehend because their concept of man is *essentially* finite. They accept the "fixed standpoint" of the Enlightenment. Like someone who complains that he is no longer able to see the feet properly when he is shown the whole body, they cannot recognize the true integrity of man's spiritual existence (the "Idea") when it is put before them. But their achievement was the making of an abstraction which completed the pattern of previous abstractions. It is no wonder, therefore, that they cannot finally let the abstractions go back into the living unity of the whole. *That* is the task of speculative thought.

## 3. KANT

One of the worst difficulties that faces the reader in seeking to understand Hegel's critique of Kant arises from the fact that Hegel uses so much terminology that derives from Kant, and uses it very freely, but in ways that contrast sharply with Kant's own interpretation and usage. "Concept," "Reason," "Idea" are all Kantian terms, in the sense that Hegel's usage of them derives in some sense from Kant. But the earnest student of Kant's "Transcendental Dialectic"—upon which Hegel's attention is largely focused—will find himself continually rubbing his eyes in bewilderment at the things that Hegel says. It is necessary to *know* what Kant thought, in order to understand what Hegel says; but it is even more necessary to grasp that Hegel begins from a flat rejection of some of Kant's most fundamental assumptions.

Take the word "Idea" for example. I have endeavoured to characterize what it means for Hegel above. Since Hegel's "Idea" is a concept that directly involves existence, we can understand why he says that "on the lower levels" of Kant's *Critique* "an Idea truly does provide the basis," for he is here referring to the *a priori* synthesis of concept and intuition in empirical knowledge. But this directly violates Kant's definition of an "Idea of Reason":

> I understand by Idea a necessary concept of Reason to which no congruent object can be given in sense-experience . . . the pure concepts of Reason are *transcendental Ideas.* They are not arbitrarily invented; they are imposed by the very nature of Reason itself, and therefore stand in necessary relation to the whole employment of understanding. Finally, they are transcendent and overstep the limits of all experience; no object adequate to the transcendental Idea can ever be found within experience.[29]

Hegel denies this last claim; and having denied it he goes on to turn Kant's whole position upside down, by pointing out that if, contrary to Kant's belief, the Ideas of Reason are *necessarily* "objective" (i.e., instantiated in experience) then all *empirically* instantiated concepts have a good claim to be regarded as Ideas precisely because the synthesis of intuition and concept is a necessary condition of experience. In the *Difference* essay Hegel claims that Kant's philosophy is "authentic idealism" "in the principle of the deduction of the categories" (i.e., in the "transcendental unity of apperception"). *Now* he says that Kant's philosophy "has the merit of being idealism" because of his doctrine of the *a priori synthesis* (68).

It is because of Kant's doctrine of the highest Ideas of Reason, on the other hand, that Hegel stigmatizes the principle of his philosophy as "formal thinking."[30] Kant's Ideas are "pure concepts" (acts of the subject) without *objects*. Or, as Kant says, their "objective employment . . . is always transcendent." Now, Kant does allow the employment of the Ideas of Reason in a practical context. The Idea of God, for example, has a fundamental role in rational ethics. But it remains, for him, a *transcendent* concept (i.e., it is beyond the limits of possible experience), and to complete Kant's "system of reflection" by resolving all the "antitheses" of the Ideas in a system of "practical faith," as Fichte does, is *not* the proper business of philosophy. If the rational concept is "empty" without an intuitive content, then it will be just as empty for practical purposes as it is for theoretical ones. And because it is empty any use of it in thought will be "formal."

Because Kant recognized the true nature of the Idea, the identity of thought and being, in his account of the *a priori* synthesis of concept and intuition in sense experience, Hegel regards the theory of the "productive imagination" that produces this *a priori* synthesis as a genuine achievement of speculation. But when we study this doctrine we must not make—and Hegel thinks that Kant did not make—the typical "reflective" error of assuming that the "synthesis" is a putting together of heterogeneous components, the uniting of a conceptual *form* with a sensible *matter*. Far from being a separate *faculty*, the intellect (which according to Kant, furnishes the forms or concepts), is just the higher "potency" of the productive imagination. Once it has *achieved* sense and intuition—which already involves an *a priori* synthesis of matter and form—the intelligence can advance to pure concepts. Having arrived at "red," brown," "green," etc., it can advance to "color."[31] The "identity" of the visual field is "color," the "difference" of the visual field is "colors." Thus the identity discovered by the intellect is the same as the differences discovered by the visual sense. There is, of course, an evident *antithesis* which does *not* disappear, between the abstract universal "color" and the particular colors of the field. As Aristotle would have said, the universal "color" *exists* in one way in the mind, and in another way in the different colors of the field. Sense and intellect are thus two forms of "intuiting." Intellectual intuition is the thinking that fills time, and sense intuition is the being that fills space. But we should say rather that "the Ego" exists in these two ways. If I think of the red, brown, green, etc., that I perceive, as "colored patches," then "the synthetic unity" which is what makes them a "visual field" "steps outside" of the colored field "and faces it in relative antithesis"—it becomes the abstract universal "color." This is an "empty" identity. It is not an "intuition," for there *is* no universal color, there are only particular colors; but when we turn all this into its proper idealist form, we realize that although there is no "abstract Ego," no "empty" form of the "unity of apperception," no self without some definite thoughts and intuitions, still the thinking and intuiting *activity* of the Ego *is* the concrete universal which is the "principle" of experience. Thinking and intuiting are quite "heterogeneous." But intelligent consciousness is "the original absolute identity of the heterogeneous."

Just as the universal concept of color is "immersed" in the differences of the perceived colors, so at the higher level where concepts have been abstracted, the *category*, the constitutive principle by which Reason unifies experience is "immersed" in the variety of the phenomena that are conceptualized in judgments. The rational principles involved only become apparent when we begin to reason syllogistically from our conceptual judgments. The *categories* have to be abstracted then, because the ultimate major premises of scientific syllogizing are formations of categorical principle. But we are not normally *conscious* of the legislative function of our intelligence, when we constitute our sense-intuitions into a world of objects. It is this activity of our own Reason—and at its most primitive level the activity of the "productive imagination" that produces the synthesis of sense-intuition—which is the "sole In-itself" (73). The reflective split into subject and object, self and world, is logically *posterior* to this original unity. Kant himself did not recognize this, he did not perceive that the thing-in-itself must be the necessary origin of appearing and being appeared to as an *a priori* synthesis, *not* the problematic origin of the objective appearance. Thus "he turned the true *a priori* back into a pure unity, i.e., one that is not originally synthetic."

Because of this mistake, the rational (necessary) and the empirical (accidental) aspects of experience were reflectively separated at their point of origin. As a result only "relative identities" of the pure concepts (the categories) and empirical data were possible. Reason lays down categorical laws which "govern" the "relations" of phenomena, but the categories and the intuited data remain obstinately heterogeneous. Hence Kant simply does not realize that in the "Transcendental Dialectic" he is investigating the nature of the "In-itself." Instead, he takes the organizing activity of Reason in experience to be the contribution of the human mind regarded as if it were something *separate* from the objective world which it organizes for cognition. The empirical aspect of experience is assigned one problematic origin, the rational aspect another.

Speculation puts the two problems of origin together into the one absolute certainty (the ground of the *a priori* synthesis) and accounts for the dialectical character of pure Reason (the one reality-in-itself) by a sort of "principle of complementarity." Thus gravity has an intuitive (subjective or particular) aspect as *body* and a *conceptual* (objective or universal) aspect as *motion*. This is an example from the philosophy of Nature. In transcendental philosophy, the activity of imagination has an intuitive (subjective, particular) side as the Ego, and a conceptual (objective, universal) side as experience.[32] The subjective side is the finite and existential side, the objective side is the infinite (hence conceptual) side. The *existing source* or "center" of gravity is a physical body. Bodies are *seen* to move. But motion is the conceptual or universal side of gravity because the resting equilibrium of a gravitational system of moving bodies is only comprehended in thought. It is not abstracted like "color" but grasped as a "periodicity *of motion*." On the transcendental side, the Ego is the existing source of Reason, and the infinity of experience is its realized (or "immersed") concept. As soon as we *stabilize* the infinity of possible experience—for example, by considering a color-wheel instead of the indefinite play of color, light and shade in our primitive sense experience—the "universal" (or conceptual) character of the "infinite" even at this "immersed" level of imagination, becomes obvious enough.[33]

Having given us these examples of the subjective side as *particular* (intuitive) and the objective side as *universal* (conceptual), Hegel now makes one of those switches of perspective that renders his discussion of the Identity theory so hard to follow. Within either one of the "philosophical sciences" the "subjective" side is *particular* and the *objective* side is "universal." But when we consider the ultimate speculative "identity" of the two sciences with one another, the situation is reversed: Natural philosophy, the science of the *object*, is the sphere of *reality*, where the moment of particular existence, of intuition, is dominant; and transcendental philosophy, the science of the subject, is the sphere of *ideality*, where the universal, the concept, is no longer "immersed" in the manifold.[34] Having shown that Kant got his *transcendental* theory right, Hegel now moves on to discuss his failure to grasp the identity of self (the concept) and nature (the empirical particulars). The "rational identity" which Kant has uncovered in his theory of the synthetic *a priori* judgment, is the "substance" of the world just as much as it is the "necessity" of the judgment. *This* identity Kant did not recognize. Or more precisely, he had an inkling of it in his doctrine of the use of the "Ideas" as *regulative* principles of teleological judgment. But this "regulative" use only preserves the "identity," the rationality of the *transcendental* science. Kant's "thing-in-itself" on the side of nature is the "composite" king in Goethe's allegorical presentation of the different philosophies of Nature, *Das Märchen*.[35]

Kant's deliberate restriction of perspective to the "transcendental" side springs from his initial commitment to the psychological standpoint of Locke, the standpoint of "reflective subjectivity." In his distinction of the "secondary" from the "primary" qualities of bodies, Locke had advanced to the recognition of the "productive imagination." By regarding "secondary" qualities as "subjective," Locke "transfers perceiving . . . into the subject" (78). Kant developed this fundamental insight into a *complete* theory of subjectivity. But he ignored the fact that he was accepting human finitude as if it were an absolute unconditioned reality. The upshot of the Critical Philosophy is that we *know absolutely* (rationally) that our experience is phenomenal, etc. This absolute knowledge of finitude has its "infinite" side. But Kant prefers not to pursue his occasional intimations of that. His "formal idealism" rests on an *uncritical* dualism. The *Ding-an-sich* is Locke's substantial "something I know not what."

We might object here that it is unfair to charge Kant with retaining an uncritical, dogmatic, conception of the *Ding-an-sich*. He consistently maintains that its status is *problematic*. Thus, for example, it cannot be numbered either as a singular falling together lump or as a falling apart many. We cannot ask *how many* there are, or whether there is *more than one type*. Hegel generally recognizes and admits this. The Kant of the first Critique is, in his view, a consistent *sceptic* because of his strictly *problematic* conception of the *Ding-an-sich*. But in *Faith and Knowledge* Hegel is concerned ultimately with the "rational faith" for which Kant explicitly claims to have "made room." This faith does make an *absolute* out of finite human individuality, for the law of duty is laid upon *me*, the hope of immortality is mine, and I am an *autonomous member* of the Kingdom of Ends —a Kingdom which is "beyond" the order of Nature that has the *Ding-an-sich* so problematically *behind* it. In Kant's philosophy as a whole the "In-itself of Reason" *does* get distinguished from the "In-itself of things" precisely because it proves to be capable of this practical development. But this distinction of the two sides (the practical faith and the theoretical problem) violates or is false to Kant's original comprehension of experience as an *a priori* synthesis.

Thus Kant's theory of the synthesis of imagination is a truer expression of his speculative genius, than the "deduction of the categories." The "deduction of the categories" was the speculative *completion* of his transcendental science, as we have seen. But he only *half* grasped the significance of the "deduction" because he did not grasp the true import of his "necessary Idea" of an "intuitive intellect" at all.

Of course, if all "universals" are conceived *reflectively* as possibilities or ranges of possibility for experience and existence, their function can only be regulative. Thus, within his own perspective, Kant is quite consistent and correct in regarding the Ideas in this way. The trouble is that, within that perspective, the autonomous development of *practical* Reason cannot be justified. In his practical philosophy, the pure Reason which, *qua* theoretical, is condemned as "dialetictical" and allowed only to "regulate" our phenomenal experience, is permitted to *constitute* the noumenal realm. The "pure form" of the "transcendental unity of apperception" becomes a "rational being" which imposes the law of duty upon itself, etc. This is inconsistent with Kant's critique of the "paralogisms," just as the postulate of immortality and the "infinite progress" violates his theoretical solution of the "mathematical antinomies." But the way to this "practical faith" *is* opened by his theoretical solution of the "dynamic antinomies." Here he momentarily abandons his sceptical stance, and at least *suggests* the dogmatic acceptance of two distinct worlds, the phenomenal and the noumenal, the realm of necessity and the realm of freedom. Hegel admits that in the first *Critique* Kant only asserts his solution of the antinomies in a properly "critical" fashion. But he claims that in his attack on the Ontological Argument Kant emerges as a dogmatic dualist. I confess that I cannot see why he says this. The reflective separation of thought and being is evident enough in Kant's argument; but this only gives rise to "dualism" when we have admitted that Reason is an "In-itself." Now, even if it be true that the first *Critique* shows this, Kant certainly did not recognize it. So he is, at most, an *unconscious* dogmatist.

Hegel deliberately postpones discussion of Kant's practical philosophy, because it is in Fichte that we shall see "rational faith" developed systematically. For this reason, he can pass straight to the *Critique of Judgment* and preserve his consistent image of Kant as a purely "critical" (i.e., sceptical) thinker. The polemical imputation of dogmatism is a distortion of this image, called forth by Kant's critique of the Ontological Argument, because of Hegel's emotional overreaction against Kant's failure of historical comprehension with respect to the great tradition of speculative rationalism. Kant overthrows Mendelssohn; and he thinks that, in doing so, he has overthrown Spinoza.

The two sections of the *Critique of Judgment*, aesthetic judgment and teleological judgment, deal with "beauty as conscious intuition" and "beauty as non-conscious intuition" (86). This characterization of Kant's theory of organism is very puzzling, because it is not at all evident what a "non-conscious intuition" can be. But if we remember the "non-conscious rational" in the synthetic *a priori* judgment earlier, we have the clue that we need. Just as "the rational" was the *necessary, a priori* element in sense-experience, os the "beauty" of it is the aspect of *freedom* in it. An organism is a self-determining, self-maintaining individual entity. Thus to perceive something as an organism, is to make "unconscious" use of the category of freedom, to "imagine" or be sensibly aware of a *practical* concept "immersed" in intuition. But this practical concept is one which, according to Kant's theory, cannot be "immersed" in intuition as "color" or "causality" is, because no "demonstration" of it in intuition could possibly be adequate. Hence Kant regards the *conscious* intuition of beauty as non-cognitive; and he restricts the employment of "free" organic categories in our cognitive science to their use as "regulative maxims." Actually the conceptual *exposition* of the "Idea of Reason" in the Transcendental Dialectic has its intuitive *demonstration* in our aesthetic experience. This is Hegel's version of Schelling's dictum that "Art is the organon of philosophy." The best illustratioin of what he means by it is his claim in the *System of Ethical Life*, that the "intuition" of "ethical life" is "das Volk."[36] Unfortunately it is very difficult to unpack the "speculative" meaning of that claim. But, at least, the relation between Athens and Athena provides a simple illustration of the function of art as an intuitive expression of the "absolute indifference point" in religious experience. We shall return to the problem of "speculative demonstration" later.[37]

Of course, this "intuition" is not finite; that is why an adequate exposition of it is so difficult. But this *exposition* is the task of speculative Reason, not of the intellect as it is (correctly) delimited by Kant. We have the "intuition" before us in objective form in the living organism. But the natural organism is not conscious of itself; and for an intellect which *is* conscious of itself, but only as finite, the necessary ground of explanation for the unconscious system of organic nature can only be *another problematic* noumenal entity, the "intuitive intellect" of the Creator. This Idea is therefore subjectively necessary for us, we can only unify and organize our science of nature, living and non-living, by regarding nature as a whole *as if* it were the creation of such an intellect. But, of course, we cannot dogmatically assert that any such intellect exists. Here, at least, Kant is right in his restraint, for the intuitive intellect does not *need* to be postulated; it only needs to be *discovered*, raised to consciousness in his own doctrine of the productive imagination. By returning to this, he could have found the clue through which he could have comprehended Nature and Intelligence as an *organic* whole, thus escaping from the mechanical determinism which was all that he could recognize in Spinoza.

"Kant himself recognized in the beautiful an intuition other than the sensuous" (91). This is an acknowledgement that in their abiding concern about *art*, the Identity philosophers were following a clue provided by Kant. Their "speculative" theory was intended as the completion of Kant's critical theory. Behind Hegel's brusque condemnation of Kant for not doing what Schelling and he have done, there lies a clear consciousness that Kant provided the foundations for what they have done.

In sum, then, Kant's philosophy is a "formal" theory, i.e., it is the theory of Reason as an empty concept, whether we "run along the thread of identity" (the necessary *a priori* synthesis in the *Critique of Pure Reason*) or the "thread of causality" (the free causality of the rational being in the *Critique of Practical Reason*). The "pure concept" A needs to be complemented by the "sensible manifold" B, in either case. This manifold which supplies the "matter" of experience remains an absolute mystery. The "copying of Reason by the intellect brings forth only a formal identity"[38] in Kant's great critical system, just as it does in the work of the epigones Reinhold and Bardili.[39] But unlike these lesser thinkers, Kant did begin from the very "point of union" between form and content, concept and manifold. His theory of the original synthesis of the manifold contained the "middle term" that he needed; Reason itself was here "immersed" and hence unrecognized.

Because he did not recognize it, Kant had to replace Reason by "practical faith" in a "noumenal world." The unity of thought and being became an *ideal*, a *Sollen*. Although the *systematic* development of this solution was Fichte's contribution, Hegel ends his reconstructive account of Kant's philosophy very properly with a brief summary of Kant's theory of the *summum bonum*. Even here, as he emphasizes, Kant remains tentative. His "practical faith" is not proposed as the ultimate ground and explanation for the very existence of finite consciousness—as it is by Fichte—but as a *regulative* use of the "Ideas of Reason" like the employment of the concept of organism in the life sciences. Just what this "subjective" *faith* amounts to, remains unclear. But the objectivity of the *law* of Reason admits no doubt at all. This is the "formal" (i.e., empty universal) aspect of speculative Reason, the infinity which is *opposed* to the finite. We shall see in the theory of Fichte, how disastrous the consequences of this reflective opposition between the infinite "concept" and the finite "intuition" are.

## 4. JACOBI

The discussion of Jacobi forms the longest section of *Faith and Knowledge* and the one that has the smallest positive content. Many pages are here devoted to the ironic exposure of "unphilosophy." Here Hegel deploys a sarcastic wit and a polemic gift which become in the end repellent because they are so unrelieved by that appreciation of positive achievement which he had himself declared to be the first essential of genuinely philosophical criticism. Yet Hegel *did* appreciate Jacobi's positive contribution. He always continued to allot to Jacobi a place of prominence in the development of the speculative viewpoint, a prominence which Jacobi has not managed to retain in the general history of philosophy. In the introduction to the *Encyclopædia Logic* (an introduction which remaps much of the ground first traversed in *Faith and Knowledge*) Hegel repeats his critical appreciation of Jacobi without the interminable polemic.[40] We shall endeavour to do the same here, and further to explicate, as far as possible, the occurrence of the interludes concerning Herder and Schleiermacher in this section of the essay.

Jacobi accepts the basic position that "all our knowledge is derived from experience"; and the further view that all our so-called "science" is a rational construction based on the comparing and relating of sense impressions. With respect to all this "finite" knowledge he was in essence a disciple of Hume, a radical empiricist of a distinctly pre-Critical type. But his account of the "immediate" knowledge from which the comparing and relating activity of empirical reflection begins, though it was inspired by his study of Hume, was quite distinctive. He regarded all "immediate" knowledge as a direct "revelation" of being. The mark of this "revelation" was an unshakeable *faith*, a feeling of immediate certainty, an inescapable conviction of real existence.[41]

According to Jacobi, we should therefore turn away from all the constructions of abstract argument, which can never be more convincing, or even as convincing, as their intuitive foundations. It is these foundations that we must seek out. Now, among the certainties of faith, some "rational" principles are found, notably the "laws of thought" and the principle that "the whole is prior to the part." This latter axiom is fundamental to "speculation" as the Identity philosophers understood it, and the importance that Jacobi gave to it is one of the main reasons for Hegel's continued interest in him. Jacobi derived our *a priori* certainty of causal necessity in experience, from this deeper certainty of the "ground."

Jacobi's conception of immediate sense-experience as *revelation* abolishes the barrier between "appearance" and "reality," or between phenomena and things-in-themselves, without any formalities of argument and discussion. But the "things" that are thus "revealed" are "in-themselves" finite and transient; and no use of the "principle of sufficient reason" can enable us to *reach* the infinite unconditioned whole by linking these conditioned, finite things in causal chains. Here in its simplest "dogmatic" form we can recognize the criticism which the Identity philosophers raised against the "copying of Reason by the intellect."

Thus Jacobi asserts that faith has cognitive value and that it is, indeed, the *only* source of true cognition. In this way he forms the bridge between Kant's appeal to a non-cognitive faith at the limit of knowledge, and Fichte's firm declaration that practical faith is not the limit but the ground of knowledge. But because of his pre-Critical dogmatism, Jacobi himself cannot find any path from finite cognition to the cognition of the absolute or unconditioned reality, like the one that practical "postulation" opened up for Fichte. Hegel's critique consists essentially in the direct *exposure* of the pre-Critical character of Jacobi's thought.

Thus Hegel's discussion continues almost all the time to be as much concerned with Kant as it is with Jacobi. But Jacobi had also been the great critic of Spinoza from the standpoint of finite reflection. So it was inevitable that Hegel should devote some attention to this aspect of Jacobi's philosophical work. Indeed, the hints that Hegel gives in this connection, about his own interpretation of Spinoza, and so about the character of his own debt to Spinoza are among the most valuable precipitates of the whole Jacobi section.

Jacobi believes that Spinoza had to move illicitly from an infinite causal sequence in time to an infinite eternal relation of whole and parts (this is the transition from an "empirical" to a "logical" use of the principle of sufficient reason which is never possible in human cognition). The crux of the Spinoza discussion, therefore, concerns the place of time in Spinoza's system. Hegel scornfully rejects Jacobi's claim that the "infinite finitude" of a temporal sequence of causes is present in Spinoza's system (except at the level of *imagination*). But Jacobi's problem about the relation of temporal sequence to eternity remained one of the most important growing points of Hegel's own speculation. Time is, after all, the "form of inner intuition." Hence it is necesssary that it *should* be conceived as a "true infinite" and not just as the "bad infinite" of imagination. If that was the only concept of time that Spinoza had, then Spinoza *was* deficient, even if not in the way that Jacobi claimed. For the moment, however, it is Hegel's defence of Spinoza's system that is important. According to Hegel, Spinoza grasped the true or speculative concept of the infinite, as the identity of thought and being, or of the abstract infinite and the finite. The "pure Reason" of Kant is only the abstract infinite, the empty form of thought (the infinity of *"possible* experience") which is just one of the opposed terms of this identity. This "nothing" of the empty concept, is thought as negative. Both of these infinites—the "full" infinite of speculation, and the "empty" infinite of "pure Reason"—are to be distinguished from the empirical infinity of an infinite *series* (the "infinite finitude" which is the only form of infinity that Jacobi can conceive). This last is what Hegel later calls the "bad" infinite.

Jacobi himself can only admit immediate intuitions, not rational expositions, of the true infinite. Thus speculative Reason is reduced in his work to flashes of insight. With respect to "absolute knowledge" he is in the position of a "common sense" philosopher. Every attempt that he makes to explicate his momentary "intuitions" contradicts what is asserted in the intuition itself. Thus he claims to intuit human nature *undivided*, but he tells us that what he intuits is a fundamental division between the finite (sensible, cognitive) aspect and the infinite (rational, intuitive) aspect of man's nature. This "identity of opposites" is just what the Identity Philosophy seeks to expound rationally. Thus although Hegel pokes a lot of very sarcastic fun at Jacobi's "flashes of insight," we should not overlook the essential soundness of some of the most important ones—for instance, "Unity is therefore both beginning and end of this eternal circle and is called—*individuality, organism, object-subjectivity*" (117)

At the opposite pole from Jacobi, as far as the interpretation of Spinoza was concerned, stood Herder, who ascribed to that severe rationalist a romantic sense of life that is quite alien to Spinoza's text. Jacobi called Herder's *God* "Spinozistic froth"; and this harsh verdict seems to me better grounded than Hegel's own attempt to "unify opposites" by portraying Herder's work as a "slight modification" of Jacobi's intuitivism. The "intuitive" character of Herder's method of presentation is undeniable. But even though Herder does leap from "insight" to "insight," leaving the reader to do a lot of the arguing for himself, there is no mistaking his *systematic* urge, or the argumentatively connected character of his thought. According to Hegel himself Herder "puts a reflective concept in the place of rational thought" (118). This seems to me to be very *different* from "veiling the rational" in "the expression of feeling, subjectivity of instinct, etc.," as Jacobi does. So the little interlude about Herder must, I think, be adjudged a superfluous excrescence upon the outer surface of Hegel's argument.[42]

Hegel was, no doubt, led to include it because Herder had published a second edition of *God* in 1800; and during 1801 Hegel promised to review it for the *Erlanger Literatur-Zeitung*. He had still not finished the review at the end of March 1802 (because he needed his copy of the first edition for comparison). He certainly did finish it, for Rosenkranz saw the manuscript after Hegel's death.[43] But for some reason—perhaps because it was so late—the review was never published; and it is now lost. It must, however, have been fresh in Hegel's mind, when he wrote *Faith and Knowledge*; and Herder's *God* was more nearly current than most of the literature surveyed in the essay. The Spinoza connection made it marginally relevant, and this tempted Hegel to exaggerate the stylistic affinity between Jacobi and Herder into a deeper affinity which does not really exist.[44]

After this not very relevant interlude comes something obviously relevant, yet far easier to dispense with than the critique of Herder: a long polemic discussion of Jacobi's essay on Kant. Hegel mentioned in the "announcement" of *Faith and Knowledge* that he would deal with Jacobi's "characteristic polemic against Spinoza and also with that against Kant (Reinhold's *Contributions*, no. 3)."[45] The article in the *Contributions*, together with the article in the *Pocketbook for 1802*, edited by Jacobi's brother, is the most completely current literature that is touched on in the essay. But they do not merit critical notice on the scale that Hegel accords to them; and no articles of this type could deserve to be savaged at such length. Hegel has already said everything important that needed saying about Jacobi's interpretation of Kant in side references before he begins his formal critique. Except for the evidence it supplies of Hegel's positive commitment to the Critical Philosophy—which one might sometimes lose sight of when he is talking directly about Kant—there is little to interest us in this diatribe. Fortunately there is not much here that will cause difficulty either. Hegel's own exposition of Kant will be found much easier to follow here than his systematic reconstruction of Kant's position in the previous section; for Jacobi had at least the merit of buttressing his misunderstandings with copious references, so that Hegel's task was reduced to the quotation and explication of definite texts.

Unluckily, Jacobi was prevented by ill health from completing the Kant essay himself. He handed it over half-finished, with a mass of notes for the continuation, to his enthusiastic follower Friedrich Koeppen. Koeppen was a young man—five years younger than Hegel—and, like Hegel, he was a candidate for an academic career. For him, Hegel has nothing but contempt, tinged perhaps with an envious fear that he may get his foot on the ladder first,[46] and with an angry consciousness that many people classed Koeppen and himself together as the servile dependents of more original minds.[47] So his irony at Koeppen's expense overflows without any conscientious checks or scruples.

The *Pocketbook*—which Hegel delights to call by its earlier title *Superfluous Pocketbook*—was intended for a popular audience. So we might expect that the philosophical articles in it would indeed be superfluous. But behind Hegel's sarcasm here, we can catch a glimpse of the ultimate "ground" of Jacobi's intuitive philosophy. The most fundamental "revelation" of immediate feeling is the direct awareness of God. This is the revelation of *Reason* in us—though it is a Reason which *cannot* become discursive, because all discursive consciousness belongs to the sphere of the intellect. Hegel criticizes this immediate consciousness of God formally at some length in the Introduction to the *Logic*. In *Faith and Knowledge* he simply ridicules it, but there is a certain embarrassment about the ridicule, because Jacobi's intuition of God is also the "intellectual intuition" of the Identity Philosophy. What Hegel objects to is Jacobi's claim that the intuition *cannot* be expressed without being turned into a "universality cut off from the particular" (136). By reducing *all* intuitive knowledge to faith, Jacobi muddies everything together and obscures the essential task of speculation, which is precisely to build a bridge between intellectual and empirical intuition. For Jacobi all the efforts of critical Reason to distinguish the different *forms* of certainty—by insisting, for example, that empirical intuition is objective but phenomenal, while practical faith, though noumenal is "subjective" and not properly cognitive—is a tissue of sophistries that seeks to deprive us in one way of the real world, and in another way of our real contact with God. To Jacobi, all this is quite simply intolerable; the remedy for it is to clarify our awareness of what really is for us immediate and undubitable, and then to keep this intuitive certainty unsullied by intellectual elaborations. But this means that Jacobi's faith in the Absolute, when it is purified and set beside the intuitive certainty of our own finitude, is the conscious awareness of our own impotence. The *undivided* humanity, that Jacobi boasts of comprehending, is a hopeless *yearning* to know or to have what it cannot, to be what it is not. The unreflective faith of the old time might suffer from a sense of being cut off from God by sin; but it had the hope and the promise of redemption. Jacobi's *rational* man is cut off from God by metaphysics, by Reason itself, in virtue of that very finiteness of experience which Jacobi obstinately refuses to surrender to the hell-fire of the Critical Philosophy.

This is a topic to which Hegel will return in his final note on Schleiermacher. But before he can come to that he has to deal briefly with Jacobi's ethics. Jacobi's ethics, again, can only be comprehended through the contrast with Kant. Hegel is therefore obliged to anticipate some of the points that belong properly to the Fichte section. In Kantian ethics, reason and feeling, law and impulse are rent apart and set in opposition to one another. Jacobi rebels against this reflective opposition, and against the moral tyranny of the Categorical Imperative. His is the ethics of noble feeling, which can dignify even an act that is formally immoral such as lying, or a violation of the sacred, like the Sabbath-breaking of Jesus. Hegel had himself rebelled in the same way in earlier years.[48] But Hegel was always conscious of the excesses of the beautiful soul,[49] and from the moment that he comprehended Schelling's breakthrough to the speculative standpoint, his attitude towards all ethics of feeling and "the heart" became predominantly negative. "Beauty" *is* an ethical standard, but ethical beauty is an "Idea," i.e., it consciously contains the law of Reason, the pure concept. It is not the sort of intuitive "particular" experience that can be reflectively opposed to the command of duty. Jacobi simply overlooks the objective aspect of ethical beauty in his examples, or worse still, he downgrades it into something accidental—for instance he has no real understanding of what "Sparta" means for Spertias and Bulis (145–6). In Hegel's view the purely subjective consciousness of the beautiful soul is the speculative equivalent of religious damnation. Thus there is "original sin" in Jacobi's immediate feeling, corruption where he least suspects it. Man is already out of Eden, and any sense of contentment with himself that he may feel is sinful. Thus "Jacobi's principle tarnishes the beauty of individuality . . . through reflection on personality" (148–9).

"Jacobi's principle" also tarnishes the "beauty of individuality" (the ethical *Idea*) in other more theoretical ways. His reduction of all "intuitions" to the same level, effectively abolishes the Protestant opposition between the things of this world and the things of God. But it does so without opening any way by which the things of this world can be made holy. Since—as we saw in his critique of Spinoza —Jacobi does not admit the possibility of viewing Nature as a whole *sub specie æternitatis*, there cannot be any Jacobian intuition of Nature as "universe." Any "reconciliation" of the finite spirit with God must therefore be of the old eudæmonist "reward" type. But the "Protestant principle" itself is capable of something higher than this.

In the midst of this discussion of Jacobi's religion, Hegel suddenly feels it incumbent upon him to explain why he chose Jacobi to represent the religious consciousness of Protestantism generally. This is because he is about to go on to show that the "Protestant principle" has achieved its highest expression in the thought of Schleiermacher. The reason why Jacobi is, nevertheless, the most appropriate spokesman for the "Protestant principle" is that Jacobi has given the most *comprehensive* exposition of the principle: "the same emphasis is also evident in other philosophical efforts, but in some it is more feeble and in others less ambitious" (148). Schleiermacher is less ambitious because he has offered no critique of finite Reason. But then, of course, Schleiermacher's expression of the "Protestant principle" is *higher* largely because he is a genuinely post-Critical thinker, and could not be guilty of the dogmatism of Jacobi, or of the "common-sense" philosophers (who are, perhaps, Jacobi's "more feeble" brethren?).

Protestantism is essentially a *private* religion (according to Hegel, at least). "It makes communion with God and consciousness of the divine into something inward" (148). But although it "does not admit . . . a consciousness of the divine . . . in which *this* nature and *this* universe are enjoyed in the present," Protestant sensibility can rise to an intuition of "the universe." This it does in Schleiermacher's *Speeches.* Here we find a genuine intuition of nature as an organic whole—an intuition which Hegel calls "infinite love" (150)[50] Just as the Greek artist created an "intuitive" focus for the religious emotion of the community in "the saturating objectivity of a cult" (148) so Schleiermacher's ideal Protestant minister is a "religious artist" who by his "virtuosity" creates a focus in *inward* consciousness for his whole congregation. But this artistic creation must remain inward, in order not to violate the "Protestant principle" of subjectivity. Hence it can only be evanescent at best. Schleiermacher's religious art is "forever without works of art" (151), and it is the bond only of a small group for a brief period. Such a Church as this can hardly rise to the intuition of the universal spirit of Christian tradition, for it is inevitably concerned about the definition of its own *distinctive* (i.e., particular) identity. The contrast with the absolute *universality* of the rational community in Kant and Fichte is quite stark.

## 5. FICHTE

In Fichte's philosophy, as we have several times said, practical faith becomes the explanatory ground of finite cognition. This is made fully explicit in *The Vocation of Man*, where, as Schelling told A. W. Schlegel, "Fichte has expressed his whole universe."[51] Schelling was only repeating the argument of Hegel himself, who said in his announcement that he would take Fichte's exposition in the *Vocation of Man* as the basis for his discussion "because this both unveils the essence of [Fichte's] philosophy most completely for a popular audience, and is also the only one among all his expositions that sets forth his philosophy in its totality as a system."[52] This was slightly disingenuous because *The Vocation of Man* does not set forth the *speculative* philosophy of absolute self-positing, oppositing and their synthesis. In *The Vocation of Man* Fichte's speculative Reason is first given the *mythic* form of a conversation between the author and a "Spirit," and then carried on as an inward but very personal meditation. One can very properly say therefore that Fichte has chosen here to present his views within the confines of "subjective reflection." This was what made the work peculiarly suitable for Hegel's present purpose.

In Kant's philosophy the "absolute identity" makes two appearances, one at the unconscious level of the synthesis of imagination, and one at the level of "subjective" consciousness—as something "conceivable" but not known to be real. The "antithesis" of infinite reality (God) and finite reflective awareness (man) does not become "objective" in Kant, because we are nowhere permitted to affirm God's *existence* categorically. Even "practical faith" is "subjective." In Jacobi, on the other hand, "faith" is the basic mode of all "objective" experience. All the "objectivity" that Kant carefully explains by means of the synthesis and the categories, Jacobi regards as belonging primitively to sensation as such, which is itself an immediate "revelation." This means that, for Jacobi, human consciousness *is* just the *antithesis*, the placing against one another of the two modes of immediate revelation, the empirical revelation of self and the world, and the revelation of Reason or the Absolute. The "yearning" that arises from this "undivided" division must look for solace to a "beyond" which cannot be articulated at all. Fichte provides an articulation for it which depends on the Kantian theory of objectivity. But it is the yearning, the *unsatisfied* consciousness, that is "objectified," i.e., it is admitted to be quite real and quite unsatisfiable. The Ego (of the finite revelation) *ought* to be equal to the Ego (of the infinite one). This *ought* is the end of the matter conceptually, and the *existence of the ought* is the endlessness of an *infinite progress.*

The conceptual side is a grasping of the "pure" infinite, the infinite abstracted in thought, and opposed altogether to the finitude of existence. Thus Fichte's "idealism" is *formal* because it is concerned with this abstracted concept (the "absolute" Ego which does not *have* experience but *is the condition* of the experience had by the finite Ego). In the account of finite experience there is an unresolved residue of realism, in the shape of the *Anstoss*, the "impact" in which the self-positing of the Ego encounters its own oppositing of the non-Ego. The "intellectual intuition" of which Fichte speaks is just an immediate awareness of the absolute Ego as "activity." This intuition remains quite distinct from all intuition of the *content* of experience which arises from the "impact" or shock with which that activity meets itself. As far as the "impact" is concerned, the absolute Ego is just the postulated *cause* of it; and the Ego causes the shock *for the sake* of having a sphere for its free causal agency. Thus "the only identity here is the relative identity of the causal nexus."

Kant was confident that his "Copernican revolution" had solved the problem of defining the "limits" of our knowledge as posed by Locke. That we do have knowledge, and that it is finite, was for him (as for Locke) an indubitable fact. But he showed that this indubitability arises from the structure of the mind itself. Thus it appeared that philosophy could afford to forget about the order of the natural world, the order of the reality within which we *come into* being as finite consciousness. Fichte's theory of the absolute Ego merely gives a definitive warrant to philosophy to forget about this, and so turn away from its original and proper task. In the *Difference* essay Hegel presented Fichte's theory as the opening for a *return* to the speculative task by way of Kant's work. But even there he focussed attention on the unsatisfactoriness of the "deduction of nature" as the growing point for future speculation. Here, he treats Fichte as the *culmination* of reflective philosophy, the final *closure* of all possibility of speculation, precisely because of the consistent *formal* character of that same "deduction of nature." Even our own "nature," the immediacy of *feeling* on which Jacobi's rebellion was based, is treated formally by Fichte (i.e., the differentiation of the *content* is regarded as entirely accidental and arbitrary, as having *no* rational significance).

Thus theoretical knowledge has, in Fichte, the two sides of "absolute identity"—the intuition of our own *activity* in sensing, feeling, thinking, etc.—and the endless *difference* of sense-*content*, emotional mood, thought process, etc. "The one self-certifying certainty . . . is that there exists a thinking subject, a Reason affected with finitude." (64) This is now *conceptualized* as "the knowing of all knowledge, pure consciousness . . . [which] shows itself immediately to be the principle of deduction only because it is strictly incomplete and finite." (158).

But this argument from incompleteness presupposes an immediate or intuitive knowledge of what completeness is. This is Jacobi's "principle of sufficient reason"—the principle of the priority of "the whole." Thus Fichte ought to find out where this intuition of perfection comes from, and then make that source into his philosophical foundation. Jacobi *finds* the intuition of perfection everywhere, Fichte *finds* it nowhere. But Jacobi cannot *relate* the absoluteness of being (its perfection) to its transitoriness (or imperfection). Fichte can show the relation, and by doing so, he justifies the *postulation* of the perfection that he cannot *find*. But in showing the relation, Fichte turns Jacobi's *simple* faith in the finite "revelation" of being into a *practical* faith. Our finite experience is shown to be necessary because finite existence is an *infinite progress* toward a moral ideal. This infinite progress is existence *with a minus sign*, it is the perpetual *perishing* of finite being. Jacobi's "empirical revelation" is "finite" and hence transient too, but he takes the sense-world as a revelation of being *while it lasts*, i.e., it is the *endurance* of the finite that reveals to Jacobi the eternal perfection of being. So for Jacobi existence has a *plus sign*.

Fichte has grasped the transience, the perishing, of existence as the *existing concept* of the infinite—"the Nothing." But the concept *needs* to have an empirical content (which is the *plus* that Jacobi hangs on to). So Fichte's theory begins "in the atmosphere [of thought] where the very same thing [empirical content] is encountered, but only negatively and ideally" (160). As soon as Fichte moves from the theoretical sphere to the practical sphere the signs change, for in moral experience it is the content which *does* exist (and so has a *plus*) while the concept (the moral imperative) is for ever striving to exist (and getting a *minus*). This switching of signs according to one's point of view is the only *totality* that Fichte has to offer. This is the way things are bound to be as long as "the one self-certifying certainty . . . is . . . a Reason affected with finitude."

The true starting point is the *actual* infinite. Existence, nature, the infinite moral progress, or the infinite causal sequence, must be recognized as the concept, grasped as a totality that thinks itself. This was "the cube of Spinoza" which neither Jacobi nor Fichte could invert as they claimed to do because (according to Hegel at this stage of his development) it cannot be inverted. He did change his mind about that, but not about the failure of Jacobi and Fichte to do the trick.

The movement from the finite "self-certifying certainty" to "practical faith" is displayed by Fichte in the second book of the *Vocation of Man*. Hegel summarizes the argument straightforwardly, adding only a comment which highlights the reduction of the natural world to a flux of immediate sense-impressions (163). When he resumes the discussion in his own terms he points up the superiority of Kant's *Critique of Judgment* in this respect (164).[53] But this superiority is bought at the expense of the "purity" of Kant's idealism.

Because of the "purity" of Fichte's idealism, the "identity" of "pure" and "empirical" consciousness in Fichte's view is always "relative," i.e., *causal* (whereas Kant does at least formulate the "Idea" of the *substantial* identity of the organism). Form and content, Ego and non-Ego are related in the infinite causal chain on the side of necessity, and in the "infinite progress" of free causality on the side of action. But the *absolute* identity of thought and existence is beyond cognition altogether. Hegel has already criticized the hypothetical, provisory character of Fichte's procedure in the *Science of Knowledge* in the *Difference* essay. The same criticism is repeated briefly in *Faith and Knowledge* (166–7; compare D 123–6). Now, however, the claim is made that Fichte does not really get beyond the position of common sense, which knows that "there is no smoke without fire" or that "murder will out." In passing, Hegel refers to his own view expressed in the *Difference* essay, as the "prejudicial" verdict that Fichte had produced a "speculative" system. He takes the appearance of the *Vocation of Man* as conclusive evidence that that was *not* what Fichte meant to do. Jacobi had given the same "prejudicial" interpretation of Fichte two years earlier (in the *Letter to Fichte*, 1799). This provides the occasion for another brief attack on Jacobi at this point.

Hegel's polemic (167–171) is unfair to all three of them, for Fichte's starting point in the *Science of Knowledge* was not the finite "I" of *The Vocation of Man*. We are bound here to agree with A. W. Schlegel's complaint to Schelling.[54] Hegel ought not to treat the *Vocation of Man* as if it superseded Fichte's *systematic* works. Hegel does, though, rather grudgingly, admit in his lectures on the history of philosophy that the starting point of the *Science of Knowledge* is speculative.[55] I find it impossible to doubt that he recognizes the difference between Fichte and Jacobi all along. He expects us to recognize the exaggeration in his claim that "Fichte's philosophy is in full agreement with Jacobi's" (167). Fichte's philosophy does abstract "the absolute nothing" in a way that Jacobi's does not; so Jacobi has some right to despise Fichte from his point of view. But I see no point in prolonging the discussion of this.

Fichte's "faith" is that the opposite signs will be made coincident, that the law of Reason will finally have the *plus* in mundane experience, that it always has in the heaven of the intellect. Then we shall have "$+ 1 = + 1$" which would express the coincidence of self-positing and opposing, instead of "$+1 - 1 = 0$" which represents the opposition between self positing and opposing on the part of the Ego. For our theoretical consciousness, the absolute Ego is the zero in the middle of this second equation, it is the *nothing* that abides in the transience of the finite. But through the changing of the signs, the transience would become illusory, and what abides at all times would be visibly and tangibly the same "law of Reason." Transience, the nothing, would then become conscious freedom, the absolute something. In practical experience, however, freedom continues to involve the *abolition* of one visible and tangible situation, and the establishment of another. The absolute stability never becomes visible. Heaven is not brought to earth; and the awful thing is that, if it were, there would be nothing left to do. The activity of the Ego, its self-positing, would abolish itself if it achieved perfect self-equivalence. Instead of "$+ 1 = + 1$" we would have "$0 = 0$."[56]

To escape from this impasse we have to see the task of Reason as the establishment of a finite system of stability. We need an account of the moral life as a systematic pattern of coherent virtuous activities. We need an *empirical image* of the Kingdom of Ends, for that is the only form in which "freedom" can be made visible and tangible. In his endeavours to make his ethics into a *systematic* theory of the ideal society, Fichte is thus taking the only way out of the "bad infinity" of his "infinite progress." Unluckily for him the relation between form and content, law and life, is too labile to allow his kind of "system." Fichte would have to approach the "hallowed and strict necessity" of our natural existence in quite a different spirit from that which he actually adopts in order to find a viable answer. This is what Hegel does for the Identity Philosophy in his *System of Ethical Life*.[57]

The third Book of the *Vocation of Man* actually contains an application of the theory of the infinite progress to nature conceived as purposive and organic, even though Fichte, unlike Kant, has not given any justification of this aspect of nature. Here Fichte appears as a kind of latter-day Wolff, deducing the purposes of animate organisms generally from the needs of the rational organism, and forming a picture of the whole earth evolving toward the perfect harmony of the Kingdom of Ends. The assumed purpose of everything in

Wolff's Eudæmonism was human happiness; in Fichte's scheme the end is rational morality. I am not sure that the status of the organic world really is (as Hegel claims) *worse* in Fichte than it was in Wolff —for in the *Vocation of Man* nature does not "fall in ruins" ultimately (177–8)—but it is certainly not in principle different. The Lisbon earthquake and *Candide* stand equally against Wolff's Reason and Fichte's "faith."

When I said that the relation of concept and life was too labile to allow the creation of a *reflective* system of ethics I was anticipating a little. But Hegel's earliest criticisms of Kantian ethics were directed at this point. In those early days he complained that Kant's reinstatement of casuistry in the *Metaphysics of Ethics* was the index of his failure.[58] Here it is taken rather as the index of Kant's good sense. For Kant is now seen as the consistently *critical* thinker who does not transgress the bounds of subjective reflection. It is Fichte now, who is mired in the multiplicity of aspects that any situation has, and the corresponding multiplicity of duties that can be generated from different but equally accurate descriptions of it. (The criticism of Fichte's philosophy of law as a totalitarian dictatorship has already been given at greater length in the *Difference* essay. In *Faith and Knowledge* it is the moral experience of the individual that is the appropriate focus of attention because it is in the "inner heart" that the "Protestant principle" is to be found.)

From the point of view of genuine ethical life the evil of this reflective situation is twofold. In the first place, to the extent that he is reflective, a genuinely ethical individual who *wants* to do his duty is thrown into a state of doubt and anxiety. For insofar as he is sensitively intelligent the moral man will be aware of how many ways of viewing his situation there are, and will recognize the impossibility of giving rationally decisive grounds for choosing among them. In the second place, the hypocrite will be provided with a ready means of justifying whatever he wants to do as done for the "good cause." The naive self-satisfaction of Jacobi's intuitive morality develops in Fichte into these more complex forms of moral evil. The way to escape from this morass of subjective motives and descriptions would be to begin from the ethical "whole" of which the "intuition" is the *Volk*. For then we can know whether an action is *objectively* good or not; though even then the threat of death—the "Nothing" in its unmistakable existential form—is needed to decide whether the agent is "noble" or not.[59]

The "Kingdom of Ends" is the "reality of the Ideal" (186). In the phenomenal world, however, a perfectly moral action may be frustrated of its intended effect; or it may even become the occasion of unhappiness, its overt effects may be bad. Hence the unachievable "Ought" has its true realization in the noumenal realm. The noumenal world becomes a kingdom of immortal but finite spirits. The will of God *is* done in a heaven which is just a projected image of this world as it *ought* to be. This realm of faith is the ultimate triumph of the bad infinite over the speculative Idea. God, the absolute Identity, disappears from view altogether by being thus "splintered" into the "moral order." Hegel seems to agree (though from a point of view far removed from that of "common sense") that Fichte was *properly* accused of atheism. But the proof of this in Hegel's eyes is a "presentation" of Fichte's view that was both meant to be, and was, entirely acceptable to all orthodox religious opinion.

## 6. CONCLUSION: THE SPECULATIVE RELIGION

The *Vocation of Man* completes the transformation of the old "dogmatism of being" (by which Hegel means not the rationalism of Spinoza and Leibniz but that of Wolff and his followers) into the "dogmatism of thinking." The whole process is a cultural one, not properly "speculative" like the rationalism of Spinoza and Leibniz, or even the materialism of D'Holbach. But if we take the manifestations together, eudæmonism from Locke to Wolff on one side, and the philosophy of duty in Kant, Jacobi and Fichte on the other, we can see in the latter the cultural reconciliation of two great spiritual movements, the flight from the world of the Protestant reformers and the acceptance of the world by the enlighteners. Now that the whole movement is complete it can be expressed speculatively by a different kind of "reflection"—one which does not set thought in opposition to existence, or abstract the infinite from the finite.

This philosophical reflection "suspends" all the particular phenomena that have perished to reveal their finiteness, in a thinking that is their own "inwardizing," or the revealing of their *immortal* essence. This is a process of conceptualization *(ein Begriff)* which comprehends *(begreift)* the particulars. Speculative philosophy cannot possibly be "abstract," it cannot be independent of, or indifferent to, particular existence, because it is a special kind of *remembering* (Hegel plays on the German word *Erinnerung*). The infinite that is within the finite, and reveals itself negatively in the perpetual perishing of the finite, reveals itself positively in the resurrection and perpetuation of the finite as a pattern of "inwardized" or "remembered" conceptual significance. Thus "out of this nothing and pure night of infinity, as out of the secret abyss that is its birthplace, the truth lifts itself upward." The Ego is both the "nothing" of present sense-consciousness which is the perpetual perishing of being, and the speculative memory, the thought in which all being is essentially preserved. But it is necessary to become conscious of the "nothing" in abstraction, no longer "immersed" in sensation but opposed to it, before we can properly "comprehend" the All.

And the "nothing" itself, having been abstracted as the "concept" of the infinite substance that abides in all transience, must be actually "intuited"—i.e., it must be lived and experienced as the *negative*, as universal mortality, as death. That is why, although the subtitle of the essay directs us to expect a philosophical treatise, the title itself indicates that the essay is about the relation of philosophy to religion. Religion is, for Hegel in 1802, still the absolute mode of experience, or the mode in which we *consciously* have *experience* of the Absolute. In his introduction Hegel sketches for us the hyper-religious Reformation and the irreligious Enlightenment. The body of the essay shows the reconciliation of the two, and it is the "protestant principle" that predominates throughout, even though Kant with his scrupulous respect for the bounds of finite experience emerges as the true prince of the Enlightenment. Each section of the essay concludes with a discussion of religious experience; and since Fichte's religion is found to be a degeneration back into the "external teleology" of "enlightened" eudæmonism, it is Jacobi (or more accurately Schleiermacher) who emerges as the true voice of the "protestant principle." Speaking of the philosophical connections, Hegel remarks with evident truth, that the link between Jacobi and true speculation is more defective than that between the critical philosophers and speculative thought. Hegel's continual polemic against Jacobi, which even invades the Fichte section, is the testimony of this. But on the *religious* side, i.e., with respect to what it aims to *comprehend*, I hope that my analysis has shown how close the affinity of Jacobi with the Identity Philosophy is.

The comprehensive intuition of the negative infinite, of the Nothing, is the "infinite grief." This is what is imaginatively portrayed in the story of God's "Incarnation and Passion." That God himself should become a man, suffer and die, underlines the absolute necessity and the universal significance of suffering and death. Nothing can be resurrected in the spirit, no finite particular can be "resumed" into the speculative infinite, until it has passed away into a remembering consciousness which values it, and hence mourns for it and grieves over it.

In Greece before the philosophers came, there was a religion of nature, which knew nothing of this grief for the things of the spirit.[60] Their artist portrayed for them an eternally beautiful, eternally enduring image of life as a *natural* cycle. With the advent of philosophy as the quest for human self-knowledge, this world view fell before the might of the One God who became a man and died. This is the experience that was conceptually "abstracted" by the cultural movement from the Reformation to Fichte; and it is now time for this "abstraction" to be speculatively comprehended. It must be *intuited*, it must be a lived experience, part of the *living history* of the remembering consciousness. The function of art is to make the living intuition of it possible.

Schleiermacher, who understood this, was still obsessed by the need to fly from the world. Hegel said in the *Difference* essay, that Art was the comprehension of the "point of indifference" from the non-conscious side (D 171–2). In *Faith and Knowledge* this becomes "the Idea of Reason [has] its demonstration in beauty"—demonstration being "the presentation of a concept in intuition" (86–7). The *real* contrast betwen "nature" and "spirit" is now replaced by the *ideal* contrast between "intuition" (existence) and "concept" (thinking). "Intuition" can be an inward experience—for how else could it be "intellectual"? Schleiermacher has an inward "intuition" of the "Universe." But this inward experience is inadequate because an intuition of this sort cannot be truly communal. Thus there must be a "presentation of the concept in *outward* intuition," through a religious art that is *public*.

We cannot say much more than this about the æsthetic aspect of Hegel's "absolute religion." In his lectures he laid out the historical experience that is to be "speculatively resumed" in it, and it appears from the summary we have that he found the æsthetic reconciliation of the "infinite grief" in the Catholic tradition.[61] But from a quotation, preserved by Haym we know that something more "political" than the art and literature of "Catholic Christendom" was wanted for the new speculative religion:

> This idealistic sphere forms an adventurous realm without rules;
> it has tumbled together at random from the histories and the
> imagination of all peoples and climates, without significance
> or truth for nature which is placed in subjection to it, and
> equally without allowing that the spirit of the individuals of a
> people can maintain their right within it; it is without person-
> alized (*eigentümlich*) imagination, as it is without personalized
> consecration.[62]

About the task of "reconstruction" on the speculative side, Hegel
does tell us something in *Faith and Knowledge*. The reconstruction
must first "expound how nature reflects itself in the free spirit. Nature takes itself back into itself and lifts its original unborrowed real
beauty, into the ideal realm, the realm of possibility" (182). This is
the *theological* aspect of natural philosophy. Nothing is said now
about there being an exact parallelism between nature and spirit (a
point which was firmly insisted on in the *Difference* essay). Of
course, the parallelism may still be there, but it looks rather as if the
developmental exigency has triumphed over the mirror-image one.
The "original, unborrowed, real beauty" of nature is the *internal*
teleology of the living organism. The association of the terms ("beauty" and "teleology") comes from the *Critique of Judgment*.

"Thus nature rises as spirit. This is the moment which—when the
identity as the original fount, is compared with the totality—appears
through the comparison alone as movement and disintegration of the
identity and as its reconstruction." This moment of comparison between the "indifference point as unity" and the "indifference point
as totality" is the religious experience of "infinite grief" and the
philosophical discovery of thought, the concept, as the "absolute
nothing." The apex of natural philosophy is the rational organism
that is aware of its own mortality, and the mortality of all life. But
the totality which thus dissolves itself is reconstituted in philosophical memory.

Now we come to the level of communal life. For the reconstruction
must show "how . . . spirit has enjoyment of itself as a living Ideal
in visible and active reality." This is what Hegel attempts to demonstrate in the *System of Ethical Life*. That work, like his description
of the "reconstruction" here, breaks off before the level of religious
experience is properly reached. Hegel is content, at this point, to describe the two forms of the "real spirit," unconscious and conscious,

which are finally "resumed" into the Idea through religious experience.[63]

But he has spoken of religion just a little earlier:

> Religion offers a possible reconciliation with nature viewed as finite and particular. The original possibility of this reconciliation lies in the original image of God on the subjective side; its actuality, the objective side, lies in God's eternal Incarnation in man, and the identity of the possibility with the actuality through the spirit is the union of the subjective side with God made man (181).

Now, it is true that this is a statement of the orthodox faith of Christianity as against Fichte's heresies. It still needs speculative interpretation. But the interpretation is not hard to supply. "The image of God on the subjective side" is the "pure Reason" that Kant has so exactly mapped on *its* subjective side. "Nature viewed as finite" includes both the unconscious and the conscious world of "real spirit" —this is evident from the way the Incarnation dogma is employed. We know that at some stage during the Jena period Hegel definitely regarded the whole of nature as the "incarnation of the Logos."[64] But we do not need to import this rather heretical doctrine here, since man is the "indifference point as totality" for natural philosophy as such.[65] Hence the reconciliation of God with a particular man *is* reconciliation of God with nature as "finite and particular." In the peculiar perspective of *Faith and Knowledge,* the *whole* of nature, spread out in space would not *be* "finite and particular." It would be the "*concept* immersed in intuition." Whereas man who as a subject is "the image of God," is objectively "nature as finite and particular." This "particular," mortal, organism is "the original fount" of Reason which Fichte did not recognize (181). Thus full human self-knowledge and self-comprehension would be "the union of the subjective side with God made man."

What Hegel objected to in the traditional religion was the fact that "consecration" and "grace" were thought of as coming from a divine source that was alien and transcendent. The existence of man in the world is a "speculative" Good Friday. That is the "infinite grief." The "speculative" Easter must come from man's own triumph in the effort to "know himself." Rosenkranz reports Hegel's hope thus:

Once the alien consecration has been withdrawn from Protestantism, the spirit can venture to hallow itself as spirit in its own shape, and reestablish the original reconciliation with itself in a *new religion,* in which the infinite grief and the whole burden of its antithesis is taken up. But it will be resolved purely and without trouble, when there is a *free people* and Reason has found once more its reality as an *ethical* spirit, a spirit which is bold enough to *assume its religious shape on its own soil and in its own majesty.* Every single man is a blind link in the chain of absolute necessity, on which the world develops. Every single man can extend his dominion over a greater length of this chain only if he recognizes the direction in which the great necessity will go, and learns from this cognition to utter the magic word that conjures up its shape. This cognition, which can both embrace in itself the whole energy of the suffering and the antithesis that has ruled the world and all the forms of its development for a couple of thousand years, and can raise itself above it all, this cognition only philosophy can give.[66]

*H. S. Harris*

1. The issues of the *Critical Journal* varied in size. Subscriptions were for the volume (three issues). Two volumes a year were promised. Only two volumes were in fact published over a period of about eighteen months (December 1801–May 1803). The *Glauben und Wissen* issue contained 192 pages. The next longest was the first issue with 158. The final issue was also the shortest, with only 64 pages.

2. Jacobi wrote to Reinhold on 10 August 1802: "Because of the bad style I am certain that he [Hegel] and not Schelling has been the pen-pusher here" (Nicolin, report 65). We know from Hegel's *curriculum vitae* of 1804 (see the next note) that Jacobi's hypothesis was correct.

3. This is how he designates it in the *curriculum vitae* of 1804 which includes a list of his contributions to

the *Critical Journal.* See *N.K.A.* IV, 541 or *Briefe* IV, 92.

4. Letter 459, 2 December 1800 (Schulz II, 302).

5. See Schelling to A. W. Schlegel, 6 July 1800 (Fuhrmans I, 197).

6. Letter 439, 18 August 1800 (Schulz, 11, 255). What happened to any part of the critical survey that Schelling had already "worked out" it is difficult to say. Reinhold is "taken to pieces" in his dialogue "On the Absolute Identity-System" in the first issue of the *Critical Journal.* But the occasion for that was an article in the third issue of the *Beiträge* which did not appear until September 1801.

7. We cannot say exactly when this was. Schelling was still hoping to collaborate with Fichte at the end of May 1801 (Letter 475, 24 May 1801, Schulz II, 321–2) and may have gone

on hoping till he received Fichte's long delayed reply in August (ibid., Letter 476).

8. We cannot suppose that Schelling actually contributed to this (though he may very likely have suggested it). For he confessed to Fichte in May that he had *never* read Bardili's philosophical work and had read Reinhold "only cursorily" (Schulz II, 321). (Fichte himself "took Bardili to pieces" in the *Erlanger Literatur Zeitung* in 1800.)

9. Hegel claimed the "Introduction" as his in the *curriculum vitae* of 1804. In 1838 Schelling wrote that "many passages, which at this moment I could not precisely identify, are mine, along with the main ideas; there is probably no passage that I did not at least revise" (cited in *N.K.A.* IV, 542).

10. Hence the showing up of Reinhold's conception of the history of philosophy as "unphilosophical" at the beginning of the *Difference* essay is balanced in the last pages of the same essay by an attempt to estimate the positive significance of his (and Bardili's) "reduction of philosophy to logic." (I have indicated in my introduction to the *Difference* essay that I do not believe Hegel's effort is successful, but his object is clear enough.)

11. *N.K.A.* IV, 120.

12. The first hint of this recognition is at the very end, in Hegel's final disposition of Reinhold and Bardili's "reduction of philosophy to logic": "The *founding-program* aims to reduce philosophy to logic. In it *one side of the universal need of philosophy appears* and fixes itself; and as an appearance it must take its necessary, definite, and objective place, in the manifold of cultural tendencies which are connected with philosophy, but which assume a rigid shape before they arrive at philosophy itself. At

every point on the line of its development, which it produces until it reaches its own completion and perfection, the Absolute must curb itself and organize itself into a pattern; and it appears as self-forming in this manifold" (D 192).

13. See the discussion in the introduction to the *Difference* essay, pp. 7–9, 33–37.

14. Jacobi to Bouterwek, 22 March 1802 (Nicolin, report 58).

15. In 1803 he published: *Schelling's Doctrine, or the whole philosophy of the absolute Nothing*. So he took his revenge on Hegel as Schelling's "assistant."

16. Schlegel's letter is lost, but see Schelling's reply, 19 August 1802. Schelling dissented from this complaint saying "In the first place he has at least shown that from a philosophical point of view it is really of no account; in the second place it deserves this critique . . . because as yet Fichte has only expressed his whole universe in this book" (Fuhrmans II, 421). For a partial justification of Schlegel's view—in spite of what is argued here—see p. 36 below.

17. "Yearning thus reflected in itself could find a higher level than Jacobi expounds . . . Jacobi's principle has in fact attained this highest level in the *Speeches on Religion*" (167–8). The "Announcement" which Hegel wrote for this issue of the *Critical Journal* specifically mentions this discussion of the "higher level (*höhere Potenzirung*) which the Jacobian philosophy has reached in the *Speeches on Religion*" (see *N.K.A.* IV, 505).

18. There may be a glancing reference to the theology of G. C. Storr in Hegel's remark that "a struggle of philosophy against the positive, against miracles and suchlike, is now regarded as obsolete and unenlight-

ened" (1). For he had spent several years of the previous decade in a "struggle against the positive" represented by Storr's theology of prophecies fulfilled and wonders performed. (It was Schelling who first insisted that all that was a waste of time. See *Toward the Sunlight*, pp. 186–7 and *Briefe* I, 14).

19. The opening pages of *Faith and Knowledge* should be compared with the longer analysis of "the Enlightenment" in the *Phenomenology* (Hoffmeister, pp. 383–413; Baillie, pp. 559–98).

20. *Hegel-Studien* IV, 53.

21. Rosenkranz, pp. 190–2.

22. For the Summer Semester of 1802, Hegel's course was advertised as "Logic and Metaphysics, or the System of Reflection" (*Hegel-Studien* IV, 53).

23. "The entire totality of limitations is to be found in [the intellect], but not the Absolute itself. . . . The intellect copies Reason's absolute positing and through the form it gives itself the semblance of Reason" (D 89–90). I suggested in the Introduction there (D 19–20), that the principal reference of the whole discussion at this point is to Kant's characterization of experience as "phenomenal."

24. I take this to be the meaning of the cryptic remark "Only the objectivity of the intellect can attain the concept" (59). Reection can produce the "law of reason," but it cannot show us how to deserve happiness by obeying it.

25. This is an echo of the *Difference* essay, p. 172.

26. Hobbes does "abstract the concept" of the eudaemonist life: for he defines the natural life not as "satisfaction" but as "power": "*a perpetual and restless desire of power after power* [this is life abstracted as concept] that ceaseth only in death"; and

Hobbes puts the intuition of this "ceasing" at the foundation of this theory of *rational* life. Death is always *intuitively* present to the rational man's mind in Hobbes (i.e., not the idea of death generally, but *his own* death): "and the life of man, solitary, poor, nasty, brutish and *short*." The felt imminence of our own death is what brings us to (Hobbesian) Reason. The ceaseless campaign to refute Hobbes and "Hobbism" is the best illustration of what Hegel means by "the concept is not posited in purity."

27. See his open letter "To Fichte," *Werke* III, 29; compare *Difference*, p. 00.

28. We should notice that in *Faith and Knowledge* Hegel does not discuss Kant's practical philosophy independently at all; and he hardly admits that Jacobi *has* a practical philosophy worthy of the name.

29. *Critique of Pure Reason*, A 327, B 383–4.

30. For Kant's own distinction of the "formal" and the "real" use of Reason see *Critique of Pure Reason*, A 299, B 355.

31. Compare Kant: ". . . intolerable to hear the representation of the color, red, called an idea [as it is by Locke]. It ought not even to be called a concept of understanding, a notion" (*Critique of Pure Reason*, A 320, B 377). Looking at this in Hegel's perspective we must say that the productive imagination organizes our visual field into reds, browns, greens, etc.; then we reflect on the "visual field" as a whole and ask what the *abstract* "identity" of it is, and so discover that it is all "colored." But we must remember that the "visual field" was not there as an *unorganized* field to begin with. The *organization* into red, brown, green, etc., is the *genesis* of the field itself as a total "field." The subsequent move from

imagination to intellect is a new mode of being for this *whole*. The "identity which in intuition is totally immersed in the manifold [of red, brown, green, etc.], now simultaneously sets itself against the manifold [as the *concept* of 'color']" (70).

32. I have borrowed the opposition of "intuition" and "concept" from the *System of Ethical Life* (almost contemporaneous with *Faith and Knowledge*) because the peculiar usages are obviously related and I think that they throw light on one another.

33. Knowing from these examples what "the rational" is we can readily see how "the rational is immersed in the judgement" as its "unconscious" side. When we say "the earth is a moving body," or "I am an imaginative power," the "rational identity" is not conscious. In one case we are apt to think we are classifying the earth within the universal category of "bodies"; in the other case we tend rather to the view that we are stating an "accidental" property of the "substantial" self. (Thus the second case also illustrates the thesis that the "speculative relation" is the substance-accident relation [D 116]. In the first case "gravity," which is the "substance," does not "appear" in the judgment at all.)

34. This creates problems for the translation. Thus the opposition between *intellektualisiert* and *realisiert* on page 00 is not simply that of "concept" and existence, but of an *empty concept* and a *filled* or "realized" concept. But the empty concept is the concept that *exists for itself*, it *intuits itself* as intelligence; and the filled or "realized" concept *is intuited* as Nature, the objective *world*.

35. See pp. 76–7, where Hegel's "tenacious memory" has let him down slightly. Hegel earlier suggested that we must think Kant's "manifold" as "falling to pieces'" (74); here he suggests that we must "think" the thing-in-itself as "falling-together." But either way we are illicitly employing one of the categories of "reality." The lesson of his two examples taken together is that we can only "think" the thing-in-itself as an "identity of opposites"—neither a "falling together" unity nor a "falling apart" plurality but a "dialectical" totality.

36. *System der Sittlichkeit*, p. 54.

37. See pp. 39–44 below.

38. See the passage quoted from Rosenkranz on pp. 9–11 above.

39. Compare the analysis of Reinhold's *Versuch* and Bardili's *Grundriss* at the end of the *Difference* essay (D 183–92).

40. *Encyclopaedia*, sections 61–78 (Wallace, pp. 121–42). There is also an interesting essay by Croce, translated in *Philosophy, Poetry, History*, pp. 145–69.

41. The fountain-head of this highly original development of Hume's theory of belief was apparently Hamann. In a letter to Jacobi he wrote: "I was full of Hume when I wrote the Socratic Memorabilia and the following passage of my little book has reference to that:

Our own existence and the existence of all things outside us must be believed, and cannot be determined in any other way. What is more certain than the end of man, and of what truth is there a more general and better attested knowledge? Nevertheless, no one is wise enough to believe it except the one who, as Moses makes clear, is taught by God himself to number his days. What one believes does not, therefore, have to be proved, and a proposition can be ever so incontrovertibly proven without on that account being believed.

There are proofs of truths which are of as little value as the application which can be made of the truths themselves; indeed, one can believe the proof of a proposition without giving approval to the proposition itself. The reasons of a Hume may be ever so cogent, and the refutations of them only assumptions and doubts; thus faith gains and loses equally with the cleverest pettifogger and most honorable attorney. Faith is not the work of reason, and therefore cannot succumb to its attack, because faith arises just as little from reason as tasting and seeing do. (O'Flaherty, pp. 167, 169).

42. Many modern students have emphasized the anti-systematic character of Herder's thought. His insistence on the historical uniqueness of every culture might be appealed to in defense of Hegel's verdict. But I do not think that the subsumption of Herder under "Jacobian philosophy" can be justified by this line of interpretation. If Herder did belong in the same camp as Jacobi, then he was neither "more feeble" nor "less ambitious" than Jacobi (few writers have been more ambitious, except perhaps Hegel himself). So if we take this line we must ask why Hegel did not choose Herder, rather than Jacobi, to represent the antithetic moment of the "reflective philosophy of subjectivity."

Kant's view of Herder is, in this respect, instructive. In his 1785 review of Herder's *Ideen* (Part 1) Kant wrote:

His is not a logical precision in the definition of concepts or careful adherence to principles, but rather a fleeting, sweeping view, an adroitness in unearthing analogies in the wielding of which he shows a bold imagination. This is combined with cleverness in soliciting sympathy for his subject—kept in increasingly hazy remoteness—by means of sentiment and sensation. Further suspicion is stimulated as to whether these emotions are effects of a prodigious system of thought or only equivocal hints which cool critical examination would uncover in them (*Akad.* VII, 45; *On History*, ed. Beck, 27–28).

This verdict—which seems to me fair—brings out very clearly the affinity between Herder and Jacobi; and it may very well be the origin of Hegel's view. But Kant goes on to show how Herder's purpose is to provide an empirical argument for human immortality through his chain of analogies: "The spiritual nature of the human soul, its performance and progress toward perfection, is to be proved by analogy with the natural forms of matter, particularly in their structure, with no recourse to metaphysics" (*Akad.* VII, 52; *On History*, p. 36). Kant criticizes the argument in two ways. In the first place, the "great chain of being"—if it exists—does not imply human immortality, but rather the existence of higher, more spiritual, beings. In the second place, "the unity of organic force . . . is an Idea which lies wholly outside the field of empirical natural science. This Idea of organic force belongs solely to speculative philosophy . . ." (*Akad.* VII, 54; *On History*, p. 38). Unlike Herder, Jacobi understood, and accepted, this last point. It was the basis of his sharp distinction between the causal and the logical employment of the "principle of sufficient reason"; and because he accepted this boundary line of empirical knowledge, Jacobi *is* the proper representative of the reflective philosophy of subjectivity. But no one can properly say that Herder's refusal to accept it, was

merely a "slight modification of Jacobi's manner of doing philosophy."
Hegel cannot have meant that. To give
Hegel's comments on Herder any
plausibility at all, we have to empha-
size the word "manner," and concentrate our attention on the style of
Herder's work (as characterized by
Kant in my first quotation). But when
we do that, we are obliged to recognize that what Hegel says does not
apply to Herder's concept of the *aim
and object* of philosophical speculation, or to his beliefs about its feasi-
bility. Herder, we must conclude, does
not rightly belong within the sphere
of the "reflective philosophy of subjectivity" at all. With all his logical
naiveties he was a *speculative* thinker.

43. Rosenkranz, p. 223; compare
*Briefe* I, 63, 66 (all the relevant testi-
monia are gathered in *N.K.A.* IV,
517).

44. We should add, perhaps, that
Hegel's debt to Herder may well be as
great, or greater than his debt to
Jacobi—though it is very difficult to
document (see *Hegel's Development*,
pp. 271–2 n.) Also that Schelling
(whose first publication—*On Myths*,
1794—was influenced by Herder) was
extremely contemptuous of Herder
from the time of his public adherence
to Fichte's Critical Idealism. Herder,
like Jacobi, had attempted to over-
throw the Critical Philosophy.

45. *N.K.A.* IV, 505.

46. Koeppen gained a professorship
at Landshut in 1807, just when Hegel
had finally been driven to abandon
his professorial aspirations. For
Hegel's comments at that point, see
his letter to Niethammer, 30 May
1807, *Briefe* I, 166.

47. Schleiermacher wrote to K. G.
von Brinkmann, 26 November 1803:
"The slavery [involved in discipleship]
seems to me equally hard on both
sides. Do but look how Schelling is

hung up with Hegel, A. W. Schlegel
with Bernhardi, Jacobi with Koeppen"
(Nicolin, report 53). Friedrich Schlegel
wrote to his brother on 20 March
1804 that he could no longer be bothered to read Hegel—his time was too
valuable (Nicolin, report 83a). Hegel
can hardly have known Schleiermacher's opinion—but since A. W. Schlegel
was in regular correspondence with
Schelling he probably had some notion
6—END notes 8 on 10 Palatino . . . . .
of the Schlegels' feelings. He was
certainly outraged when he was pub-
licly designated as Schelling's "stout
warrior from home" by K. A. Böttinger (see the Introduction to *Difference*,
p. 00).

48. The influence of Jacobi on
Hegel's own ethical reflections at
Berne and Frankfurt is shown by his
borrowing of Jacobi's examples. Compare further *Toward the Sunlight*, pp.
98, 335, 508–9.

49. Compare *Toward the Sunlight*,
pp. 353–5, 381.

50. This usage is no doubt influenced by Spinoza's doctrine of the
"intellectual love of God."

51. Fuhrmans II 421 (compare
further note 16 above).

52. *N.K.A.* IV, 505.

53. Hegel recurs to this theme
several times. See for instance (175–
6), (179), (182).

54. See above, p. 6.

55. See the introduction to the
*Difference* essay, p. 8; and Haldane-
Simson III, 483).

56. Hence "being one with the eternal . . . would have to be the bad"
(182).

57. He gives a hint here of how
speculative ethics is founded on the
Philosophy of Nature in his echo
from Plato's *Timaeus* (180).

58. See "The Spirit of Christianity,"
Nohl, p. 294 (Knox-Kroner, pp. 244–
5); and *Toward the Sunlight*, pp. 336–

41. Compare also Nohl 19–20 (*Toward the Sunlight*, p. 497) where there is, however, no explicit reference to Kant.

59. Hegel makes one or two explicit references to genuine *Sittlichkeit* (see especially 183–4). But they can only be securely interpreted by reference to the *System of Ethical Life*.

60. Hegel was certainly aware of the general nature of the Eleusis cult, and he probably knew of the Adonis cult. But I assume he would have said that this was not a portrayal of the "infinite grief" for *spiritual* things. It was not God as such, or Man as such, who died with Persephone or Adonis, but only Nature in the cycle of the seasons, or the beauty of youth in the coming of manhood, etc.

61. "In Catholicism this religion has come to be a beautiful one" (Rosenkranz, p. 139).

62. Haym, p. 165.

63. See the "structural outline" of his system at this time, given in the *Difference* essay, pp. 59–60.

64. Compare his attempt to lay out his whole philosophy of Nature as a "divine Triangle" (Rosenkranz, pp. 101–2). The date of this endeavour cannot be precisely fixed—Kimmerle believes it was later—but it seems to me to be in perfect accord with the references to the dogma of the Trinity in those two essays. I think, therefore, that the "Divine Triangle" belongs to 1801 (or even 1800) and represents the earliest form of Hegel's *independent* speculation about natural philosophy.

65. See the exposition of the "indifference point" theory in the introduction to the *Difference* essay, p. 42. Compare *Difference* p. 172 and *Faith and Knowledge*, pp. 24, 41.

66. Rosenkranz, p. 141.

# Note on the Text
# and on Conventions

THE TEXT:

Two editions of the text were used in making this translation: that of Georg Lasson (Philosophische Bibliothek, Leipzig: F. Meiner, 1928; reprinted, Hamburg, 1962), and that of Hartmut Buchner and Otto Pöggeler (*Gesammelte Werke*, Band 4, Hamburg: Meiner, 1968). The latter was taken as basic, and the pagination of this authoritative critical edition is indicated in square brackets in the translation.

## THE TREATMENT OF HEGEL'S QUOTATIONS

When Hegel quotes from other authors, he rarely uses quotation marks. We have added quotation marks wherever we were able to trace the quotation (a task which has generally been made easy by the editors of the two German texts that we have used). In the relatively rare cases where Hegel himself used quotation marks we indicate this in the footnotes.

But whether they are marked by him or by us, Hegel's quotations from other authors are apt, like those of most other (German?) authors of the period, to fall short of perfect scholarly precision. He rarely marks his omissions. We have marked his unacknowledged elisions by inserting "[. . .]". Also, Hegel's emphases are almost always different from those of the original text quoted. Here, we have not tried to be precise ourselves. Instead of noting every change in emphasis we rest content with a general warning to the reader that the emphases in quotations are usually Hegel's, and not those of the author quoted. Other major deviations are indicated in our footnotes. Occasionally we have also furnished a translation of the original text from which Hegel's quotations and summaries are taken.

*Abbreviations and References:*

The following abbreviations are employed regularly:

D=*The Difference Between Fichte's and Schelling's System of Philosophy*, translated by H. S. Harris and Walter Cerf, Albany: State University of New York Press, 1977.

*N.K.A.*=Hegel, *Gesammelte Werke*, Hamburg: Meiner, 1968 ff.

*Akad.*=*Kants Gesammelte Schriften*, herausgegeben von der Königlich Preussischen Akademie der Wissenschaften, Berlin.

Other references in the notes are usually confined to the author (editor, translator) and short title where needed. The Bibliographic Index supplies the full details of the work cited.

Concerning the use of the dagger (†), see the Translators' Preface.

# Faith and Knowledge

or the *Reflective Philosophy of Subjectivity*
in the complete range of its forms as
Kantian, Jacobian, and Fichtean Philosophy
by Ge. Wilhelm Fr. Hegel

published in the *Critical Journal of Philosophy*
edited by F. W. J. Schelling and G. W. F. Hegel
Volume II, part 1, Tübingen 1802

# Introduction

[315] Civilization has raised this latest era so far above the ancient antithesis of Reason and faith, of philosophy and positive religion that this opposition of faith and knowledge has acquired quite a different sense and has now been transferred into the field of philosophy itself. In earlier times philosophy was said to be the handmaid of faith. Ideas and expressions of this sort have vanished and philosophy has irresistibly affirmed its absolute autonomy. Reason, if it is in fact Reason that appropriates this name, has made itself into such an authority within positive religion that a philosophical struggle against the positive, against miracles and suchlike, is now regarded as obsolete and unenlightened. Kant tried to put new life into the positive form of religion with a meaning derived from his philosophy, but his attempt was received poorly, not because it would have changed the meaning peculiar to these forms, but because they no longer appeared to be worth the bother.[1] The question arises, however, whether victorious Reason has not suffered the same fate that the barbarous nations in their victorious strength have usually suffered at the hands of civilized nations that weakly succumbed to them. As rulers the barbarians may have held the upper hand outwardly, but they surrendered to the defeated spiritually. Enlightened Reason won a glorious victory over what it believed, in its limited conception of religion, to be faith as opposed to Reason. Yet seen in a clear light the victory comes to no more than this: the positive element with which Reason busied itself to do battle, is no longer religion, and victorious Reason is no longer Reason. The new born peace that hovers triumphantly over the corpse of Reason and faith, uniting them as the child of both, has as little of Reason in it as it has of authentic faith.

Reason had already gone to seed in and for itself[2] when it envisaged religion merely as something positive and not idealistically. And after its battle with religion the best that Reason could manage was

---

1. Hegel is here referring to *Religion within the Bounds of Reason Alone* (Königsberg, 1793; *Akad.* VI, 1–202); English translation by T. M. Greene and H. H. Hudson, 1934 (New York: Harper Torchbooks, 1960).

2. *An und für sich*: this may here have the meaning that it usually has nowadays in ordinary German. In that case the sentence should be translated: "Reason, though, had already gone to seed when. . . ."

to take a look at itself and come to self-awareness. Reason, having in this way become mere intellect, acknowledges its own nothingness by placing that which is better than it in a *faith outside and above* itself, as a *beyond* [to be believed in]. This is what has happened in the *philosophies of Kant,* [316] *Jacobi, and Fichte.* Philosophy has made itself the handmaid of a faith once more.

According to Kant, the supersensuous is incapable of being known by Reason; the highest Idea does not at the same time have reality. According to Jacobi, "Reason is ashamed to beg and has no hands and feet for digging."[3] Only the feeling and consciousness of his ignorance of the True is given to man, only an inkling, a divination of the True in Reason, Reason being something subjective, though universal—an instinct. According to *Fichte,* God is something incomprehensible and unthinkable. Knowledge knows nothing save that it knows nothing; it must take refuge in faith.[4] All of them agree that, as the old distinction put it, the Absolute is no more against Reason than it is for it; it is beyond Reason.[5]

The Enlightenment, in its positive aspect, was a hubbub of vanity without a firm core. It obtained a core in its negative procedure by grasping its own negativity. Through the purity and infinity of the negative it freed itself from its insipidity but precisely for this reason it could admit positive knowledge only of the finite and empirical. The eternal remained in a realm beyond, a beyond too vacuous for cognition so that this infinite void of knowledge could only be filled with the subjectivity of longing and divining. Thus what used to be regarded as the death of philosophy, that Reason should renounce its existence in the Absolute, excluding itself totally from it and relating itself to it only negatively, became now the zenith of philosophy. By coming to consciousness of its own nothingness, the Enlightenment turns this nothingness into a system.

In general, imperfect philosophies immediately pertain to [i.e., arise from] an empirical necessity just because they are imperfect. So it is through and in this empirical necessity that their imperfect aspect is to be comprehended. The empirical is what is there in the world

3. Friedrich Heinrich Jacobi, *Letters on the Teaching of Spinoza* (1786); see *Werke,* IV, i, 214: "Reason has no hands and feet for digging and is ashamed to beg." The metaphor comes from Luke 16, 3.

4. See especially *The Vocation of Man* (1800) in *Sämmtliche Werke* II, 254–5 (Chisholm, pp. 89–90).

5. The *locus classicus* for the "old distinction" is Thomas Aquinas, *Summa contra Gentiles,* Book I, chapters 3–8.

as ordinary existence (*Wirklichkeit*). In empirical philosophies it is present in conceptual form, as one with consciousness, and therefore justified. [But] on the one hand, the subjective principle shared by the philosophies of Kant, Jacobi and Fichte [does not pertain to empirical necessity because it] is by no means a restricted expression of the spirit of a brief epoch or a small group. [And] on the other hand, [these philosophies taken together are not empirical or imperfect because] the mighty spiritual form that is their principle achieved in them perfect self-consciousness, perfect philosophical formation and definitive self-expression as cognition.

The great form of the world spirit that has come to cognizance of itself in these philosophies, is the principle of the North, and from the religious point of view, of Protestantism. This principle is subjectivity for which beauty and truth present themselves in feelings and persuasions, in love and intellect. Religion builds its temples and altars in the heart of the individual. In sighs and prayers he seeks for the God whom [317] he denies to himself in intuition, because of the risk that the intellect will cognize what is intuited as a mere thing, reducing the sacred grove to mere timber.[6] Of course, the inner must be externalized; intention must become effective in action; immediate religious sentiment must be expressed in external gesture; and faith, though it flees from the objectivity of cognition, must become objective to itself in thoughts, concepts, and words. But the intellect scrupulously distinguishes the objective from the subjective, and the objective is what is accounted worthless and null. The struggle of subjective beauty must be directed precisely to this end: to defend itself properly against the necessity through which the subjective becomes objective. That beauty should become real in objective form, and fall captive to objectivity, that consciousness should seek to be directed at exposition and objectivity themselves, that it should want to shape appearance or, shaped in it, to be at home there—all this should cease; for it would be a dangerous superfluity, and an evil, as the intellect could turn it into a thing (*zu einem Etwas*). Equally, if the beautiful feeling passed over into an intuition that was without grief, it would be superstition.

That it is subjective beauty which grants this might to the intel-

6. An echo of Horace (Epistles I, 6, 31–2); the theme recurs more than once in Hegel's early manuscripts—first in 1794 (Nohl, p. 37); and again, with reference to stone statues, in 1798 (Nohl, 300–1; Knox-Kroner, p. 252). It recurs also in the *Phenomenology* (Baillie, pp. 571–2). Compare p. 145 note 157 below.

lect seems at first glance to contradict its yearning which flies beyond the finite and to which the finite is nothing. But the grant is as much a necessary aspect [of its relation to the intellect] as is its striving against the intellect. This will be brought out more fully in our exposition of the philosophies of this subjectivity. It is precisely through its flight from the finite and through its rigidity that subjectivity turns the beautiful into things—the grove into timber, the images into things that have eyes and do not see, ears and do not hear.[7] And if the Ideals cannot be reduced to the block and stones of a wholly explicable (*verständig*) reality, they are made into fictions. Any connection with the Ideals will then appear as a play without substance, or as dependence upon objects and as superstition.

Yet alongside of this intellect which everywhere sees nothing but finitude in the truth of being, religion has its sublime aspect as feeling (*Empfindung*), the love filled with eternal longing; for it does not get hung up on any transitory sight (*Anschauung*) or enjoyment, it yearns for eternal beauty and bliss. Religion, as this longing, is subjective; but what it seeks and what is not given to it in intuition, is the Absolute and the eternal. For if the longing were to find its object, then the temporal beauty of a subject in his singularity would be its happiness, it would be the perfection of a being belonging to the world; but to the extent that religion as longing actually singularized beauty it would be nothing beautiful [as far as the longing itself is concerned].[8] But [what the longing does not recognize is that] when empirical existence is the pure body of inward beauty, it ceases to be something temporal and on its own. The intention abides unpolluted by its objective existence as an action; and neither the deed nor the enjoyment will be built up by the intellect into something that is opposed to the true identity of the inner and the outer. The highest cognition [318] would be the cognition of what that body is wherein the individual would not be single [and separate], and wherein longing reaches perfect vision and blissful enjoyment.

When the time had come, the infinite longing that yearns beyond body and world, reconciled itself with existence.[9] But the reality with

7. See the preceding note; and compare Psalm 115, 4–8.

8. The text reads simply: "aber soweit als *sie* wirklich *sie* vereinzelte so würde *sie* nichts Schönes sein" (our italics).

9. Hegel deals with this "reconciliation" at length in the *Phenomenology*. The whole section on "Enlightenment" is relevant to his discussion of the general principle of "eudæmonism" here, and the section on "the moral view of the world" is a proof of the "eudæmonism" of Kant, and Fichte (Baillie, pp. 559–98, 615–27).

which it became reconciled, the objective sphere acknowledged by subjectivity, was in fact merely empirical existence, the ordinary world and ordinary matters of fact (*Wirklichkeit*). Hence, this reconciliation did not itself lose the character of absolute opposition implicit in beautiful longing. Rather, it flung itself upon the other pole of the antithesis, the empirical world. Although the reconciliation was sure of itself and firm in its inner ground because of the absolute and blind natural necessity [of empirical existence] it was still in need of an objective form for this [inner] ground. Being immersed in the reality of empirical existence this reconciliation has an unconscious certainty which must, by the same necessity of nature, seek to secure justification and a good conscience. At the conscious level it was the doctrine of happiness that brought about this reconciliation. The fixed point of departure here is the empirical subject, just as what it becomes reconciled with is ordinary life (*Wirklichkeit*): the empirical subject is allowed to confide in ordinary life and surrender to it without sin. The utter crudity and vulgarity that are at the bottom of this doctrine of eudæmonism are redeemed only by its striving toward justification and good conscience. But Reason cannot achieve this justification and good conscience through the Idea, since the empirical is [here] absolute. Only the objectivity of the intellect can attain the concept, which has presented itself in its most highly abstract form as so-called pure Reason.

So the dogmatism of the Enlightenment flurry and of eudæmonism did not consist in declaring virtuous happiness and enjoyment to be the highest good; for when happiness is conceived as Idea, it ceases to be something empirical and contingent, and it ceases to be something sensuous. In the highest being (*Dasein*) rational action and highest enjoyment are one. Only if we isolate the ideal aspect of the highest being, can we then call it rational action. And only if we isolate the real aspect can we call it enjoyment and feeling. It does not matter whether we wish to apprehend the highest being from the side of its ideality or from the side of its reality; [for] if highest bliss is highest Idea, then rational action and highest enjoyment, ideality and reality, are equally contained in it and are identical. Every philosophy sets forth nothing else but the construction of highest bliss as Idea. In Reason's cognition of the highest enjoyment, the possibility of distinguishing them [rational action and enjoyment] vanishes immediately; concept and infinity which dominate action, and reality and finitude which dominate enjoyment are absorbed into one another. Polemics against happiness will be dismissed as empty chatter when this happiness is recognized to be the blissful enjoyment of eternal [319] intuition. But of course what is nowadays called eudæmonism refers to a happiness that is empirical, a sensual enjoyment, not the bliss of eternal vision.[10]

Infinity or the concept is so directly opposed to this absoluteness of the empirical and finite being (*Wesen*) that they condition one another and they are one with each other.[11] Since the one is absolute in its being-for-itself, so is the other; and the third, which is the true first, the eternal, is beyond this antithesis. The infinite, the concept, being in itself empty, the nothing, receives its content from what it is connected with as its opposite, that is, the empirical happiness of the individual. What is called wisdom and science consists in positing everything under the unity of the concept whose content is absolute singularity, and in calculating [the worth of] each and every form of beauty and expression of an Idea, wisdom and virtue, art and science from this point of view. That is to say, all this has to be treated as something that does not exist in itself, for the only thing that is in itself is the abstract concept of something that is not Idea but absolute singularity.

The fixed principle of this system of culture is that the finite is in and for itself, that it is absolute, and is the sole reality. According to this principle, the finite and singular stands on one side, in the form of manifoldness; and anything religious, ethical and beautiful is thrown onto this side because it can be conceived as singular by the intellect. On the other side there is this very same absolute finitude but in the form of the infinite as concept of happiness. The infinite and the finite are here not to be posited as identical in the Idea; for each of them is for itself absolute. So they stand opposed to each other in the connection of domination; for in the absolute antithesis of infinite and finite the concept is what does the determining. However, above this absolute antithesis and above the relative identities of domination and empirical conceivability, there is the eternal. Because the antithesis [between the infinite and the finite] is absolute, the sphere of the eternal is the incalculable, the inconceivable, the empty—an incognizable God beyond the boundary stakes of Reason. It is a sphere that is nothing for intuition since intuition is only allowed to be sensuous and limited. Equally, it is nothing for enjoyment

10. Literally "not eternal intuition and bliss."
11. In context "*eins mit dem andern*" may mean no more than "they are together."

since only empirical happiness exists, and nothing for cognition since what is here called Reason consists solely in calculating the worth of each and every thing with respect to the singularity, and in positing [i.e., subsuming] every Idea under finitude.

This is the basic character of eudæmonism and the Enlightenment. The beautiful subjectivity of Protestantism is transformed into empirical subjectivity; the poetry of Protestant grief that scorns all reconciliation with empirical existence is transformed into the prose of satisfaction with the finite and of good conscience about it. What is the relation of this basic character to the philosophies of Kant, Jacobi and Fichte? So little do these philosophies step out of this basic character that, on the contrary, they have merely perfected it to the highest degree. Their [320] conscious direction is flatly opposed to the principle of eudæmonism. However, because they are nothing but this direction, their positive character is just this principle itself; so that the way these philosophies modify eudæmonism merely gives it a perfection of formation, which has no importance in principle, no significance for Reason and philosophy. The absoluteness of the finite and of empirical reality is still maintained in these philosophies. The infinite and the finite remain absolutely opposed. Ideality (*das Idealische*) is conceived only as the concept. And in particular, when this concept is posited affirmatively, the only identity of the finite and infinite that remains possible is a relative identity, the domination of the concept over what appears as the real and the finite—everything beautiful and ethical being here included. And on the other hand, when the concept is posited negatively, the subjectivity of the individual is present in empirical form, and the domination is not that of the intellect but is a matter of the natural strength and weakness of the subjectivities opposed to one another. Above this absolute finitude and absolute infinity there remains the Absolute as an emptiness of Reason, a fixed realm of the incomprehensible, of a faith which is in itself non-rational (*vernunftlos*), but which is called rational because the Reason that is restricted to its absolute opposite recognizes something higher above itself from which it is self-excluded.

In the form of eudæmonism the principle of an absolute finitude has not yet achieved perfect abstraction. For on the side of infinity, the concept is not posited in purity; because it is filled with content it stays fixed as happiness. Because the concept is not pure, it has positive equality with its opposite; for its content is precisely the same reality, which is manifoldness on the other side [the side of finitude]—but on the side of infinity it is posited in conceptual form.

Hence, there is no reflection on the opposition, which is to say that the opposition is not objective: the empirical is not posited as negativity for the concept nor the concept as negativity for the empirical nor the concept as that which is in itself negative. When abstraction achieves perfection, there is reflection on this opposition, the ideal opposition becomes objective, and each of the opposites is posited as something which is not what the other is. Unity and the manifold now confront one another as abstractions, with the result that the opposites have both positive and negative aspects for one another: the empirical is both an absolute something and absolute nothing for the concept. In the former perspective the opposites are the preceding empiricism;[12] in the latter they are at the same time idealism and scepticism. The former is called practical philosophy, the latter theoretical philosophy. In practical philosophy, the empirical has absolute reality for the concept, that is, it has absolute reality in and for itself; in theoretical philosophy knowledge of the empirical is nothing.

[321] The fundamental principle common to the philosophies of Kant, Jacobi and Fichte is, then, the absoluteness of finitude and, resulting from it, the absolute antithesis of finitude and infinity, reality and ideality, the sensuous and the supersensuous, and the beyondness of what is truly real and absolute. Within this common ground, however, *these philosophies* form antitheses among themselves, exhausting *the totality of possible forms of this principle.* The Kantian philosophy establishes the objective side of this whole [subjective] sphere: the absolute concept, existing strictly for itself as practical Reason, is the highest objectivity within the finite realm, and it is absolute as ideality postulated in and for itself. Jacobi's philosophy is the subjective side. It transposes the antithesis and the identity, postulated as absolute, into the subjectivity of feeling, into infinite longing and incurable grief. The philosophy of Fichte is the synthesis of both. It demands the form of objectivity and of basic principles as in Kant, but it posits at the same time the conflict of this pure objectivity with the subjectivity as a longing and a subjective identity. In Kant the infinite concept is posited as that which is in and for itself and as the only thing philosophy acknowledges. In Jacobi, the infinite appears as affected by subjectivity, that is, as instinct, impulse, individuality. In Fichte, the infinite as affected by subjectivity is itself objectified again, as obligation and striving.

So these philosophers are as completely confined within eudæmon-

12. Compare pp. 58–9 above.

ism as they are diametrically opposed to it. It is their exclusive, their only articulate tendency, their programmatic principle, to rise above the subjective and empirical and to justify the absoluteness of Reason, its independence from common existence (*Wirklichkeit*). But since this Reason is simply and solely directed against the empirical, the infinite has a being of its own only in its tie with the finite. Thus, although these philosophies do battle with the empirical, they have remained directly within its sphere. The Kantian and Fichtean philosophies were able to raise themselves to the concept certainly, but not to the Idea, and the pure concept is absolute ideality and emptiness. It gets its content and dimensions quite exclusively in, and hence through, its connection with the empirical. In this way their pure concept is the ground of that very same absolute moral and philosophical (*wissenschaftlich*) empiricism for which they reproach eudæmonism. Jacobi's philosophy does not take this detour. It does not first sunder the concept from empirical reality and then let the concept get its content from this very same empirical reality because outside of it there is nothing for the concept but its nullification. Instead, since the principle of his philosophy is straightforward subjectivity, Jacobi's philosophy is straightforward eudæmonism, except that it is tinged with negativity. For whereas to eudæmonism thought is not yet the ideal realm, the negative of reality, Jacobi's philosophy does reflect on thought and holds it to be nothing in itself.

The philosophy of Locke and the doctrine of happiness were the earlier philosophical manifestations (*Erscheinungen*) of this realism of finitude (to which the non-philosophical manifestations, all the hustle and bustle [322] of contemporary civilization, still belong). Locke and the eudæmonists transformed philosophy into empirical psychology. They raised the standpoint of the subject, the standpoint of absolutely existing finitude, to the first and highest place. They asked and answered the question of what the universe is for a subjectivity that feels and is conscious by way of calculations typical of the intellect, or in other words, for a Reason solely immersed in finitude, a Reason that renounces intuition and cognition of the eternal. The philosophies of Kant, Jacobi, and Fichte are the completion and idealization of this empirical psychology; they consist in coming to understand that the infinite concept is strictly opposed to the empirical. They understood the sphere of this antithesis, a finite and an infinite, to be absolute: but [they did not see that] if infinity is thus set up against finitude, each is as finite as the other. They understood the eternal to be above this [sphere of] opposition, beyond the concept and the empirical; but they understood the cognitive faculty and Reason simply to be that sphere. Now a Reason that thinks only the finite will naturally be found to be able to think only the finite; and Reason as impulse and instinct will naturally be found not to be able to think the eternal.

The idealism of which these philosophies are capable is an idealism of the finite; not in the sense that the finite is nothing in them, but in the sense that the finite is received into ideal form: they posit finite ideality, i.e., the pure concept, as infinity absolutely opposed to finitude, together with the finite that is real+ and they posit both equally absolutely. (In its subjective dimension, that is, in Jacobi's philosophy, this idealism can only have the form of scepticism, and not even of true scepticism, because Jacobi turns pure thinking into something merely subjective, whereas idealism consists in the assertion that pure thinking is objective thinking.)

The one self-certifying certainty (*das an sich und einzig Gewisse*), then, is that there exists a thinking subject, a Reason affected with finitude; and the whole of philosophy consists in determining the universe with respect to this finite Reason. Kant's so-called critique of the cognitive faculties, Fichte's [doctrine that] consciousness cannot be transcended nor become transcendent, Jacobi's refusal to undertake anything impossible for Reason, all amount to nothing but the absolute restriction of Reason to the form of finitude, [an injunction] never to forget the absoluteness of the subject in every rational cognition; they make limitedness into an eternal law and an eternal being both in itself and for philosophy. So these philosophies have to be recognized as nothing but the culture (*Kultur*) of reflection raised to a system. This is a culture of ordinary human intellect which does, to be sure, rise to the thinking of a universal; but because it remains ordinary intellect it takes the infinite concept to be absolute thought and keeps what remains of its intuition of the eternal strictly isolated from the infinite concept. [323] It does so either by renouncing that intuition altogether and sticking to concept and experience, or by keeping both [intuition and concept] although unable to unite them—for it can neither take up its intuition into the concept, nor yet nullify both concept and experience [in intuition]. The torment of a nobler nature subjected to this limitation, this absolute opposition, expresses itself in yearning and striving; and the consciousness that it is a barrier which cannot be crossed expresses itself as faith in a realm beyond the barrier. But because of its perennial incapacity this faith is simultaneously the impossibility of rising above the barrier into the realm of Reason, the realm which is intrinsically clear and free of longing.

The fixed standpoint which the all-powerful culture of our time has established for philosophy is that of a Reason affected by sensibility. In this situation philosophy cannot aim at the cognition of God, but only at what is called the cognition of man. This so-called man and his humanity conceived as a rigidly, insuperably finite sort of Reason form philosophy's absolute standpoint. Man is not a glowing spark of eternal beauty, or a spiritual focus of the universe, but an absolute sensibility. He does, however, have the faculty of faith so that he can touch himself up here and there with a spot of alien supersensuousness. It is as if art, considered simply as portraiture, were to express its ideal aspect (*ihr Idealisches*) through the longing it depicts on an ordinary face and the melancholy smile of the mouth, while it was strictly forbidden to represent the gods in their exaltation above longing and sorrow, on the grounds that the presentation of eternal images would only be possible at the expense of humanity. Similarly philosophy is not supposed to present the Idea of man, but the abstract concept of an empirical mankind all tangled up in limitations, and to stay immovably impaled on the stake of the absolute antithesis; and when it gets clear about its restriction to the sensuous—either analyzing its own abstraction or entirely abandoning it[13] in the fashion of the sentimental *bel esprit*—philosophy is supposed to prettify itself with the surface colour of the supersensuous by pointing, in faith, to something higher.

Truth, however, cannot be deceived by this sort of hallowing of a finitude that remains what it was. A true hallowing should nullify the finite. If an artist cannot give true truth to what actually exists by casting an ethereal light upon it, and taking it wholly up therein; if he is only able to represent actuality in and for itself—which is what is commonly called reality and truth, though it is neither the one nor the other—then he will take refuge in feeling, in yearning and sentimentality as his remedy against actuality, spreading tears on the cheeks of the vulgar and bringing an "Oh Lord" to their lips. Thus [324] his figures will indeed look away beyond the actual situation toward heaven, but they will do so like bats that are neither bird nor beast, and belong neither to earth nor to sky. There cannot be beauty of this sort without ugliness, nor a moral ethos of this

---

13. The text could also mean: "either analysing its own abstraction or leaving it intact [i.e., unanalysed]."

kind without weakness and perfidy, nor such intellect as here occurs without platitude; good fortune cannot come to pass without meanness, nor ill fortune without fear and cowardice, nor any kind of fortune, without being contemptible. In the same way, when philosophy after its own fashion, takes up the finite and subjectivity as absolute truth in the form of the concept, it cannot purify them [i.e., the finite and subjectivity] by connecting subjectivity with an infinite [the concept]. For this infinite is itself not the truth since it is unable to consume and consummate finitude (*die Endlichkeit aufzuzehren*).

In philosophy, however, the actual and the temporal as such disappear. This is called cruel dissection destructive of the wholeness of man, or violent abstraction that has no truth, and particularly no practical truth. This abstraction is conceived of as the painful cutting off of an essential part from the completeness of the whole. But the temporal and empirical, and privation, are thus recognized as an essential part and an absolute In-itself. It is as if someone who sees only the feet of a work of art were to complain, when the whole work is revealed to his sight, that he was being deprived of his deprivation and that the incomplete had been in-completed. Finite cognition is this sort of cognition of a part and a singular. If the absolute were *put together* out of the finite and the infinite, abstracting from the finite would indeed be a loss. In the Idea, however, finite and infinite are one, and hence finitude as such, i.e., as something that was supposed to have truth and reality in and for itself, has vanished. Yet what was negated was only the negative in finitude; and thus the true affirmation was posited.

The supreme abstraction (*Abstractum*) of this absolutized negation is the Ego-concept, just as the thing is the highest abstraction (*Abstraction*) pertaining to position [i.e., to affirmation]. Each of them is only a negation of the other. Pure being like pure thinking—an absolute thing and absolute Ego-concept—are equally finitude made absolute. Eudæmonism and the Enlightenment fuss belong to this same level—not to mention much else—and so do the philosophies of Kant, Jacobi, and Fichte. We shall now proceed to a more detailed confrontation of these three philosophers with one another.

# A. Kantian Philosophy

Because the essence of the Kantian philosophy consists in its being critical idealism, it plainly confesses that its principle is subjectivism and formal thinking. Secure in its standpoint, which makes the unity of reflection supreme, it reveals what it is and aims at, by telling its story quite frankly. The name of Reason which it gives to the concept may, at the worst, impede the disclosure or mask it. On its lower levels, in cases where an Idea truly does provide the basis, the confused way in which the Idea is expressed makes it difficult to recognize it in the first place; and secondly, the rational ground is soon transformed back into something conditional that pertains to the intellect. But, for the rest, when the Kantian philosophy happens upon Ideas in its normal course, it deals with them as mere possibilities of thought and as transcendent concepts lacking all reality, and soon drops them again as mere empty thoughts. The highest Idea which it encountered in its critical business [i.e., the Idea of God in the Ontological Argument] it treated at first as if it were empty musing, nothing but an unnatural scholastic trick for conjuring reality out of concepts.[1] Then in the final stage of its development,[2] Kant's philosophy establishes the highest Idea as a postulate which is supposed to have a necessary subjectivity, but not that absolute objectivity which would get it recognized as the only starting point of philosophy and its sole content instead of being the point where philosophy terminates in faith.

The Kantian philosophy remains entirely within the antithesis. It makes the identity of the opposites into the absolute terminus of philosophy, the pure boundary which is nothing but the negation of philosophy. We must not, by contrast, regard it as the problem of the true philosophy to resolve at that terminus the antitheses that are met with and formulated perchance as spirit and world, or soul and body, or self and nature, etc.

---

1. Compare *Critique of Pure Reason*, A 603; B 631.

2. Hegel probably means to refer to *Religion within the Bounds of Reason Alone* (1793), Book II, Section 1, subsections B and C (*Akad.* VI, 62–78). But compare also *Critique of Practical Reason*, 1 (1787), Book II, Chapter II, Section V (*Akad.* V, 124–32).

On the contrary, the sole Idea that has reality and true objectivity for philosophy, is the absolute suspendedness of the antithesis. This absolute identity is not a universal subjective postulate never to be realized. It is the only authentic reality. Nor is the cognition of it a faith, that is, something beyond all knowledge; it is, rather, philosophy's sole knowledge. Philosophy is idealism because it does not acknowledge either one of the opposites as existing for itself in its abstraction from the other. The supreme Idea is indifferent against both; and each of the opposites, considered singly, is nothing. The Kantian philosophy has the merit of being idealism [326] because it does show that neither the concept in isolation nor intuition in isolation is anything at all; that intuition by itself is blind and the concept by itself is empty;[3] and that what is called experience, i.e., the finite identity of both in consciousness is not a rational cognition either. But the Kantian philosophy declares this finite cognition to be all that is possible. It turns this negative, abstractly idealistic side [of cognition] into that which is in itself, into the positive. It turns just this empty concept into absolute Reason, both theoretical and practical. In so doing, it falls back into absolute finitude and subjectivity, and the whole task and content of this philosophy is, not the cognition of the Absolute, but the cognition of this subjectivity. In other words, it is a critique of the cognitive faculties.

> For I thought that the first step towards satisfying several in-
> quiries the mind of man was very apt to run into, was, to take
> a survey of our own understandings, examine our own powers,
> and see to what things they were adapted. [. . .] Thus men,
> extending their inquiries beyond their capacities and letting their
> thoughts wander into those depths where they can find no sure
> footing, it is no wonder that they raise questions and multiply
> disputes, which, never coming to any clear resolution, are proper
> only to continue and increase their doubts, and to confirm them
> at last in perfect scepticism. Whereas, were the capacities of
> our understanding well considered, the extent of our knowledge
> (*Erkenntnis*) once discovered, and the horizon found which sets
> the bounds between the enlightened and dark parts of things;
> between what is and what is not comprehensible by us, men
> would perhaps with less scruple acquiesce in the avowed igno-

---

3. *Critique of Pure Reason*, A 51, B 75: "Thoughts without content are empty, intuitions without concepts are blind."

rance of the one, and employ their thoughts and discourse with more advantage and satisfaction in the other.

With these words, Locke expresses in the Introduction to his *Essay*[4] the goal of his undertaking. They are words which one could just as well read in the introduction to Kant's philosophy; for it similarly confines itself to Locke's goal, that is, to an investigation of the finite intellect.

Within these bounds, however, and notwithstanding its ultimate results which are quite different, the Kantian philosophy expresses the authentic Idea of Reason in the formula, *"How are synthetic judgments a priori possible?"* Kant reproaches Hume for thinking of this task of philosophy with far too little definiteness and universality. This is exactly what happened to Kant himself; and like Hume he stopped at the *subjective* and external meaning of this question and believed he had established that rational cognition is impossible. According to his [327] conclusions all so-called philosophy comes down to a mere delusion of supposed rational insight.

How are synthetic judgments *a priori* possible? This problem expresses nothing else but the Idea that subject and predicate of the synthetic judgment are identical in the *a priori* way. That is to say, these heterogeneous elements, the subject which is the particular and in the form of being, and the predicate which is the universal and in the form of thought, are at the same time absolutely identical. It is Reason alone that is the possibility of this positing, for Reason is nothing else but the identity of heterogeneous elements of this kind. One can glimpse this Idea through the shallowness of the deduction of the categories. With respect to space and time one can glimpse it, too, though not where it should be, in the transcendental exposition of these forms,[5] but later on, in the deduction of the categories, where the original synthetic unity of apperception finally comes to the fore.[6] Here, the original synthetic unity of apperception is recognized also as the principle of the figurative synthesis,[7] i.e., of the forms of intuition; space and time are themselves conceived as synthetic unities, and spontaneity, the absolute synthetic activity of the productive

4. Hegel quotes from the German translation by H. E. Poleyen (Altenburg, 1757). We give the text from Book I, chapter 1, section 7 (ed. Yolton, London, Everyman, 1961, I, 8–9).

5. *Critique of Pure Reason*, Transcendental Aesthetic, sections 3, 5.

6. Ibid., B 131–9 (compare A 115–25).

7. Ibid., B 150–3, 160–1.

imagination, is conceived as the principle of the very sensibility which was previously characterized only as receptivity.

This original synthetic unity must be conceived, not as produced out of opposites, but as a truly necessary, absolute, original identity of opposites. As such, it is the principle both of productive imagination, which is the unity that is blind, i.e., immersed in the difference and not detaching itself from it; and of the intellect, which is the unity that posits the difference as identical but distinguishes itself from the different. This shows that the Kantian forms of intuition and the forms of thought cannot be kept apart at all as the particular, isolated faculties which they are usually represented as. One and the same synthetic unity—we have just now determined what this means here—is the principle of intuition and of the intellect. The intellect is only the higher potency; in it the identity which in intuition is totally immersed in the manifold, simultaneously sets itself against the manifold, and constitutes itself within itself as universality, which is what makes it the higher potency. Kant is therefore quite right in calling intuition without form [i.e., concept] blind. For in [mere] intuition [without form][8] there is no relative antithesis, and hence there is no relative identity of unity and difference. This relative identity and antithesis is what seeing or being conscious consists in; but the identity[9] is completely identical with the difference just as it is in the magnet. The antithesis is not suspended in sensuous intuition, as it is in intellectual intuition; in the empirical intuition *qua* sensuous the antithesis must emerge; so it keeps its standing even in this state of immersion. Hence, the antitheses step apart as two forms of intuiting, the one as identity of thinking, the other as identity of being, the one as intuition of time and the other of space.[10]—Similarly, the concept is empty [328] without intuition. For the synthetic unity is only concept because it binds the difference in such a way that it also steps outside of it, and faces it in relative antithesis. In isolation the pure concept is the empty identity. It is only as being relatively identical with that which it stands against, that it is concept; and it is [thus] plenished

8. I.e., the pure intuitions of space and time considered in separation from the functions of the intellect.

9. Hegel clearly means "the unity" here. The opposite poles of the magnet are its essential nature. Thus when it is broken they are not separated but duplicated.

10. Hegel appears here to sketch an explanation of what Kant asserted to be incapable of further explanation: "why space and time are the only forms of our intuition" (*Critique of Pure Reason*, B 145–6).

only through the manifold of intuition: sensuous intuition $A = B$, concept $A^2 = (A = B)$.[11]

The main point is that productive imagination is a truly speculative Idea, both in the form of sensuous intuition and in that of experience which is the comprehending of the intuition. For the expression "synthetic unity" might make the identity look as if it presupposes the antithesis[12] and need the manifold of the antithesis as something independent and existing for itself; the identity might look as if it was by nature posterior to the opposition. But in Kant the synthetic unity is undeniably the absolute and original identity of self-consciousness, which of itself posits the judgment absolutely and *a priori*. Or rather, as identity of subjective and objective, the original identity appears in consciousness as judgment. This original unity of apperception is called synthetic precisely because of its two-sidedness, the opposites being absolutely one in it. The absolute synthesis is absolute insofar as it is not an aggregate of manifolds which are first picked up, and then the synthesis supervenes upon them afterwards. If we sunder the absolute synthesis and reflect upon its opposites, one of them is the empty ego, the concept, and the other is the manifold, body, matter or what you will. Kant puts it very well (*Critique of Pure Reason* [second edition, 1787], p. 135): "through the empty Ego as simple representation nothing manifold is given."[13] The true synthetic unity or rational identity is just that identity which is the connecting of the manifold with the empty identity, the Ego. It is from this connnection, as original synthesis that the Ego as thinking subject, and the manifold as body and world first detach themselves. Thus Kant himself distinguishes the abstract Ego or the abstract

---

11. This formula says that the judgment is the second "power" ($A^2$) of productive imagination, the first "power" being sensuous intuition ($A = B$). In its appearance as judgment the intellect is the reflective awareness of the identity of Subject and Predicate in their difference. Hegel's present paradigm of judgment is the subsumption of a particular under a universal (cf. above p. 69). As he takes the particulars to have the form of being and the universals to have the form of thought, he can now say that the judgment is the reflective awareness of the identity of being and thought in their difference. The next step would lead from particular beings to objects and from concepts to the subject. So we get judgments as the reflective awareness of the identity of object and subject in their difference.

12. Hegel here uses the Kantian term *Antithesis*, not his own *Gegensatz*.

13. Kant says: "through the I as simple representation, nothing manifold is given."

identity of the intellect from the true Ego, the absolute, original synthetic identity, which is the principle.

This is how Kant truly solved his problem, "How are synthetic judgments *a priori* possible?" They are possible through the original, absolute identity of the heterogeneous. This identity, as the unconditioned, sunders itself, and appears as separated into the form of a judgment, as subject and predicate, or particular and universal. Still, the rational or, as Kant calls it, the *a priori* nature of this judgment, the absolute identity as the mediating concept (*Mittelbegriff*) manifests itself, not in the judgment, but in the [syllogistic] inference.[14] In the judgment the absolute identity is merely the copula "is," without consciousness. It is the difference whose appearance prevails in the judgment itself. Here, the [329] rational is, for cognition, just as much immersed in the antithesis as the identity is immersed in intuition for consciousness in general. The copula is not something thought, something cognized; on the contrary it expresses precisely our non-cognizance of the rational. What comes to the fore and enters consciousness is only the product, i.e., the subject and predicate as terms of the antithesis. Only these terms are posited as object of thought in the form of judgment, and not their being one. In sensuous intuition concept and real thing do not confront each other. At the same time in the judgment the identity extricates itself as the universal from its immersion in the difference, so that the difference appears as the particular; the identity confronts this immersion as its opposite. Yet the rational identity of identity as [the identity] of the universal and the particular[15] is the non-conscious in the judgment, and the judgment itself is only the appearing of this non-conscious identity.

The whole transcendental deduction both of the forms of intuition and of the category in general cannot be understood without distin-

14. *The Critique of Pure Reason* (A 298–309; B 355–66) relates the pure principles of understanding, i.e., of the "intellect" to the forms of judgment, and the Ideas of Reason to the forms of syllogism.

15. This is a literal translation. Perhaps we should read "*die vernünftige Identität als die Identität des Allgemeinen und Besonderen*": "the rational identity as the identity of the universal and the particular." Or else, "*die vernünftige Identität der Identität und der Differenz (des Allgemeinen und Besonderen)*": "the rational identity of the identity and the difference (between the universal and the particular)," which would agree with formulations on p. 74 below, and in the *Difference between Fichte's and Schelling's System* (compare D 156).

guishing what Kant calls the faculty of the original synthetic unity of apperception from the Ego which does the representing and is the subject—the Ego which, as Kant says, merely accompanies all representations. [Secondly,] we must not take the faculty of [productive] imagination as the middle term that gets inserted between an existing absolute subject and an absolute existing world. The productive imagination must rather be recognized as what is primary and original, as that out of which subjective Ego and objective world first sunder themselves into the necessarily bipartite appearance and product, and as the sole In-itself. This power of imagination is the original two-sided identity. The identity becomes subject in general on one side, and object on the other; but originally it is both. And the imagination is nothing but Reason itself, the Idea of which was determined above.[16] But it is only Reason as it appears in the sphere of empirical consciousness. There are those who, when they hear talk of the power of imagination, do not even think of the intellect, still less of Reason, but only of unlawfulness, whim and fiction; they cannot free themselves from the idea of a qualitative manifold of faculties and capacities of the spirit. It is they above all who must grasp that the In-itself of the empirical consciousness is Reason itself; that productive imagination as intuition, and productive imagination as experience are not particular faculties quite sundered from Reason. They must grasp that this productive imagination is only called intellect because the categories, as the determinate forms of the experiential imagination, are posited under the form of the infinite, and fixated as concepts which, also, form a complete system within their [or its] own sphere. Productive imagination [330] has been allowed to get by easily in the Kantian philosophy, first because its pure Idea is set forth in a rather mixed-up way like other potencies, almost in the ordinary form of a psychological faculty, though an *a priori* one, and secondly because Kant did not recognize Reason as the one and only *a priori*, whether it be of sensibility, of intellect, or what have you. Instead he conceived of the *a priori* only under formal concepts of universality and necessity. As we shall now see, he turned the true *a priori* back into a pure unity, i.e., one that is not originally synthetic.

Thus the In-itself was established in the power (*Potenz*) of imagination, but the duplication of this power was conceived as a reflected

16. See pp. 69–70.

one, namely as judgment, and the identity of this power was likewise conceived as intellect and category, that is, as similarly reflected and relative. Because the relative identity was fixated as the universal or the category and the relative duplication as that of the universal and the particular, their absolute identity—that is, the identity of the relative identity and the relative duplication—was also bound to be cognized in reflected form, that is, as Reason. Imagination, however, which is Reason immersed in difference, is at this level raised only to the form of infinitude and fixated as intellect. This merely relative identity necessarily opposes itself to, and is radically affected by, the particular as something alien to it and empirical. The In-itself of both, the identity of this intellect and the empirical, i.e., the *a priori* aspect of judgment, does not come to the fore; philosophy does not go on from judgment to *a priori* inference,[17] from the acknowledgement that the judgment is the appearing of the In-itself to the cognition of the In-itself. It is for this reason that the absolute judgment of idealism as expounded by Kant [i.e., the synthetic judgment *a priori*] may, and, on this level [the *Potenz* of Reason as intellect], must be grasped in such a way that the manifold of sensibility, empirical consciousness as intuition and sensation, is in itself something unintegrated, that the world is in itself falling to pieces, and only gets objective coherence and support, substantiality, multiplicity, even actuality and possibility, through the good offices of human self-consciousness and intellect. All this is an objective determinateness that is man's own perspective and projection. Thus the whole deduction gets the easily grasped meaning that the things in themselves and the sensations are without objective determinateness—and with respect to the sensations and their empirical reality nothing remains but to think that sensation comes from the things in themselves. For the incomprehensible determinateness of the empirical consciousness comes altogether from the things in themselves, and they can be neither intuited nor yet cognized. In experience, the form of intuition belongs to the figurative synthesis, the concept to the intellectual synthesis.[18] No other organ remains for the things in themselves but sensation; for sensation alone is not *a priori*, or in other words, it is not grounded in man's cognitive faculty for which only appearances exist. [331] The objective determinateness of sensations is their unity, and this unity is merely the self-consciousness of an experiencing

17. Compare p. 72 note 14 above.
18. *Critique of Pure Reason*, B 151.

subject. So it is no more something truly *a priori* and existing in itself than any other subjectivity.

It would seem, then, as if critical idealism consisted in nothing but the formal knowledge that the subject and the things or the non-Ego exist each for itself[19]—the Ego of the I think, and the thing in itself. They do not, however, exist for themselves in the sense of each being a substance, one posited as soul-thing, the other as objective thing. Rather, the Ego of the I think is absolute *qua* subject, just as the thing in itself beyond the subject is absolute, without any further categorical determinateness in either case. Objective determinateness and its forms first come in with the connection between them [the Ego and thing-in-itself]; and this identity of theirs is the formal one that appears as causal nexus; the thing in itself becomes object insofar as it obtains from the active subject some determination which for this reason alone is one and the same in both of them. Apart from this they are completely heterogeneous, identical only as sun and stone are in respect to warmth when the sun warms the stone.[20] The absolute identity of the subject and the object has passed into this formal identity, and transcendental idealism into this formal or more properly, psychological idealism.

Once subject and object have been separated, the judgment reappears doubled on the subjective and the objective side. On the objective side it appears as transition from one objective [fact] to another, these objectivities themselves being posited in the relation of subject and object, and in that of the identity of both; and [on the subjective side] it appears likewise as a transition from one subjective phenomenon to another. Thus, gravity is the objective [fact] which *qua* subjective, or particular, is body, but *qua* objective or universal is motion. Or imagination is the subjective which *qua* subjective or particular is Ego and *qua* objective or universal is experience.

On their objective side Kant has set up these relations of appearance as judgments in the system of the principles of judgment.[21] This must be recognized as true idealism inasmuch as the identity of what

19. *Für sich* does not here have the special sense that Hegel gives to it; it is simply Kant's *an sich*.

20. See Kant's *Prolegomena*, section 20. (*Akad.* IV, 301n); compare also p. 93 below.

21. Hegel must be referring either to the whole "System of all Principles of Pure Understanding" (*Critique of Pure Reason*, A 148–235; B 187–294) or to that part of it which is called "Systematic Representation of all the Synthetic Principles of Pure Understanding" (A 158–235; B 197–294).

appears as heterogeneous in one of these relations of judgment is a necessary identity; or in other words, it is an absolute and therefore transcendental identity. For example, the cause is posited as necessarily, i.e., absolutely bound to the effect. However, this whole system of principles makes its own appearance as conscious human intellect and so belongs to the subjective side; and the question now arises: what sort of relation does this judgment, i.e., this subjectivity of the intellect have to objectivity? They are identical, but only formally so, since the heterogeneity of appearance has here been left out: the form A is present as the same in subject and object. It is not simultaneously posited in a heterogeneous way, i.e., on one side as something subjective, and on the other side as something objective, here as unity, there as manifold, which is the one and only way in which [332] oppositeness and appearance must be cognized; it is not posited as 1=2, here as point, there as line. Rather, if the subjective is point, then the objective is point; and if the subjective is line, then the objective is line. The same thing is regarded, first as idea, then as existing thing: the tree as my idea and as thing; warmth, light, red, sweet, etc. as my sensations and as qualities of a thing, and the category, similarly, is posited once as a relation of my thinking and then again as a relation of the things. It is the essence of formal or psychological idealism to regard a distinction of the kind here represented as being just distinct aspects of my subjective viewpoint, and not to regard them in their turn as objectively posited, in the positing of opposites as cognition of appearance, but to allow that formal identity to appear to be the main thing. This sort of idealism can no more cognize the *appearance* of the Absolute in *its* truth than it can cognize the absolute identity, the one being completely inseparable from the other. Kantian, and more particularly Fichtean philosophy are forever sliding into this psychological idealism.

Identity of this formal kind finds itself immediately confronted by or next to an infinite non-identity, with which it must coalesce in some incomprehensible way. On one side there is the Ego, with its productive imagination or rather with its synthetic unity which, taken thus in isolation, is formal unity of the manifold. But next to it there is an infinity of sensations and, if you like, of things in themselves. Once it is abandoned by the categories, this realm cannot be anything but a formless lump, even though, according to *The Critique of Judgment*, it is a realm of beauteous nature and contains determinations with respect to which judgment cannot be subsumptive but only reflecting.[22] Objectivity and stability derive solely from the categories; the realm of things in themselves is without categories; yet it is something for itself and for reflection. The only idea we can form of this realm is like that of the iron king in the fairy tale[23] whom a human self-consciousness permeates with the veins of objectivity so that he can stand erect. But then formal transcendental idealism sucks these veins out of the king so that the upright shape collapses and becomes something in between form and lump, repulsive to look at. For the cognition of nature, without the veins injected into nature by self-consciousness, there remains nothing but sensation.

In this way, then, the objectivity of the categories in experience and the necessity of these relations become once more something contingent and subjective. This intellect is human intellect, part of the cognitive faculty, the intellect of a fixed Ego-point. The things, as they are cognized by the intellect, are only appearances. They are nothing in themselves, which is a perfectly truthful result. The obvious conclusion, however, is that an intellect which [333] has cognizance only of appearances and of nothing in itself, is itself only appearance and is nothing in itself. But, on the contrary, Kant regards discursive intellect, with this sort of cognition, as in itself and absolute. Cognition of appearances is dogmatically regarded as the only kind of cognition there is, and rational cognition is denied. If the forms through which the object exists are nothing in themselves, they must also be nothing in themselves for cognitive Reason. Yet Kant never seems to have had the slightest doubt that the intellect is the absolute of the human spirit. The intellect is (for him) the absolute immovable, insuperable finitude of human Reason. —

In dealing with the problem of *"explaining* the community of the soul with the body" Kant correctly locates "the difficulty"—which is not one of explanation but of cognition—"in the assumed heterogeneity of [. . .] the soul and the objects of the outer senses." The difficulty would disappear [according to Kant] "if we considered that the two kinds of objects thus differ from each other, not inwardly but only as one outwardly appears with the other, and hence that what, as thing in itself, underlies the appearance of matter perhaps, after

22. See *Critique of Judgment*, Introduction (especially sections IV and V, *Akad.* V, 179–86).

23. The reference is to Goethe's *Das Märchen* (published in *Die Horen* 1795). It is the "composite" king, not the "iron" one in the story, which supplies the appropriate model. See *Werke*, Berlin edition, xii, 379.

all, may not be so heterogeneous. The only remaining difficulty would then concern the general possibility of a community of substances (it was superfluous to shift the difficulty)[24] and the solution of this problem lies *without doubt* beyond the field of *human* knowledge."[25] As can be seen, it is for the sake of dear mankind and its cognitive faculty, that Kant so little esteems his thought that maybe the two kinds of things are not so heterogeneous in themselves, but only in appearance. He regards this thought as a chance idea about a maybe and not as a rational thought at all.

A formal idealism which in this way sets an absolute Ego-point and its intellect on one side, and an absolute manifold, or sensation, on the other side, is a dualism. Its idealistic side—which claims for the subject certain relations, called categories—is nothing but an extension of Locke's view. The latter allows the concept and forms to be given by the object, and transfers only perceiving (*Wahrnehmen*) *in general*, a universal intellect, into the subject. In Kant's idealism, on the other hand, the perceiving as immanent form is further determined; and it certainly does make an infinite gain thereby. The emptiness of perceiving (*Percipieren*) or of *a priori* spontaneity is filled with content absolutely: the determinateness of form is nothing but the identity of opposites. As a result the *a priori* intellect becomes, at least in principle, *a posteriori* as well; for a *posteriority* is nothing but the positing of the opposite. Thus the formalt concept of Reason is obtained; Reason has to be *a priori* and *a posteriori*, identical and not identical, in absolute unity. [334] This Idea, however, remains intellect and only the product of the Idea is recognized as a synthetic *judgment a priori*. Inwardly, then, the intellect is, and should be, a speculative Idea, inasmuch as universal and particular are one in it. For the positing of the opposites in the judgment should be *a priori*, i.e., necessary and universal, which is to say that the opposites should be absolutely identical. But the matter comes to rest with the "should." For as opposed to empirical sensibility, this thinking [as conceived by Kant] is once more [only] an [activity of] intellect. The entire deduction is [merely] an analysis of experience and it posits an absolute antithesis (*Antithesis*) and a dualism.

There is, then, a double meaning to the proposition that the intellect is something subjective and that there are only appearances for

24. But it was in the tradition of the rational cosmologies of Wolff, Baumgarten, etc.

25. *Critique of Pure Reason*, B 427–8. Where Hegel has "as one outwardly appears with the other," Kant wrote "as one outwardly appears to the other."

it, and not things in themselves. There is the quite correct meaning that the intellect expresses the principle of opposition and the abstraction of finitude. But there is also the other meaning according to which this finitude and appearance are an absolute in man:[26] it is not the In-itself of things, but that of cognitive Reason. The intellect is supposed to be absolute as a subjective quality of the spirit. But in general, simply by being posited as something subjective, the intellect is acknowledged to be nothing absolute. Even for formal idealism it must not matter whether the intellect which is the necessary, and the dimensions of whose form have been cognized, is subjectively or objectively posited. If the intellect is to be considered for itself as abstraction of the form in its triplicity,[27] it is all one whether it be regarded as intellect of consciousness or as intellect of nature, as the form of conscious or of non-conscious intelligence: just as in the Ego the intellect is thought of as conceptualized,[28] so in nature it is thought of as realized. Suppose the intellect existed altogether in itself, then it would have as much reality in nature, i.e., in a world outside of intellectual cognition, yet intelligible in and for itself, as it would have in an intellect thinking of itself in the form of intellectuality outside of nature. It would be experience taken subjectively as the conscious system, and experience taken objectively as the non-conscious system of the manifoldness and coherence of the world. The world, however, is nothing in itself, not because a conscious intellect first gives form to it, but because it is nature, i.e., it is exalted above finitude and intellect. In the same way, conscious intellect is nothing in itself, not because it is human intellect, but because it is intellect at all, or in other words, because there is an absolute being of the antithesis in it.

So, then, we must not place Kant's merit in this, that he put the forms, as expressed in the categories, into the human cognitive faculty, as if it were the stake of an absolute finitude. We must find it, rather, in his having put the Idea of authentic *a priority* in the form of transcendental imagination; and also in his having put the beginning of the Idea of Reason in the intellect itself. For he regarded thinking, or the form, not as something subjective, but as something

26. The text could also be translated: "the intellect and appearance in man are an absolute."

27. Compare *Critique of Pure Reason*, B 110–111; compare also pp. 71 ff. above.

28. *Intellektualisiert.* See note 36 below.

in itself; not as something formless, [335] not as empty apperception, but as intellect, as true form, namely as triplicity. The germ of
speculation lies in this triplicity alone. For the root judgment, or
duality, is in it as well, and hence the very possibility of *a posteriority*, which in this way ceases to be absolutely opposed to the
*a priori*, while the *a priori*, for this reason, also ceases to be formal
identity. We will touch later[29] on the still purer Idea of an intellect
that is at the same time *a posteriori*, the Idea of an intuitive intellect
as the absolute middle.

Before we go on to show how this Idea of an intellect that is also
*a posteriori* or intuitive hovered very clearly before Kant, how he
expresssed it and consciously destroyed it again, we must consider
what Reason can amount to, if it refuses to pass over into this Idea.
Because of this refusal nothing remains for Reason but the pure
emptiness of identity. It considers identity only in the judgment and
conceives it as the pure universal existing for itself, i.e., as the subjective which, in a state completely purified of the manifold, establishes itself as pure abstract unity. The human intellect is the linking
together of the manifold through the unity of self-consciousness.
Analysis shows that something in the subject is the linking activity.
This spontaneity has various dimensions which yield the categories,
and it is in this regard intellect. But after abstracting both from the
content that the linking activity has through its connection with the
empirical, and from its immanent peculiarity as expressed in the dimensions, the empty unity [that remains] is Reason. The intellect is
unity of a possible experience whereas the unity of Reason relates
to the intellect and its judgments.[30] In this general determination Reason is raised above the sphere of the intellect's relative identity, to
be sure, and this negative character would allow us to conceive of it
as absolute identity. But it was raised above intellect only to let the
speculative Idea—which came out most vividly in imagination and
had already been degraded as intellect—finally sink down completely
to formal identity. Kant is quite correct in making this empty unity
a merely regulative and not a constitutive principle[31]—for how could
something that is utterly without content constitute anything?—and
he posits it as the unconditioned. But to consider how he does this

29. See pp. 86 ff. below.

30. *Critique of Pure Reason*, A 302, B 359.

31. *Critique of Pure Reason*, A 508 ff., B 536 ff.; A 616–17, B 644–5; A 642 ff.,
B 670 ff.; A 644 ff., B 692 ff.; A 671 ff.

would really be of interest from the following perspectives only. For one thing it would be interesting to see how far Kant will go in his polemic against Reason in order to constitute this emptiness—how he roots out again the rational element acknowledged as transcendental synthesis in the intellect and its Deduction; how he roots it out just so far as it should now be recognized as Reason, and not only *qua* product or in its appearance as judgment. [336] It would be of more particular interest, for another thing, to see how this empty unity, as practical Reason, is nonetheless supposed to become constitutive again, to give birth out of itself and give itself content;[32] how, moreover, the Idea of Reason is in the end re-established in its purity only to be brought to nought once more and placed in the irrationality of faith as an absolute Beyond which is a vacuum for cognition;[33] and how subjectivity, which had already come onto the stage in the account of the intellect—though in a way that looked more innocent—thus remains the absolute and the principle.

Kant always and everywhere recognizes that Reason, as the dimensionless activity, as pure concept of infinitude is held fast in its opposition to the finite. He recognizes that in this opposition Reason is an absolute, and hence a pure identity without intuition and in itself empty. But there is an immediate contradiction in this: this infinitude, strictly conditioned as it is by its abstraction from its opposite, and being strictly nothing outside of this antithesis, is yet at the same time held to be absolute spontaneity and autonomy. As freedom, Reason is supposed to be absolute, yet the essence of this freedom consists in being solely through an opposite. This contradiction, which remains insuperable in the system and destroys it, becomes a real inconsistency (*reale Inkonsequenz*) when this absolute emptiness is supposed to give itself content as practical Reason and to expand itself in the form of duties. Theoretical Reason, on the other hand, lets the intellect give it the manifold which it has only to regulate; it makes no claim to an autonomous dignity, no claim to beget the Son out of itself.[34] We must leave it to its own emptiness and the

---

32. *Critique of Practical Reason*, Part I, Book I, Chapter I, sections 1–7 (*Akad.* V, 19–33).

33. *Ibid.*, Book II, chapter II, sections IV–VIII (*Akad.* V, 122–46); compare also *Religion*, Book II, section 1, subsection C (*Akad.* VI, 66–78).

34. This is a reference to the dogma of the Trinity. The Son, or Second Person of the Trinity, has always been identified with the *Logos* or Word referred to in the first chapter of the Gospel of John. According to the Creeds, God the Father *created* the world, but the Son was "*begotten*, not made" and "begotten

unworthiness that comes from its being able to put up with this dualism of a pure unity of Reason and a manifold of the intellect, and from its not feeling any need for the middle and for immanent cognition. The Idea of Reason occurs in the Deduction of the Categories as original unity of the one and the manifold. But instead of lifting it entirely out of its appearance as intellect, Kant makes this appearance permanent with respect to one of its terms, unity, thereby also with respect to the other [the manifold]: finitude is made absolute. We get wind of the Rational again, to be sure, the word "Idea" is dragged up out of Plato once more, and virtue and beauty are recognized as Ideas. But this Reason cannot even get to the point of being able to produce an Idea.

The *polemical side* of Reason, as expressed in the *Paralogisms* [of Pure Reason][35] has no other concern save that of setting aside (*aufheben*) the concepts of the intellect [i.e., the categories] as predicates of the Ego. The Ego is to be raised up into the intelligible realm (*Intellektualität*)[36] out of the sphere of the thing, and of objective, finite

---

of the Father, *before all worlds.*" John, however, says of the Logos "by him (it) all things were made, and without him (it) was not anything made, that was made." Hegel seems to have been influenced by John rather than by Genesis or the Creeds. We know that sometime between 1800 and 1804 he attempted to lay out his philosophy of Nature schematically as a "Divine Triangle" based on the Trinitarian dogma (see Rosenkranz, *Hegels Leben*, pp. 101–2). The present passage clearly shows that he did not interpret the distinction between the "begetting of the Son" and the "creation of the world" in an orthodox way. By treating the "creation" as the "moment of difference" in the "begetting" he could legitimately assert "all things came to be through the *Logos* and apart from it not even one thing came to be that did come to be," (which is what John asserts in the most literal translation possible). Also he could avoid the philosophical inconvenience of a creation of the world *in time* (which does appear to be implied by the *priority* which the Nicene Creed gives to the begetting of the *Logos*). For the way Hegel himself distinguished "the Son" from "the world" at this time see Rosenkranz' reports of his lecture-manuscripts of Summer 1802 (Rosenkranz, pp. 131–41). Compare further p. 181 n. 59 below, and *Difference between Fichte's and Schelling's System*, p. 171.

35. *Critique of Pure Reason*, A 341–405, B 399–432.

36. As we regularly use "intellect" to translate Hegel's *Verstand*, we now have recourse to the Kantian "intelligible" and "noumenal" (over against "sensible" and "phenomenal") to translate Hegel's "intellektuell." Hegel uses *intellektuell* here in two closely related senses. He refers, in the first place, to the operations of Reason as conceived by Kant, i.e., not Hegel-Schelling's own Reason which is intellectual intuition, but a Reason which Kant accuses of illicitly applying the intellect's categories to entities of which in principle no sensuous intuition can be had. In the second place, *intellektuell* refers to the whole realm

determinations. On this level, what is to be predicated of spirit is the abstract form of finitude itself, not a determinate dimension and particular form of the intellect. The "I think" is to be transformed into an absolute noumenal (*intellektuell*) [337] point—not a real existing monad in the form of substance, but a noumenal monad, as a fixed noumenal unit conditioned by infinite opposition, and absolute in this finitude. Thus the Ego is changed from a soul-thing into a qualitative noumenal entity, a noumenal and abstract unit which, as such, is absolute; absolute finitude, which had formerly been a dogmatic object, becomes now a dogmatic subject.

The *mathematical antinomies*[37] deal with the application of Reason as mere negativity to something reflection has fixed. This application immediately produces empirical infinity. A is posited and at the same time it is not to be posited. A is posited in that it remains what it was. It is suspended in that there is a transition to something else. This empty requirement of another, and the absolute being of that for which another is required, together give rise to this empirical infinitude. The antinomy arises because being-other is posited as well as being, i.e., the contradiction in its absolute insuperability. Hence, one side of the antinomy must consist in positing the determinate point, and the refutation in positing the opposite, the being-other—and vice versa for the other side of the antinomy. Kant recognized that

---

of those entities (including the Ego of the "I think") of which in principle no sensuous intuition can be had. This is the realm which Kant's *Dissertation* of 1770 distinguished as the intelligible or noumenal world from the sensible or phenomenal world and which his *Critique of Pure Reason* proved to be unknowable to the understanding (intellect) and the source of the paralogisms (rational psychology), antinomies (rational cosmology) and of illusory proofs of the existence of God (rational theology) to Reason. As to the paralogisms, Hegel confronts Kant's teachings on the "I think" as subjective dogmatism with the objective dogmatism of Leibniz' conception of the monad. (This confrontation offers one interesting perspective among others on how Hegel will conceive his philosophical task on the new level of the spirit that was reached by way of the Leibnizian thesis and the Kantian antithesis.) Hegel criticizes Kant for conceiving of the I that thinks purely abstractly, as a mere Ego-point (*Punkt der Egoität*), as Hegel had expressed this earlier (cf. above p. 78). The I is turned into a "qualitative intellectuality." By this phrase Hegel may mean either or both of two things: 1) there must be some sort of qualitative differentiation between the Ego-points; 2) "qualitative" stands here for the first category of "quality," i.e., reality (and not existence, which is a category of "modality." Cf. A 80, B 106), so that "qualitative intellectuality" would be the same as "noumenal (supersensuous) reality."

37. *Critique of Pure Reason*, A 426–43, B 454–71; A 515–32, B 545–60.

this conflict originates only through and within finitude and is therefore a necessary illusion. Yet he did not succeed in dissolving the conflict. He did not succeed, in the first place, because he did not suspend finitude itself. On the contrary, by turning the conflict into something subjective again, he allowed it to subsist. In the second place, he did not succeed because he can only use transcendental idealism as a negative key for the solution of the antinomy inasmuch as he denies that either side of it is anything in itself. In this way what is positive in these antinomies, their middle, remains unrecognized. Reason appears pure only in its negative aspect, as suspension of reflection. It does not emerge in its own proper shape. Yet [one would think that] this negative aspect, would already be sufficient to keep practical Reason from *infinite progress*[38] at least; for there is the same antinomy in it, as there is in infinite regress, and it similarly exists only for the finite and within its realm. Practical Reason, which takes refuge in this infinite progress and means to constitute itself as absolute in freedom, confesses its finitude and its inability to validate its absoluteness precisely through this infinity of the progress. Kant' solution of the *dynamic antinomies*,[39] however, did not remain merely negative, but confesses the absolute dualism of his philosophy: it removes the conflict by making it absolute. When freedom and necessity are brought into connection with one another, the intelligible world with the sensible, or absolute with empirical necessity, they produce an antinomy. Kant's solution directs us not to relate the antinomic propositions (*Gegensätze*) [338] in this insipid fashion, but to think of them as absolutely heterogeneous and without communion at all. And indeed, in comparison with the [usual] insipid and unsubstantial connection of freedom and necessity, of the intelligible world with the sensible world their pure and complete separation has merit: [it is a step towards] the positing of their absolute identity in perfect purity. But this was not what Kant had in view when he separated them so sharply. To him, the separation [itself] was the absolute: when they are thought without any communion at all freedom and necessity do not conflict.

In this so-called solution of the antinomies the possibility of freedom and necessity being completely separated is proposed as a mere

---

38. I.e., from postulating an infinite moral progress toward the coincidence of virtue and happiness (see *Critique of Practical Reason*, Book II, Chapter II, section IV—*Akad.* V, 122–4).

39. *Critique of Pure Reason*, A 440–60, B 472–88; A 532–65, B 559–93.

thought. But it is posited categorically in another form of reflection, namely in the celebrated critique of speculative theology.[40] This critique positively asserts the absolute opposition of freedom in the form of concept and necessity in the form of being, and brings about the complete victory of nonphilosophy over the horrible delusion that deranged and blinded previous philosophy. Here blinkered intellect enjoys in complete self-confidence and complacency its triumph over Reason which is the absolute identity of the highest Idea and absolute reality. Kant made his triumph even more brilliant and comfortable for himself by taking what used to be called the ontological proof of the existence of God in the worst form it is capable of, which is the form given to it by Mendelssohn[41] and others. They turned existence into a property so that the identity of Idea and reality was made to look like the adding of one concept to another. Altogether—especially in his refutations—Kant showed a pervasive ignorance of philosophical systems and a lack of any information about them that went beyond purely historical data.

Thus Reason is crushed completely. Intellect and finitude are quite properly exultant over the decreeing of their own absolute status. Thereafter, finitude as the very highest abstraction of subjectivity or of conscious finitude, establishes itself also in its positive form, in which it is called *practical Reason*. How the emptiness, the pure formalism of this principle is set forth in contrast to an empirical fullness, and how it grows into a system, we shall show in greater detail in [our discussion of] Fichte at whose hands the mutual integration of this empty unity and its antithetic opposite receives a more thorough and consistent development.

This is, finally, the place to exhibit the most interesting point in the Kantian system, the point at which a region is recognized that is a middle between the empirical manifold and the absolute abstract unity.[42] But [339] once again, it is not a region accessible to cognition. Only the aspect in which it is appearance is called forth, and not its ground which is Reason. It is acknowledged as thought, but with respect to cognition all reality is denied to it.

40. *Ibid.*, A 567–642, B 595–670.

41. See Moses Mendelssohn, *Morgenstunden* (Berlin, 1785), Lecture XVII (Hegel used the second edition of 1786). Kant's "triumph" is in the *Critique of Pure Reason*, A 592–602, B 620–30.

42. *Critique of Judgment*, Preface, and Introduction, section III (*Akad.* V, 167–70, 176–9).

It is, namely, in the *reflecting judgment*[43] that Kant finds the middle term between the concept of nature and the concept of freedom. On one side, there is the objective manifold determined by concepts, the intellect generally[44]; and, on the other side, the intellect as pure abstraction.[45] Neither theoretical nor practical philosophy had lifted themselves above the sphere of the absolute judgment;[46] the middle ground is the region of the identity of what in the absolute judgment is subject and predicate;[47] this identity is the one and only true Reason. Yet according to Kant it belongs only to the reflecting judgment; it is nothing for Reason. Throughout Kant's reflections on Reason in its reality, that is, in his reflection on beauty as conscious intuition[48] and on beauty as non-conscious intuition, that is, on organization [in nature][49] one finds the Idea of Reason expressed in a more or less formal fashion. With respect to beauty in its conscious form (*die ideelle Form der Schönheit*) Kant sets up the Idea of an imagination lawful by itself, of lawfulness without law and of free concord of imagination and intellect[50] His explanations of this sound very empirical, however. When he tells us, for example, that "an esthetic Idea is a representation by the imagination which gives rise to much thought without any particular concept being adequate to it, so that it cannot be reached by, and made understandable in any language,"[51] there is no sign that he has even the mildest suspicion that we are here in the territory of Reason.

In resolving the antinomy of taste Kant comes upon Reason as "the key to the riddle"; but it is still nothing but "the undetermined Idea of the supersensuous in us [. . .] without any further possibility of its being made comprehensible"[52]—as if Kant himself had not given

43. Compare p. 77 n. 22 above.
44. Compare *Prolegomena*, section 21 (*Akad.* IV, 302–4).
45. *Die reine Abstraction des Verstandes*, i.e., the form of universality which the intellect, as practical Reason (or practical Reason as intellect) prescribes as moral law in the categorical imperative.
46. The synthetic judgment *a priori.*
47. Thought and being, or the universal and the particular, or the infinite and the finite.
48. *Critique of Judgment*, sections 1–22 (*Akad.* V, 203–44).
49. *Ibid.*, sections 61–68 (*Akad.* V, 359–84).
50. *Ibid.*, General Note to First Section of the Analytic (*Akad.* V, 241). Kant actually speaks of "free lawfulness" and of "purposiveness without purpose." For the "concord" see also section 9 (*Akad.* V, 218, 219) and section 57, note I (*Ibid.*, 342).
51. *Ibid.*, section 49 (*Akad.* V, 314).
52. *Ibid.*, section 57 (*Akad.* V, 341) .

[us] a concept of it in [his doctrine of] the identity of the concepts of nature and freedom.[53] "An esthetic Idea," according to Kant, "cannot become cognitive because it is an intuition of the imagination for which no concept can ever be found adequate. An Idea of Reason can never be cognitive because it contains a concept of the supersensuous for which no intuition can ever be found commensurate."[54] The esthetic Idea is a representation of the imagination for which no [conceptual] exposition can be given; the Idea of Reason is a concept of Reason for which no demonstration can be given —demonstration in the Kantian sense being the presentation of a concept in intuition.[55] As if the esthetic Idea did not have its exposition in the Idea of Reason, and the Idea of Reason did not have its demonstration in beauty. But instead of asking for an intuition of the absolute identity of the sensuous and the supersensuous, Kant [once more] reverts to what is the very ground of the mathematical antinomies:[56] an intuition for the Idea of Reason [340] in which the Idea would be experienced as purely finite and sensuous and simultaneously and contiguously experienced as a supersensuous Beyond of experience. And he demands an exposition and cognition of the esthetic [intuition, i.e., the beautiful] in which the esthetic would be exhausted by the intellect.

Since beauty is the Idea as experienced or more correctly, as intuited, the form of opposition between intuition and concept falls away. Kant recognizes this vanishing of the antithesis negatively in the concept of a supersensuous realm in general.[57] But he does not recognize that as beauty, it is positive, it is intuited, or to use his own language, it is given in experience. Nor does he see the supersensuous, the intelligible substratum of nature without and within us, the thing in itself, as Kant defines the supersensuous, is at least superficially cognized when the principle of beauty is given a [conceptual]

---

53. It is doubtful whether Hegel has any precise passage in mind here. He may well be thinking of the Introduction to the *Critique of Judgment* (especially sections II, III, IX); but the reader should also compare section 57 Note I, section 59, and section 76 *(Akad.* V, 174–9, 195–9, 341–4, 351–4, 397–401).

54. Section 57 Note I *(Akad.* V, 342).

55. In the German text, this definition of demonstration occurs in the next sentence, but it appears to belong more naturally here; compare *Critique of Judgment,* section 57, Note I *(Akad.* V, 343) and *Critique of Pure Reason,* A 734 ff., B 762 ff.

56. Compare pp. 83–4 above.

57. *Critique of Judgment,* section 57 *(Akad.* V, 341).

exposition as the identity of the concepts of nature and freedom.[58] Still less does he recognize that it is only because the perennial antithesis of the supersensuous and the sensuous is made basic once for all that the supersensuous is taken to be neither knowable nor intuitable. The rational, fixed in this rigid opposition, becomes the supersensuous and is absolutely negative with respect both to intuition and to rational cognition. Consequently, the esthetic is given a relation to the faculty of judgment, and to a subject for whom the supersensuous becomes the principle of nature's purposiveness with respect to our cognitive faculty;[59] and intuition does not present the supersensuous for the Idea, and for cognition, nor does its Idea present itself for intuition. So again, the supersensuous, insofar as it is principle of the esthetic, is unknowable; and the beautiful turns into something strictly finite and subjective because it is only connected with the human cognitive faculty and a harmonious play of its various powers.[60]

The objective side is the nonconscious intuition of the reality of Reason, that is to say, organic nature.[61] In his reflection upon it in the "Critique of Teleological Judgment," Kant expresses the Idea of Reason more definitely than in the preceding concept of a harmonious play of cognitive powers. He expresses it now in the Idea of an intuitive intellect, for which possibility and actuality are one.[62] In an intuitive intellect "concepts (which *merely* concern the possibility of an object) and sensuous intuitions (which give us something without allowing it to be known as object) equally disappear."[63] An intuitive† intellect would "not proceed from the universal to the particular and so to the singular (through concepts); and the concordance of the *particular* laws in nature's products with the intellect will not be *contingent* for it."[64] It is an "archetypal (*urbildlich*) intellect" for which "the possibility of the parts, etc., as to their character and [341]

58. Compare p. 87 n. 3 above.

59. *Critique of Judgment*, section 77 (*Akad.* V, 408–10); compare also the Introduction, *ibid.*, pp. 359–61.

60. *Ibid.*, section 9 (*Akad.* V, 218).

61. Hegel turns now from the "Critique of Aesthetic Judgment" to the "Critique of Teleological Judgment" (the second part of the *Critique of Judgment*).

62. *Critique of Judgment*, section 76 (*Akad.* V, 402). Sections 76–77 of the *Critique of Judgment* exercised an enormous and continuing influence on Hegel, for which the present passage is the earliest clear documentation.

63. *Ibid.*, section 76 (*Akad.* V, 402).

64. *Ibid.*, section 77 (*Akad.* V, 406).

integration is dependent on the whole."[65] Kant also recognizes that we are necessarily driven to this Idea. The *Idea* of this archetypal *intuitive† intellect* is at bottom nothing else but the *same Idea* of the transcendental imagination that we considered above.[66] For it is intuitive activity, and yet its inner unity is no other than the unity of the intellect itself, the category [still] immersed in extension, and becoming intellect and category only as it separates itself out of extension. Thus transcendental imagination is itself intuitive intellect.

The Idea occurs [to Kant] here only as a thought. Notwithstanding its admitted necessity, reality must not be predicated of it. On the contrary, we must once for all accept the fact that universal and particular are inevitably and necessarily distinct. "The intellect is for concepts, sensuous intuition for objects—they are two entirely heterogeneous parts" [of cognition].[67] The Idea is strictly necessary and it is yet problematic. In respect of our cognitive faculty nothing is to be acknowledged save the way it appears in its exercise (as Kant calls it)[68] in which possibility and actuality are distinguished. This its appearance is [for Kant] an absolute essence; it is the In-itself of cognition—as if it were not also an exercise of the cognitive faculty when it conceives and knows (*denkt und erkennt*) that an intellect for which possibility and actuality are not sundered, in which universal and particular are one and whose spontaneity is at the same time intuitive, is a necessary Idea. Kant has simply no ground except experience and empirical psychology for holding that the human cognitive faculty essentially consists in the way it appears, namely in this process from the universal to the particular or back again from the particular to the universal.[69] Yet he himself thinks an intuitive† intellect and is led to it as an absolutely necessary Idea. So it is he himself who establishes the opposite experience, [the experience] of thinking a nondiscursive intellect. He himself shows that his cognitive faculty is aware not only of the appearance and of the separation of the possible and the actual in it, but also of Reason and the In-itself. Kant has here before him both the Idea of a Reason in which possibility and actuality are absolutely identical and its appearance as cognitive faculty wherein they are separated. In the experience of

65. *Ibid.*, (*Akad.* V, 407).
66. Compare pp. 69 ff. above.
67. *Critique of Judgment*, section 76 (*Akad.* V, 401).
68. *Ibid.*, (*Akad.* V, 401, 402).
69. *Critique of Judgment*, Introduction, section IV, and section 77 (*Akad.* V, 179–81, 406–10).

his thinking he finds both thoughts. However, in choosing between the two his nature despised the necessity of thinking the Rational, of thinking an intuitive spontaneity and decided without reservation for appearance.[70]

He recognizes that *in and for itself* it may be possible that the mechanism of nature, the relation of causality, is at one with nature's teleological technique.[71] [342] This is not to say that nature is determined by an Idea opposite to it,[72] but rather that what from the mechanistic point of view appears as absolutely sundered, one term as cause the other as effect in an empirical nexus of necessity, absolutely coheres within an original primordial identity.[73] Kant admits the possibility of this. He admits that this is one way of looking at it. Nonetheless he sticks to the viewpoint from which it is [or they are] absolutely sundered; and what is cognizant of it [them] is thus strictly contingent,[74] an absolutely finite and subjective cognitive faculty which he calls human; and he declares that rational knowledge, for which the organism, as the [physical] reality of Reason, is the higher principle of nature and the identity of the universal and particular, is transcendent.[75] So he recognizes in Spinozism, too, "an idealism of final causes"[76]—as if Spinoza had wished to divest the Idea of final causes of all reality; and as if, without disavowing the teleological coherence of the things of nature, he had given as its principle of explanation only the unity of the subject in which they all inhere, thus turning a merely ontological abstract unity (this means a unity of the intellect like the one that Kant calls Reason) into the principle—for of course "the mere idea of the unity of the sub-

70. Careful reading of sections 76 and 77 of the *Critique of Judgment* is required for the assessment of Hegel's critique of Kant's position with respect to an archetypal intellect. Notice the quite un-Kantian ease with which Hegel (a) proceeds from conceiving (thinking) to knowing and (b) implies that the "experience" of thinking a necessary Idea is an experience of the object of that Idea. Compare also *Difference*, p. 163.

71. About Kant's use of "technique" cf. *Critique of Judgment*, section 72, (*Akad.* V, 389–92). As to the possible identity of mechanistic and final causality see, among other places, *ibid.*, section 78 (*Akad.* V, 410–5).

72. That is, by God, a non-nature making nature purposive.

73. *Ibid.*, sections 70, 78 (*Akad.* V, 382, 412).

74. *Sie* may here be feminine singular referring to *Identität* or plural referring to causality and teleology. The latter view is not ruled out by the singular verb *ist*, since Hegel often uses *ist* with a plurality of subjects.

75. *Critique of Judgment*, section 78 (*Akad.* V, 413).

76. *Ibid.*, sections 72, 73 (*Akad.* V, 391–2, 393).

stratum cannot even ground the Idea of a merely unintentional purposiveness."[77] In understanding Spinoza's unity, Kant should have
kept his eye on his own Idea of the unity of an intuitive† intellect
in which concept and intuition, possibility and actuality are one,[78]
not on that unity of the intellect which he calls theoretical and practical Reason. He would then have had to take Spinoza's unity, not as
an abstract one lacking purposiveness, that is, lacking an absolute
teleological coherence, but as the absolutely intelligible and in itself
organic unity. In this way he would have rationally and directly cognized this organic unity which is by nature purposive (*Naturzweck*)
and which he conceives as the determination of the parts by the
whole, or as identity of cause and effect.[79] But a true unity such as
this, the organic unity of an intuitive† intellect must not ever be
thought; it must not be Reason that here cognizes; it must be the
faculty of judgment that [merely] reflects; and its principle must be
to think *as if* an intellect having consciousness determined nature.
Kant recognizes very clearly that this is no objective affirmation, but
something merely subjective; yet this subjectivity and finitude of the
maxim are to stay as absolute cognition. *In itself* it is not "impossible
that the mechanism and the purposiveness of nature coincide"; but
*"for us men"* it is impossible. The cognizance of this coincidence would
require an intuition other than sensuous. It would require a determinate [343] cognition of the intelligible substratum of nature through
which it would be possible even to give a ground for the mechanism
of appearances according to particular laws. All this transcends our
capacity completely."[80]

Kant himself recognized in the beautiful an intuition other than
the sensuous. He characterized the substratum of nature as intelligible, recognized it to be rational and identical with all Reason, and
knew that the cognition in which concept and intuition are separated
was subjective, finite cognition, a [merely] phenomenal cognition.
Nonetheless, there the matter must rest; we must absolutely not go
beyond finite cognition. Although the cognitive faculty is capable
of [thinking] the Idea and the rational, it simply must not employ

77. *Ibid.*, section 73 (*Akad.* V, 394).
78. *Ibid.*, section 76 (*Akad.* V, 402–3).
79. *Ibid.*, section 65 (*Akad.* V, 372–3).
80. *Ibid.*, section 80 (*Akad.* V, 418). Hyppolite appeals to this passage in explicating the doctrine of "observing Reason" in the *Phenomenology*. See his
*Genèse et Structure* I, 233–4 (English translation, pp. 242–3) and compare Hoffmeister, pp. 196–8 (Baillie, pp. 296–300).

it as a cognitive standard; it must regard itself as absolute only when it knows the organic and itself finitely, phenomenally. The truly speculative aspect of Kant's philosophy can only consist in the Idea being thought and expressed so definitely, and the pursuit of this side of his philosophy is the only interesting aspect of it. This makes it all the harder to see the Rational being muddled up again, and not just that, but to see the highest Idea corrupted with full consciousness, while reflection and finite cognition are exalted above it.

From this exposition we may gather briefly what transcendental knowledge is in this philosophy. The deduction of the categories, setting out from the organic Idea of productive imagination,[81] loses itself in the mechanical relation of a unity of self-consciousness which stands in antithesis to the empirical manifold, either determining it or reflecting on it.[82] Thus transcendental knowledge transforms itself into formal knowledge [i.e., knowledge of the identity of form only]. The unity of self-consciousness is at the same time objective unity, category, formal identity. However, something that is not determined by this identity must supervene to it in an incomprehensible fashion; there must be an addition, a *plus*, of something empirical, something alien. This supervening of a B to the pure Ego-concept [which is A] is called experience, while the supervening of A to B, when B is posited first, is called rational action, [and the formula for both is] A : A + B.[83] The A in A + B is the objective unity of self-consciousness,

81. Compare pp. 69–73 above.

82 .These terms, which derive from the *Critique of Judgment* (Introduction, section IV: *Akad.* V, 179–81) are now applied by Hegel to the different relations Kant conceives theoretical Reason (as "reflecting") and practical Reason (as "determining") to have to what Hegel calls nature.

83. We have here transcribed what was printed in the text of the *Critical Journal*. But it is not clear to us exactly what 'A: A + B' signifies. We could read it as "A *becomes* A + B" (experience) or "A produces A + B (rational action) or "A has as correlate A + B" (neutral). However, on p. 00 above there occurs "$A^2 = (A = B)$." Perhaps what is here meant is that the second power of A is *equal* to A + B at the lower level. The explanation that follows in the text itself would fit very neatly into the hypothesis that ' : ' here is simply a mistake or a substitute for '='. An alternative possibility is that " : " stands for a peculiar combination of " $=$ " and " $\neq$ ". From the viewpoint of the "philosophy of Identity" in which A (self-consciousness) and B (nature) should both be constructed as manifesting the Absolute, that is, as rational, Kant makes the mistake of making self-consciousness the Absolute and therefore of recognizing only an identity of form between nature and self-consciousness. The content or the manifold (sensations in Kant's theoretical philosophy, desires, urges, etc. in his practical philosophy) remains something

B is the empirical, the content of experience, a manifold bound together through the unity A. But B is something foreign to A, something not contained in it. And the *plus* itself, i.e., the bond between the binding activity and the manifold, is what is incomprehensible. This *plus* was rationally cognized as productive imagination. But if this productive imagination is merely a property of the subject, of man and his intellect, it abandons of itself its [place in the] middle, which alone makes it what it is, and becomes subjective. It does not matter whether we picture this formal knowledge as running along the thread of identity or that of causality. For if A as universal [344] is posited in opposition to A + B as particular, it is the cause. On the other hand, if reflection stresses that both [A and A + B] contain one and the same A which as concept binds itself up with the particular, this causal relation appears as identity relation from the side where the cause is joined to the effect,[84] i.e., where it is cause, although on this side something else must still supervene. And saying that the causal bond belongs entirely to the analytic judgment is the same as saying that in the causal bond there is transition to an absolute opposite.

Generally speaking, then, this formal cognition takes the shape of its formal identity being confronted absolutely by a manifold; when taken to exist in itself, the formal identity is freedom, practical Reason, autonomy, law, practical Idea, etc., and its absolute opposite is necessity, the inclination and drives, heteronomy, nature, etc. The connection that is possible between the two [formal identity and the manifold] is an incomplete one within the bounds of an absolute anti-

---

totally alien to A. A: A + B, then, expresses the identity between the two As: A= A (+ B) and at the same time the absolute non-identity between A and B: A ≠ (A+) B. More specifically, in Kant's *theoretical* philosophy "the formal identity" consists in the identity of the "form" of A and the "form" of B, the categories of the understanding (intellect) being the same as the universal structure of nature: A = A (+ B). But the wealth of content experienced is due to the sensations totally alien to theoretical Reason (and caused in the subject by the unknowable things-in-themselves "in an incomprehensible way"): A ≠ (A +) B. In Kant's *practical* philosophy the formal identity lies in the form of universality prescribed by Reason to (the maxims of) our actions in all their manifoldness: A = A (+ B). But B (our "nature, that is, our desires, etc.") are as alien to Reason as the sensations are to the categories: A ≠ (A +) B. However, whereas in theoretical philosophy the causal genesis of sensations is incomprehensible, in practical philosophy it is the causality of Reason on our nature that is incomprehensible.

84. Compare p. 75 above.

thesis: the manifold gets determined by the unity [in practical philosophy] just as the emptiness of identity gets plenished by the manifold [in theoretical philosophy]. Whether active or passive, each supervenes to the other in a formal way, as something alien. This formal cognition only brings about impoverished identities, and allows the antithesis to persist in its complete absoluteness. What it lacks is the middle term (*Mittelglied*), which is Reason; for each of the two extremes is to exist within the opposition as an Absolute, so that the middle, and the coming to nothing of both extremes and of finitude is an absolute Beyond. It is recognized [by Kant] that this antithesis necessarily presupposes a middle, and that in this middle the antithesis and its content must be brought to nothing. But this is not an actual, genuine nullification; it is only a confession that the finite *ought* to be suspended. Nor is the middle any more genuine; again it is only a confession that there *ought* to be a Reason.[85] And it is all posited in a faith, whose content itself is empty because the antithesis which as absolute identity could be its content has to remain outside it; expressed positively, the content of this faith would be Reasonlessness (*Vernunftlosigkeit*) because it is an absolutely unthought, unknown and incomprehensible Beyond.

If we remove from the practical faith of the Kantian philosophy some of the popular and unphilosophical garments in which it is decked, we shall find nothing else expressed in it but the Idea that Reason does have absolute reality, that in this Idea the antithesis of freedom and necessity is completely suspended, that infinite thought [345] is at the same time absolute reality—or in short we shall find the absolute identity of thought and being. (We are here thinking only of Kant's doctrine of faith in God.[86] For his account of immortality[87] has nothing original in it to make it worthy of philosophical attention.) This Idea of the absolute identity of thought and being is the very one which the ontological proof and all true philosophy recognize as the sole and primary Idea as well as the only true and philosophical one. Kant, to be sure, recasts this speculative Idea into the humane form: morality and happiness harmonize. This harmony is made into a thought in its turn, and the realization of this thought is called the highest good in the world[88]—something as wretched as

85. *Critique of Judgment*, section 76 (*Akad.* V, 402–4).
86. *Critique of Practical Reason*, Book II, Chapter II, section V (*Akad.* V, 124–32).
87. *Ibid.*, section IV (*Akad.* V, 122–4).
88. *Ibid.*, section V (*Akad.* V, 125).

this morality and this happiness the highest good! But then, of course, Reason as active in the finite, and nature as sensed in the finite, cannot raise themselves to anything higher than a practical faith of this kind. This faith is just made to measure for the state of absolute immersion in the empirical; for it lets Reason[89] keep the finitude of thought, and action, as well as the finitude of enjoyment. If Reason were to arrive at intuition and knowledge that Reason and nature are in absolute harmony and are in themselves blissful, it would recognize its wretched morality which does not harmonize with happiness and the wretched happiness which does not harmonize with morality, as the nothings that they are. But what matters [to Kant] is that both morality and happiness be something, and something high and absolute. This morality reviles nature and its spirit, as if the order and direction (*die Einrichtung*) in nature was not itself made rational, while on the contrary this morality in its misery—it was not for this, surely, that the spirit of the universe organized itself?—existed in itself and eternally. Moreover, this morality means indeed to justify itself and do itself honor on the ground that it does set the reality of Reason before itself in faith though not as something that possesses absolute being. Yet if the absolute reality of Reason were truly certain, then limited being and the finite and this morality could not have either certainty or truth.

It should not be overlooked, however, that Kant remains within the right and proper bounds of his postulates, which Fichte does not respect. According to Kant himself the postulates and the faith that goes with them (*ihr Glauben*) are subjective;[90] the only question is how to take this "subjective." Is it the identity of infinite thought and being, of Reason and its reality, that is subjective? Or is it only the postulating and the believing of them? Is it the content or the form of the postulates? It cannot be the content that is subjective, for the negative content of the postulates immediately suspends everything subjective. Hence it is the form, or in other words it is something subjective and contingent that the Idea is only a subjective thing. There should in principle (*an sich*) be no postulating, no ought and no [mere] believing, and the postulating of the absolute reality of the highest Idea is something non-rational. Fichte did not acknowl-

---

89. The text has *ihr* which may refer to *die Vernunft* (as we think) or to *die Natur* or finally to *die Empirie* (which Méry prefers).

90. *Critique of Practical Reason*, Book II, Chapter II, section VIII (*Akad.* V, 145–6).

edge this subjectivity of postulating and believing and ought. To him, this is the In-itself. Kant, on the contrary, does acknowledge that the postulating and the ought and [346] the believing are only a subjective and finite thing. Nevertheless, the matter must simply rest there, just as with morality. Letting it rest there meets with universal approval, and what is approved is just exactly the worst thing about it, namely the form of postulating.

This, then, is the character of the Kantian philosophy. The common ground which it shares with the philosophies of reflection that we are talking about is that knowledge is formal knowledge; Reason as a pure negativity is an absolute Beyond; as a Beyond and as negativity it is conditioned by this-worldliness (*Diesseits*) and by positivity; infinity and finitude, each with its opposite, are all equally absolute. What is peculiar to the Kantian philosophy is the form in which it presents itself, its richly instructive and well-organized range; also its truth within the bounds that it sets, however, not only for itself, but for Reason in general. Then there is that interesting aspect of it in which it happens on truly speculative Ideas, though as if they were incidental ideas and mere thoughts without reality. Not counting all this, the uniqueness of the Kantian philosophy is that it establishes its absolute subjectivity in objective form, that is, as concept and law—and it is only because of its purity that subjectivity is capable of passing into its opposite, objectivity. —Of the two parts of reflection, the finite and the infinite, therefore, it raises the infinite above the finite, thus vindicating at least the formal† aspect of Reason. The highest Idea of the Kantian philosophy is the complete emptiness of subjectivity, or the purity of the infinite concept, which is also posited as what is objective in the sphere of the intellect, though there it has the dimensions of the categories; whereas on the practical side the infinite concept is posited as *objective law*. On one side there is infinity infected with finitude, on the other side, there is pure infinity, and in the middle there is posited the identity of the finite and the infinite,[91] though once more only in the form of the infinite, that is, as concept. The authentic Idea remains an absolutely subjective maxim, partly for reflecting judgment, and partly for faith; but it does not exist for the middle of cognition and of Reason.[92]

91. In the doctrines of the *Critique of Judgment* concerning beauty and natural teleology.

92. The "authentic Idea" has its real "middle" when Reason comes into its own as intellectual intuition. In Kant, however, this "middle of Reason" takes the form not of intellectual intuition, but of reflective intellect and faith.

# B. Jacobian Philosophy

*Jacobi's philosophy* shares with Kant's the common ground of absolute finitude, both in its ideal form, as formal knowledge, and in its real form as an absolute empiricism. They also agree about the integration of these two absolute finitudes by way of a faith that posits an absolute Beyond. Within this common [347] sphere, however, the philosophy of Jacobi forms the opposite pole to that of Kant. In Kant's philosophy finitude and subjectivity have an objective form, the form of the concept. Jacobi's philosophy, on the contrary, makes subjectivity entirely subjective, it turns it into individuality. This subjective core of the subjective thus regains an inner life so that it seems to be capable of the beauty of feeling (*Empfindung*).

We begin with the subjectivity of knowledge. Jacobi immediately recognizes and consciously abstracts the formal side of knowledge, and expounds it in its purity. He asserts positively that knowledge exists only in this form and he denies the objectivity of Reason in knowledge.[1] It is this formal knowledge therefore that he accepts as valid in his polemics, and he combats the science of Reason by means of it.

All that Jacobi knows of throughout is this formal knowledge, an identity of the intellect whose content is supplied by experience, a thinking to which reality in general supervenes in some inconceivable way. This is one of the few points, indeed the only point, about which Jacobi's philosophy is objective and pertains to science; and it is a point which is presented in clear concepts. Thus Jacobi says (*David Hume*, Preface, p. V): "My philosophy [. . .] limits Reason, considered by itself, to the mere faculty of perceiving relations distinctly, that is, to forming the *principle of contradiction*[2] and judging according to it. So, of course, I [Jacobi] have to admit that only the affirmation of identical propositions is apodictic and accompanied

---

1. I.e., he denies the possibility of speculative philosophy.
2. Jacobi wrote: "the principle of identity." This is the one place where Hegel's citation is not exact. It is probably a slip of the pen, since Hegel goes on to call the principle of sufficient reason "the necessary counterpart of the principle of identity"; and he expounds it as a "principle of contradiction" in Jacobi's philosophy (p. 99 below).

with absolute certainty."[3] Similarly (*Letters on Spinoza*, p. 215 seq.):
Conviction upon rational grounds[4] is a second-hand certainty (first-
hand certainty is faith, of which more later). Rational grounds are
but marks of *similarity* with something of which we are certain
(namely through faith). The conviction produced by reason emerges
"from *comparison* and can never be quite certain and perfect."[5] One
of the five theses that summarize his assertions (*ibidem.* p. 225) is:
"We can demonstrate only *similarities*"—for demonstration is advance by way of identical propositions—" . . . and every proof presupposes something already proved, of which the principle is nothing
but revelation."[6] Cf. p. 421: "The business of Reason in general is a
progressive tying together (*Verknüpfung*) and its *speculative* business is a tying together according to known (*erkannte*) laws of necessity. . . . The essential *indeterminateness of human language* and
notation and the *changeable aspect of sensuous shapes* permits almost
all these propositions to acquire an *external appearance* (*Ansehen*)
of saying something more than the mere *quidquid est, illud est*, more
than a mere fact which was perceived, observed, compared, recognized and linked with other concepts."[7] Cf. also p. 283 and *David
Hume*, p. 94.[8]

[348] The necessary counterpart to the principle of identity is the
principal of sufficient reason (*Satz des Grundes*), whether—following
Jacobi's distinctions in the *Letters on Spinoza*, p. 415[9]—we mean by
this the general principle of sufficient reason or the principle of cause
and effect or a union of both; and considering its content, whether
one proceeds from concepts to concepts or from the concept to its
reality or from some objective realities to others.

The earlier philosophical culture has deposited the testimony of its
rational endeavours in the formulation of the principle of sufficient
reason. The principle has swayed between Reason and reflection, and
passed over into the latter. All this shows up very characteristically
in the distinction that Jacobi draws between its function as logical
principle and its function as causal relation. He uses this distinction
both as a way to understand philosophy and as a way to combat it.

---

3. Jacobi did not reprint this "Preface" in his *Collected Works*, Vol. II.
4. Hegel substitutes *Gründe* for Jacobi's *Beweise*.
5. Jacobi, *Werke* IV, 1, 210.
6. *Werke* IV, 1, 223 (Hegel added the "nothing but").
7. *Ibid.*, IV, 2, 150–151.
8. The corresponding references for the *Werke* are: IV, 1, 231 and II, 193.
9. *Ibid.*, IV, 2, 144–47.

We want now to follow him upon his road. Jacobi recognizes in the principle of sufficient reason its significance as principle of rational cognition: *totum parte prius esse necesse est* [the whole is necessarily prior to the part]. (*David Hume*, p. 94).[10] In other words, the single part only gets determined in the whole. It has its reality only in the absolute identity which, insofar as discernibles are posited in it, is absolute totality. In one connection, so Jacobi says, the proposition *totum parte prius esse necesse est* is "nothing but *idem est idem*"[11] while in another it is not. It is essential [according to Jacobi] that these two contexts be distinguished and kept absolutely apart; and this is precisely the point where this basic dogmatism[12] takes its beginning. For Jacobi conceives the principle of sufficient reason as pure principle of contradiction and calls it in this sense logical—an abstract unity to which it is, of course, necessary that the difference should supervene as an empirical content. From this logical sense of the principle he distinguishes a causal relation in which the heterogeneous element, the empirical datum that is added to the identity of the concept, is reflected upon. He asserts that the causal relation is in respect of this peculiarity an empirical concept. The way in which he makes this out in *David Hume* (p. 99 seq.)[13] and which he appeals to in the *Letters on Spinoza* (p. 415)[14] is a remarkable piece of empiricism à la Locke and Hume with an equally glaring piece of German dogmatism of the analysing kind kneaded into it. This last is even worse than the Mendelssohn variety,—and the world can never be grateful enough to the Gods—next to Kant—for its salvation from that. Specifically what Jacobi misses in the principle of sufficient reason and in the totality is the parts, and he has to fetch them from somewhere outside the whole. Or, as he conceives it, all parts are already actually united in a whole and present in it; but such an intuitive cognition of the parts within and through the whole is merely *something subjective* and incomplete, *because* the objective becoming and the succession are still lacking, and for their sake [349] the causal relation must still supervene to the totality.[15] Just listen to the

10. *Ibid.*, II, 193.

11. *Ibid.*, II, 193.

12. *Grund-Dogmatismus*—i.e., dogmatism about the "principle of sufficient reason."

13. *Ibid.*, II, 199 ff.

14. *Ibid.*, IV, 2, 144 ff.

15. Hegel is here summarizing from the same context referred to above (*ibid., Werke* II, 193–200).

following series of propositions which give the deduction of what Jacobi calls the absolute necessity of the concept of cause and effect and of succession *(David Hume,* pp. 111 ff.):

"For *our human consciousness* and I may add immediately, for the consciousness of every finite being, an actual thing that is sensed is necessary, besides the thing that senses. [. . .]

"Where two created beings, which are external to each other, stand in such a relation that one acts upon the other, there is an extended being. [. . .]

"We feel the manifold of our being knitted together in a pure unity we call our Ego. The indivisible *(das Unzertrennliche)* in a being defines its individuality; it makes it an actual whole. [. . .] In corporeal extension in general we perceive something that is somewhat analogous to individuality; for the extended being as such is always indivisible, setting before us everywhere the same unity that knits a plurality together indivisibly within itself.[16]

"If [organic][17] individuals [. . .] also have the capacity to act externally, they must, in order for the effect to take place, mediately or immediately touch other beings. [. . .]

"The immediate consequence of impenetrability to the touch we call resistance. So, where there is touch, there is impenetrability on both sides, and hence also resistance, action and reaction; *both are the source*[18] *of the successive and of time,* which is the idea of the successive."[19]

[In sum,] this deduction of the concepts of extension, of cause and effect, and of succession, in other words, the deduction of the absoluteness of finitude results from the presupposition that "there exist single beings that are aware of themselves and in community with one another."[20] At the same time the deduction shows that these concepts "must be common to all self-aware finite beings, and that these concepts have their objective correlate independent of the con-

---

16. In a footnote *(ibid.,* II, 212) Jacobi connects this analogy between the wholeness of individuals and that of "the extended being" with Link's now forgotten book on the *Philosophy of Nature;* but in another context he connects it with the "Metaphysical Exposition of Space" in Kant's *Critique of Pure Reason* (A 25; B 39).

17. That Jacobi's *Individua* are primarily organisms is made clear in the preceding omission.

18. Jacobi wrote "Resistance in space, *action and reaction,* is the source. . . ."

19. *Ibid.,* II, 208–213 (Hegel's quotation marks).

20. *Ibid.,* II, 213.

cept *in the things in themselves* and consequently that they have a true objective significance."[21]

"These concepts are concepts which must be given completely in any experience, and they are so basic that without their object no concept would have an object, and without them no cognition would be possible at all. Such concepts are called strictly universal or necessary concepts, and the judgments and conclusions originating from them are called *a priori cognitions*."—[22]

We note that this deduction was supposed to concern the causal relation in its entire scope and to deliver something more compelling than the Kantian deduction. This deduction of Jacobi's, however, is so little deserving of the name that it cannot even be called an ordinary analysis of its presupposition, which is the concept of a community of single things. It is surely something [350] which all speculation must recoil at, to see the absoluteness of a human consciousness, of a thing that senses, a thing that is sensed, and of their community, presupposed straight off, in the spirit of the most vulgar empiricism. By way of superfluous mediating concepts they [the singles in their community] are analytically messed up into action and reaction, and *this*—here even the analyzing runs out—is the *source* of the successive. One cannot see what all the elaborate artifice is supposed to be good for at all; for all philosophy is already driven from the field by the unanalyzed and absolute assumption of a thing that senses and a thing sensed. There is a noteworthy difference between Jacobi's presupposition and result, and the result of the Kantian deduction of the categories. According to Kant, all these concepts of cause and effect, succession, etc., are strictly limited to appearance; the things in which these forms are objective as well as any cognition of them are simply nothing at all *in themselves*. The In-itself and Reason are wholly raised above these forms of finitude and kept clear of them. This is the very result which gives Kant the immortal merit of having really made the beginning of a philosophy. Yet it is precisely in this nothingness of finitude that Jacobi sees an absolute in-itself. With this dream as his weapon he fights Spinoza wide awake.

We previously located the inadequacy of Kant's annihilation of the intellect in his treating the intellect and its forms as something which, though subjective, is still positive and absolute even in that

---

21. *Ibid.*, II, 114.
22. *Ibid.*, II, 214 (Hegel's quotation marks).

shape. Jacobi, after having so felicitously squeezed action and re-action, succession, time, etc. out of the community of finite things, opines, on the contrary, that "to become independent of experience, these basic concepts and judgments do not need to be turned into prejudices of the intellect, from which we have to be cured by learn-ing to recognize that they are not connected with anything in itself and consequently have no true objective significance. For the basic concepts and judgments lose neither their universality nor their ne-cessity if they are taken from what must be common and basic to all experiences. Rather they gain a far higher degree of unconditioned universality"—does the unconditioned have degrees?—"if they can be derived [not merely as valid for man and his peculiar sensibility, but]²³ from the essence and community of singular things in general. [. . .] —[According to Kant] our senses teach us nothing of the qualities of things, nothing of their mutual relations and connections, they do not even teach us that, in a transcendental sense, things are actually there.²⁴ This would be a sensibility that represented *nothing at all of the things themselves*, [351] a sensibility that is decidedly empty of objective reference. Our intellect is supposed to connect with this sensibility in order to give radically subjective forms to radically subjective intuitions according to radically subjective rules. [. . .] In that case I am everything and, properly speaking, nothing exists outside me. I, and everything of mine, am in the end also nothing but a mere delusion of something or other, the form of a form, [. . .] a ghost. [. . .] A system of this sort completely uproots all claims to the cognition of truth and leaves for the most important matters only a faith more blind and utterly devoid of cognition than anyone ever imputed to man before."²⁵

We should do well to make a distinction here. Kant's view that faith is non-cognitive is grounded only in his misjudgment of the ra-tional as such, and not in his great theory *that the intellect cognizes nothing in itself*. What Jacobi enriches the human cognition with, on the other hand, is such discoveries as the absoluteness of finite things and their community, the absoluteness of time and succession and the causal nexus, each of which (*Hume*, p. 119) "has an objective

---

23. The words here bracketed were inserted by Hegel. They are not in Jacobi's text.

24. Here Jacobi wrote "do not even teach us that things are actually there outside of us."

25. *Ibid.*, II, 214–7 (Hegel's quotation marks).

correlate independent of the concept in the things-in-themselves."[26] Jacobi finds it shocking and horrifying that these absolutes of objective finitude should be negated and recognized as nothing in themselves, and that in consequence subjective finitude, the Ego that is sensuous and thinks reflectively, *my* whole world, should likewise be only an empty illusion of something-in-itself. He finds it shocking and horrifying that *my* finite world should perish in the face of Reason, no less than the world of finite objects. His abhorrence of the nullification of the finite is as fixed as his corresponding absolute certainty of the finite; and this abhorrence will everywhere show itself to be the basic character of Jacobi's philosophy. If what we have quoted above could be called a deduction at all, it might at first be considered an improvement upon Kant's because Jacobi conceives of succession and causality as relation in general, that is, as a merely relative connection, restricted to finite things, and in that the deduction proceeds not merely from a conscious intellect, as Kant does, but also from a non-conscious intellect.[27] In Jacobi, however, relation regarded as subjective, that is, the conscious intellect, stands quite independently and dualistically alongside relation regarded as objective, that is, as intellect and relation of things; whereas in Kant relation is one and one only—without any distinction between a subjective intellect and a separate objective intellect. For though we must conceive the intellect as something subjective in Kant, still there is no external and alien relation of things; so that there is only *one* intellect, and in this Kant expresses at least the formal aspect of philosophy. But even if we pass over all that, Kant's most important result [as against Jacobi] will always remain this: these relations of the finite (whether they are relations within the sphere of the subject alone, or relations of things as well) are nothing in themselves, and cognition in accordance with them is only [352] a cognition of appearances, (even though it becomes absolute because it is not to be transcended). The *apriority* of Jacobi's relations, on the contrary, consists in their belonging also to the *things-in-themselves*, which is to say that the finite things, both the thing that senses and, apart from it, the actual thing that is sensed, are *things-in-themselves*. Relations of these things, relations such as succession, causal nexus, resistance, etc. are [in Jacobi] true rational relations, that is, Ideas. As a result the apparent improvement, according to which the rela-

---

26. *Ibid.*, II, 214.

27. Compare Jacobi's account of "the extended being" on p. 100 above.

tions are not merely subjective, belonging to the conscious intellect, but also something objective and non-conscious, is really the establishment of an absolute dogmatism, the elevation of the finite to an In-itself.

[As we have seen] the important distinction of the principle of sufficient reason from the principle of causality resulted, for Jacobi, in a founding of the absoluteness of the finite.[28] [We shall see now how] he applies this result to Spinoza's system in two ways. He argues, on the one hand, that Spinoza lacks the concept of succession; and, on the other, that in the last analysis Spinoza does have it, but in the absurd form of an eternal time.

As to the first point, the lack [of the concept] of time, Jacobi understands Spinoza's philosophy as meaning to achieve a *"natural explanation of the existence of finite and successive things."*[29] But because, by the standard of the concept of Reason, Spinoza regarded things as present at once—"for in the concept of Reason there is no before and after, everything is necessary and simultaneous"[30]—and because he cognized the universe *sub specie æterni*, he mistook the principle of sufficient reason for a merely logical principle and thus established "not an objective and actual succession, but only a subjective and ideational one. But in fact there could not even be an ideational succession if it were not grounded on an *actual* succession in the subject that produces it in thought."[31] In the logical principle of sufficient reason succession itself is what is inconceivable.[32]

It is not worth talking about a psychological reminder of this kind —to the effect that a subjective and ideational succession presupposes an actual succession in the subject. It either says nothing or it says something false. The reason for this is that ideational succession is connected with Spinoza's mathematical similes (which we shall discuss later);[33] and that in its truth it can only be something real because it is the absolute simultaneity of the totality and not a succession

---

28. Compare p. 98 ff. above, and Jacobi, *Werke* II, pp. 197–217.

29. *Ibid.*, IV, 2, 135. Jacobi's' complaint about "eternal time" is *ibid.*, p. 136.

30. *Ibid.*, IV, 2, 140.

31. *Ibid.*, IV, 2, 136; compare II, 198. We take the main strand of the meaning of Jacobi's term *idealisch* ("ideational") to be "pertaining to mere ideas." Thus "succession" as *idealisch* is the mere idea of succession; but this mere idea of succession would have to be grounded on an actual succession of ideas. Compare, however, Méry, p. 306.

32. *Ibid.*, II, 199.

33. See p. 110 ff. below.

at all. Jacobi, however, ascribes this absolute simultaneity of the totality, and the cognition of things as they are, not temporally but *sub specie æterni*, to the principle of sufficient reason and to neglect of the principle of causality, the latter so understood that time is posited in it. Causality and time should not be neglected, the absolute ground for this being that according to Jacobi time is in itself and absolute. He calls the principle of sufficient reason, that is, the totality, logical, because cause and effect are simultaneous in it, and no time is posited. [353] Of course, if we do *not* forget the principle of causality as distinct from the principle of sufficient reason, we are immovably enthroned in time,[34] which is Jacobi's absolute demand. Jacobi insistently admonishes us not to forget his distinctions, because from the rational concept in which there is no before and no after, and everything is necessary and simultaneous, a misfortune arises: finitude and time and succession perish in the highest Idea, the Idea of the eternal. These warnings are very much like the famous signals of that worthy sentry of the Town Walls, who shouted to the approaching enemy who was ready to fire, not to shoot because this might cause misfortunes—as if such misfortune was not what was intended in the first place.

In the concept of Reason everything is simultaneous. From this, Jacobi drew the simple and correct conclusion that "we are forced to accept that in nature everything is simultaneous and what we call succession is mere appearance." Jacobi calls this proposition paradoxical and he is amazed that Mendelssohn was the first who thought its admission unobjectionable,[35]—Mendelssohn says very rightly that "succession and duration are *necessary* determinations of a thinking that is restricted"[36]—while he, Jacobi, had to defend the thesis [that succession is an appearance] against the other philosophers (!) to whom he submitted it.[37] But he did not propound the proposition seriously [he says], but only as a necessary consequence of the principle of sufficient reason. Anyway, it is quite incomprehensible how Jacobi can pride himself on having discovered this proposition; for it surely belongs to Spinoza. Can it possibly be the case that Jacobi, the commentator on Spinoza, understood Spinoza to have placed time in God, when according to Spinoza it belongs only to *natura*

34. Jacobi, *Werke* IV, 2, 146–7.

35. *Ibid.*, II, 195–7.

36. Cited by Jacobi, *ibid.*, IV, 1, 109.

37. Jacobi says that he has defended it "for fifteen years or longer against many philosophers" (*ibid.*, II, 197).

naturata? We shall in fact see in a moment that after having concluded that Spinoza must really affirm time to be nothing but appearance, Jacobi still manages to find it in Spinoza, and in the absurd
form of an eternal time at that. Spinoza does talk about the subordinate form of succession incidentally in a few places—for example,
in the second book of the *Ethics* and in his letters,[38] where he marks
off the infinite series of finite things under this form of abstraction.
But the word he uses for it is 'imaginari,' not 'think,' and he calls it
quite definitely an *auxilium imaginationis*; now surely Jacobi is familiar enough with Spinoza's distinction between *intellectus* and *imagi-
natio*? The doctrine of the absolute *simul*, the doctrine that God is
not the transient cause, but the eternal cause of things, and that the
things outside God are nothing in themselves, and hence things in
time, and time itself are nothing—every line of Spinoza's system
makes the proposition that time and succession are mere appearance
so utterly trivial that not the slightest trace of novelty and paradox
is to be seen in it. Jacobi (*Letters* [354] *on Spinoza*, p. 409) cites
Spinoza's conviction that "everything must be considered solely *se-
cundum modum quo a rebus æternis fluit*" [according to the mode in
which it flows from eternal things] and that "time, measure and
number must be considered as kinds of idea abstracted from this
mode, and hence, as entities of the imagination."[39] So how could the
proposition that succession is mere appearance not belong to Spinoza?
Jacobi finds it so paradoxical that he not only does not entertain it
in earnest, he simply turns this most finite form of finitude into something absolute. And he bases his whole refutation of Spinoza and
his explanation of Spinoza's delusion about philosophy on Spinoza's
supposed failure to formulate the principle of sufficient reason in such
a way that it includes time. It is just on account of this finitude that
Jacobi himself recognizes that the enterprise of Reason is impossible
and contingent.

Jacobi actually does find Spinoza guilty of the inconsistency of
positing time as something in-itself. He finds that "the infinite series
of single things where one after (!) the other becomes real, is basically (where is this basis, this ground?) *an eternal time*, an infinite
finitude." This assertion—to which there is no rhyme or reason—

---

38. Hegel appears to have the following two passages in mind throughout his
discussion: *Ethics*, Part II, Prop. 44; Epistle XII (Gebhardt) (= Epistle XXIX in
the traditional ordering of the Paulus edition which Hegel used).

39. Jacobi, *Werke* IV, 2, 141.

Jacobi believes impossible to push aside with any mathematical figure: here, Spinoza allowed himself to be "deceived by his imagination."[40]

We first want to elucidate Spinoza's infinite series of finite things, and then the eternal time which Jacobi makes of it, and the [supposed] inadmissibility of mathematical similes.

Spinoza explains the *infinitum actu* [actual infinite] in the 29th letter (which Jacobi takes into consideration too). Spinoza says of the *infinitum actu* that "it is denied by those who, because they are ignorant of the true nature of things, confuse the things of imagination, that is, number, measure and time, with the things themselves."[41] It is precisely the actual infinite that Jacobi himself confuses with the infinite of imagination. Spinoza defines the infinite (*Ethics*, Part I, Prop. VIII, Sch. I) as "the absolute affirmation of the existence of any nature"; and contrariwise he defines the finite as partial negation. Thus this simple definition makes the infinite into the absolute and true concept, equal to itself and indivisible, which of its essence includes the particular or finite in itself at the same time, and is unique and indivisible. Spinoza calls this infinite, in which nothing is negated and determined, the infinity of the intellect. It is the infinity of substance, and the cognition of it is intellectual intuition. In this intuitive cognition, the particular and finite are not excluded [from the infinite] as opposites, as [they are] from the empty concept and from the infinity of abstraction. This infinite is the Idea itself. The infinite of imagination, on the other hand, originates in an entirely different way. Spinoza's way of putting it is this: "we can at will determine and divide the existence and duration of the modes if we consider, not the order of nature itself, but the particular essence [of the modes] insofar as [355] their concept is not the concept of the substance itself."[42] "Measure and time originate for us when we conceive quantity in abstraction from substance, and duration in abstraction from the way it flows from the eternal things."[43] In other words, it is only imagination, as Spinoza calls it, or, in general, only reflection that posits and partially negates the finite; and this partially negated thing, which, when posited for itself and opposed to

40. *Ibid.*, IV, 2, 135–6.
41. Spinoza, *Opera* (ed. Paulus) I, 530 (= Epistle XII in *Opera*, ed. Gebhardt, IV, 58–9).
42. *Opera* (ed. Paulus) I, 528–9; or (ed. Gebhardt) IV, 55–6.
43. *Ibid.*

what is in itself not negated, to what is strictly affirmative, turns this infinite itself into something partially negated. The infinite, being thus brought into antithesis with the finite becomes an abstraction, the pure Reason, or the infinite of Kant. The eternal is to be posited as the absolute identity of both; and in the eternal the infinite on one side, the finite on the other, are once more nullified as to the antithesis between them.[44] It is quite another matter when the finite and infinite in their abstractness are to remain what they are and each is to be taken up into the form of an opposite. Here, the one is determined as not being what the other is, and each is posited and not posited, as being this determinate being and as something else. Anything posited in this fashion runs to empirical infinity. Duration, simply as it is posited by imagination, is a time moment, a finite; fixed as such, it is something partially negated, something that is in and for itself determined as being also another moment; and this other moment which likewise receives its actual being through the imagination, is yet another moment. This negation, remaining what it is, and made positive through imagination, results in the empirical infinite, that is, in an absolute, unresolved contradiction.

This empirical infinity is posited only insofar as single things are posited (*Ethics*, Part I, Proposition XXVIII). But, as against Jacobi who posits them in the deduction above as absolute, in the form of a thing that senses and a thing that is sensed, Spinoza takes single things to be strictly nothing in themselves. Jacobi makes Spinoza responsible for this empirical infinite with no more ado, although no philosopher was ever farther removed from assuming anything of the sort than Spinoza was; for since he regards finite things as nothing in themselves, this empirical infinite and time disappear at once. According to Jacobi, Spinoza "asserts that it is merely due to our imagination that we represent an infinite series of *single things that follow one another, and actually, objectively arise from one another* as an eternal time."[45] But how could Spinoza ever have allowed *such a series of single things that follow one another, and actually, objectively arise from one another* to count as *something self-existent* or seen as it truly is? The mistake is already there in this series of single and successive things, which Jacobi regards as an absolute, and it is Jacobi who introduces the single thing and time into Spinoza's infinity. An Idea, considered from its negative side, *vis-à-vis* [356]

44. *Nach ihrem Gegensatz*: Méry translates, "après leur opposition."
45. Jacobi, *Werke* IV, 2, 135–6.

imagination or reflection, is an Idea because imagination or reflection can transform it into an absurdity. This transformation is of the simplest; [for] imagination, or reflection, is only concerned with single things or with abstractions and the finite—they have absolute validity for it. But in the Idea this singularity and finitude is brought to nought, because the opposite of reflection or of imagination, the mental or the empirical opposite[46] is thought as one [with the Idea]. Reflection can comprehend this much: that things which it posits as particulars are posited as identical. What it cannot comprehend is that in the identity they are nullified; for since it is only reflection that is active, its products are absolute. So, to its delight, it detects an absurdity: it posits both the identity of what exists for it, only in separation, and the absolute standing of those same separate entities in this identity. This is Jacobi's case. He posits the abstract entity "time" and the abstract entity "single thing," which are products of imagination or reflection, as existing in themselves; and then he finds that, if the absolute *simul* of the eternal substance is posited, the single thing and time, which only are in virtue of having been removed from it, are equally posited along with it. He fails to reflect on the fact that when the single thing and time are restored to the eternal substance from which they were taken, they cease to be what they only are if torn away from it. So he retains time and singularity and [finite] actuality within infinity and eternity itself.

The fashionable urge for explanation is not satisfied with time being nothing in itself and being lost in eternity; and Jacobi imputes to Spinoza the intention of furnishing in his philosophy "*a natural explanation of the existence of finite and successive things.*"[47] What should properly be called an explanation of time, however, emerges from the above: time is an abstraction made in an eternal Idea. So Jacobi could have made the abstraction of time directly in the totality, that is, in the principle of sufficient reason, and could thus have comprehended it through this principle. But the finding of the abstraction as such and in this form in the totality is immediately self-suspending.

46. *Das ideell oder empirisch Entgegengesetzte* can be translated in a dozen different ways according to (1) how one understands *ideell*, (2) whether one takes the adverbial use of *ideell* and *empirisch* seriously or not, and (3) what function one assigns to *oder*. Perhaps the phrase stands for "whether the opposites are conceived as being mere ideas in the mind or as objects of experience" (Méry treats the *oder* as *und*, and gets "les opposés dus à l'imagination et à la réflexion, les opposés idéel et empirique, sont pensés comme ne faisant qu'un").
47. *Ibid.*, IV, 2, 135.

We obtain the abstraction of time if we do not conceive thinking as attribute of absolute substance (for as attribute it expresses the substance itself) but isolate it from the attributes, and abstract it from the substance, i.e., if we fixate thinking as empty thinking, as subjective infinity, and place this abstraction in relative connection with the particularity (*Einzelheit*) of being. Through this abstraction, eternity will then truly be the basis of the cognition of time and, if you like, of the explanation of time, whereas its deduction from a community of single things will give a more natural explanation, because the single things, which are presupposed, are already something quite natural. As is obvious throughout, what Jacobi means by the naturalism (*Natürlichkeit*) that philosophy wants to achieve in its mode of explanation [357] is nothing but formal knowledge, reflective thinking and cognition according to imagination. The passages that we have cited about Jacobi's concept of knowledge are relevant at this point.[48] No philosophical comprehension is possible on the pattern of this kind of naturalism; and not many lines of it will be found in Spinoza. On the contrary, well-nigh everything is [by this criterion] supernatural in Spinoza, since Jacobi means by natural explanation cognition according to imagination. Thus Jacobi's assertion that there is no natural explanation of the world[49] could find its strongest confirmation in Spinoza who not only affirmed it but worked it out. But as a result all so-called naturalism vanishes entirely, and Jacobi's supernaturalism goes with it, too; for it is supernaturalism only insofar as something natural stands opposed to it. The point is not that, as Jacobi says (*Letters on Spinoza*, p. 419)[50] Reason "seeks to transform the extra-natural or supernatural into something natural"; nor is it that Reason "tries to transform the natural into a supernatural." The point is that this naturalism, that is, mechanism, the causal nexus and time, like the knowledge that proceeds by way of pure identity and by analyzing facts, just are not there at all for Reason.

Finally, as to Spinoza's mathematical similes for an actual infinite: Spinoza set them up against the deception of imagination; but, according to Jacobi, he must have been deceived here by his imagination. Spinoza, however, is so certain of his case that he says: "the mathematicians might well be the judges of how miserably those

48. See pp. 98–9 and 101–4 above.
49. Jacobi, *Werke* IV, 2, 147.
50. *Ibid.*, IV, 2, 148–9.

have reasoned" who declare the actual infinite to be absurd; "for the mathematicians have never allowed themselves to be delayed by arguments of this sort in [the case of] things which they cognized clearly and distinctly." Spinoza's example is the space enclosed by two circles that do not have a common centre. This is also the figure which he took as his own authentic symbol and he had it put at the front of his *Principles of the Cartesian Philosophy,* because by means of it he had dragged the empirical infinite back from imagination's endless pushing on and on and conjured it into facing him. "The mathematicians conclude that the inequalities possible in this space are infinite, and they conclude this, because it is the nature of the thing that surpasses any numerical determination"—and not because of the infinite multitude of the parts, for the area is determinate and bounded and I can posit bigger and smaller spaces, that is, bigger and smaller infinities.[51] There is in this bounded space an *actual* infinite,

51. The full context of Hegel's citation and reference is: "Further, as it is evident from what has been said, that neither number, nor measure, nor time, since they are only aids of the imagination, can be infinite (for otherwise number would not be number, nor measure measure, nor time time); hence it can clearly be seen why many who confused these three abstractions with realities, because they were ignorant of the true nature of things, have denied the actuality of the infinite. Let the mathematicians judge how wretchedly they have reasoned, for they have never allowed themselves to be delayed by arguments of this sort in [the case of] things which they clearly and distinctly perceived. For apart from the fact that they have discovered many things which cannot be expressed (*explicari*) by any number; which makes the inadequacy of numbers for determining everything plain enough; they even have many things which cannot be equalled by any number, but surpass every possible number. But still

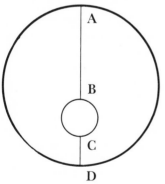

they do not conclude that such things surpass all number because of the multitude of their parts; but because the nature of the thing cannot suffer to be numbered without manifest contradiction. Thus, for instance, all inequalities of the space AB and CD interposed between two circles, and all the variations which matter moved in it must undergo surpass all number. This is not concluded from the excessive magnitude of the interposed space: for however small a portion of it we take, the inequalities of this small portion will surpass all number. Nor is it concluded as happens in other cases, because we do not have the maximum and minimum of the space, for in our example here we have both, the maximum is AB, the minimum CD; but it is concluded just from this, that the nature of the space be-an *infinitum actu*. In this example we behold the infinite, which was defined above as absolute affirmation or absolute concept,[52] set forth at the same time for intuition, and hence in the particular; here the absolute concept is the identity of opposites *actu*. If these parts are kept apart and as parts posited as identical; if this particular *qua* particular is posited as actual and expressed in numbers, and if it is to be posited in its incommensurability according to the concept as identical, then [358] the empirical infinity arises in the infinite series of the mathematicians. But the incommensurability consists in this: [1] the particular is set free from subsumption under the concept and broken up into parts; [2] these parts are absolutely determinate and absolutely unequal [or unlike] among themselves; [3] previously, in the intuitive† concept they had been equal, but now, when they are compared, they are no longer in the identity, they are only in relation. In one word, all this is nothing but the transformation of geometry into analysis; or more precisely it is the transformation of the Pythagorean theorem, which contains all authentic geometry, into the series of functions of curved lines.

This yields the true character of thought which is infinity. For the absolute concept is infinity, is in itself the absolute affirmation, but since the concept is turned against the opposite and finite as their [its?] identity, thought is absolute negation;[53] and this negation, posited as existent, as real, is the positing of opposites: $+ A - A = 0$. The nothing exists as $+ A - A$, and is in its essence infinity, thought, absolute concept, absolute pure affirmation. This abstracted infinity of the absolute substance is the infinity which Fichte brought home to our more subjective modern civilization as the Ego, or pure self-consciousness—the pure thinking, which is the eternal act, the eternal producing of the difference which reflected thinking is aware of always and only as product. What is kept separate in appearance, the incommensurable, the difference as product, is self-identical in the ultimate relation, i.e., in the infinity which is where the opposites

---

tween two circles having different centres, cannot suffer anything of the sort. And so, if anyone wanted to determine all those inequalities by some certain number he would have to bring it about at the same time, that a circle should not be a circle" (Epistle XXIX, *Opera*, ed. Paulus, I, 530–1; Epistle XII, *Opera*, ed. Gebhardt, IV, 59–60).

52. See p. 107 above.

53. We have followed the *Critical Journal* text; the editors of the *Werke* of 1832 changed *es* (*das Denken*) to *er* (= *der Begriff*, "the concept").

vanish both together. And in regard to the incommensurables, posited as existing for themselves (in numbers), the identity is an infinite one, it is a nothing. But if the incommensurables are posited, not as these abstractions, existing for themselves (in numbers), nor as parts having standing apart from the whole, but according to what they are in themselves; that is, if they are posited only in the whole, then the authentic concept, the true equality of whole and parts, and the affirmative infinity, the *actual* infinite, is present for intuitive,† i.e., geometrical, cognition. This Idea of the infinite is one of the most important in Spinoza's system. It should play a greater role in any exposition of the system, than that which is allotted to it in Jacobi's propositions,[54] where it is always just an idle predicate of thinking, extension, etc. For in this Idea there lies just what is most crucial: the cognition of the point of union of the attributes. Lacking this Idea Jacobi expounds Spinoza's highest Ideas in a formal, historical fashion. In his fourteenth thesis, for example, he ascribes the attributes and modes to the absolute substance as *qualities*, in the ordinary reflective sense.[55]

We will briefly bring together the forms of infinity. The true infinite is [359] the absolute Idea, identity of the universal and particular, or identity of the infinite and finite themselves (i.e., of the infinite as opposed to a finite). This [opposed] infinite is pure thinking. Posited as this abstraction, it is pure, absolutely formal identity, pure concept, Kant's Reason, Fichte's Ego. But when it is set against the finite, it is for this very reason, the absolute nothing of the finite: $+ A - A = 0.$[56] It is the negative side of the absolute Idea. If this nothing is posited as reality, if infinity itself is taken, not as subject or as producing—where infinity is pure identity as well as nothing— but as object or product, infinity is the $+ A - A$, the positing of opposites. But none of these forms of infinity is empirical infinity, the infinity of imagination. The first infinity is that of absolute Reason. The infinity of pure identity or of negativity is that of formal or negative Reason. But the infinite in its reality as $+ A - A$, where one term is itself determined as infinite and the other as finite, this

---

54. Jacobi offers forty-four propositions (*Werke* IV, 1, 172–205) as a result of his resolution "to spare neither effort nor patience" in the attempt to present Spinoza's edifice of doctrines.

55. *Ibid.*, IV, 1, 183–4.

56. Compare p. 172 below.

finitude in general is the infinite of reflection or imagination. The infinity mentioned above[57] belongs to it, in case a finite is to be posited as absolute, or in other words it is to be posited at the same time as something other [than itself]. In Jacobi, infinity occurs either as something otiose or as the empirical infinite of imagination, and this misleads him into the belief that Spinoza wanted in his mathematical example to present an empirical infinite as existing *actu*. Jacobi, for his part, is satisfied by the example up to a point. He does not find an objective and real infinity in it, to be sure, but he does find a subjective, ideational one. (He speaks of 'mathematical examples,' in the plural but in Letter XXIX[58] there is only one, and in *Ethics*, Part I, Proposition XIX Schol. the example is not Spinoza's—he adduces it from his opponents.)

"Where we perceive a linkage of ground and consequence we become conscious of the manifold in an idea" (*David Hume*, p. 94),[59] and this occurs in time. This ideational succession is itself an *actual* succession in the subject that produces it.—On this view, Spinoza did more than he meant to. For he was not thinking of succession at all in his example, and succession is not to be seen in it. But Jacobi finds at least a subjective succession in it, so the example has for him a psychological and empirical significance, instead of a philosophical one. Still, he does not find *enough* of the empirical in it; he wanted to find an objective, actual succession beside the psychological one, even though this ideational succession is itself an actual succession in the subject.

The nature of Jacobi's polemical procedure is this then: he either complains about the absence of succession and finitude [in Spinoza] and simply demands their presence in speculation, [360] or he reads them into Spinoza and then finds absurdities. The positive side of this fixation on the finite we have seen above[60] in its ideal form, that is, with regard to knowledge: knowledge is conceived as proceeding by way of similarity and identity, and as being in need of a fact that must be given to it as an alien datum, the $+$ B upon which the identity of the concept is regarded as supervening. Jacobi occasionally makes remarks that are full of sense and wit about this experi-

57. Compare the analysis of the moment of tiime on p. 107 above. This is a paradigm of what the formula '$+$ A $-$ A' stands for.
58. Compare note 51 above.
59. Jacobi, *Werke* II, 193.
60. See p. 96 above.

ence in general; about the individuality of the sense that determines the scope and beauty of this experience; about how Reason gives to the experience of man a different character from that of the beast; and also about the empirical setting forth of subjective individuality, that is, of sense. In Reinhold's *Contributions*, Vol. III, p. 92, however, we find: "Space and time are matters of fact, because motion is matter of fact; *a human being who had never moved would be unable to have an idea of space; one who had never changed would not be acquainted with any concept of time*; [. . .] we could no more arrive at it in an *a priori* way than we can arrive at the pure manifold, the binding bond or the productive spontaneity of the intellect."[61] This sort of thing about the connection between experience and knowledge may perhaps belong to his assistant Koeppen, rather than to Jacobi.

The utterances of experience and about experience have esprit because there is the allusive echo of speculative Ideas in them. The interest of Jacobi's writings rests on this musical consonance and resonance of speculative Ideas. But the music remains an echo; for the Ideas are refracted in the medium of reflection's absoluteness; the music must not blossom into *Logos*, the scientifically articulated word which is what one expects where the issue is philosophical. If it were permitted that the resonance of Ideas should be taken up into the concept as something objective, and be apprehended and held onto as a common good and property of thought, then one could not mistake the presence of an exposition of Reason in expressions of this kind if one concentrated only on their significance. But objectivity of Ideas is not to be. For example, after the passage from the *Letters on Spinoza* which we quoted above[62] where Jacobi allows to Reason only the capacity to analyze a fact and to link facts in accordance with pure identity, he tells us about his basic thought (p. 423). He says that *"he* takes man without dividing him, and *he* finds that human consciousness is put together out of two original ideas, that of the conditioned and that of the unconditioned, which are inseparably linked."[63] But the fact that according to Jacobi consciousness is a composite of two absolutely opposite ideas, is this not a division? On

---

61. See Jacobi, *Werke* III, 172. For the ground of Hegel's surmise that Koeppen is the author of this passage see *ibid.*, p. 158.

62. See p. 98 above.

63. Jacobi, *Werke* IV, 2, 152 (Hegel has turned the citation from the first to the third personal form, but it is otherwise almost verbatim).

the following page Jacobi says that "as long as we understand [nature] we remain within a chain of conditioned conditions, i.e., within comprehensible nature;"[64] but this nexus of concepts and of nature comes to an end, and absolutely [361] beyond it, hence quite out of its context, there is the supernatural, the inconceivable and unconditioned. How can Jacobi say, then, that he does *not* divide man, since he allows human consciousness to consist of two absolute opposites? Or rather, he already takes man as divided, in that he deals with him as he appears in consciousness. —If we actually do mean to take man and his consciousness with its compositeness as undivided, as Jacobi wants to, then we must comprehend what Jacobi calls the principle of cognition and Reason as the undivided identity of the conditioned and unconditioned; and since, according to Jacobi, the conditioned is the natural and the unconditioned the supernatural, we must comprehend the principle as identity of the natural and the supernatural. In this conditioned unconditionedness or unconditioned conditionedness we would have the same absurdity of finite infinity which Jacobi finds in Spinoza; but at least we would also have the nullification of the antithesis between the natural and the supernatural, the finite and the infinite; and thus we would be free at least from reflection, which absolutizes the opposition and makes the opposites into things-in-themselves.

In the same way, we could easily interpret the note on page 30 of the *Superfluous Pocketbook* for 1802[65] as a speculative Idea: "Where there is sense [i.e., sensation] there is beginning and end, there is separation and integration, there is one and an other, and the sense is the third." Or again in Reinhold's *Contributions*, number 3, page 70: "The characteristic mark of a sense is [. . .] this bipolarity, and its standing in the middle between subject and object."[66] Page 95 provides still another example: "Sensibility does not do any determining, nor does the intellect; the principle of individuation lies outside them. This principle contains the mystery of the one and the

64. *Ibid.*, p. 154. The rest of the sentence is paraphrased from p. 155.

65. Actually *Pocketbook for the Year 1802*, edited by J. G. Jacobi (Hamburg). This publication—which did appear in earlier years as the *Superfluous Pocketbook*—contained an article by F. H. Jacobi, "Ueber eine Weissagung Lichtenbergs" (*Werke* III, 196–243), to which Hegel refers here. The quotation is *ibid.*, p. 225 n.

66. Hegel himself marked this quotation from an essay "On the Undertaking of the Critical Philosophy to reduce Reason to the Intellect and give Philosophy a New Aim" (now in *Werke* III, 58–195); see *ibid.*, 143–4.

manifold in their indissoluble integration; [that is, of] *being, reality, substance.* Our *concepts* of it are all reciprocal ones: Unity presupposes totality, totality multiplicity, and multiplicity unity. Unity is therefore both beginning and end of this eternal circle and is called —*individuality, organism, object-subjectivity.*"[67] The middle of this circle, however,—which is both centre and periphery at once and sustains[68] the reciprocity because it will not let one disappear when the other steps forth—would be the Idea of Reason, the Idea of the absolute yet bi-polar identity of the one and the many. But an Idea of this kind is quite a different kind of knowledge and cognition from that which merely analyzes given facts and proceeds by way of similarities.

This aphoristic guise in which Jacobi raises reflection above itself is the sole outlet for Reason to express itself, once finitude and subjectivity are made into something absolute. Presented as aphoristic esprit Reason guards itself against lifting itself up into the infinity of the concept,[69] against becoming a common good, and science. [362] Instead, it remains affected by subjectivity, it remains something personal and particular. Attached to the ring, which it offers as a symbol of Reason, there is a piece of the skin from the hand that offers it; and if Reason is scientific connection, and has to do with concepts, we can very well do without that piece of skin. Ingenuity of this kind, proceeding by way of the absurdity of a finite infinity, of something being beginning and end at the same time, of a composite of the conditioned and the unconditioned, etc., comes rather close once more to being a formalism of Reason, which can be had cheap enough. Since the form of this philosophizing is subjective, its object must be equally subjective and finite; for finitude is [here taken to be] some-

67. *Ibid.*, 176 (Hegel's quotation marks). As printed in the *Critical Journal*: the passage read "Unity presupposes totality (*Allheit*), totality multiplicity and multiplicity totality." But it is clear this was a slip of the pen or the typesetter (since it is the circular return to unity which interests Hegel here). We have followed Lasson in correcting it. Hegel took this quote from the section of Jacobi's essay that the despised Koeppen worked over.

68. *Festhalten.* This word, like the more notorious *aufheben,* has many meanings: sustain, give support, hold fast, tie together, arrest, etc.

69. The *Critical Journal* reads "hütet die Vernunft sich, das Unendliche des Begriffs aufzunehmen"; Buchner reads "hütet die Vernunft sich, in sich das Unendliche aufzunehmen," which makes explicit the only sense the text as it stands will bear. Lasson reads: "hütet sich die Vernunft, sich in das Unendliche aufzunehmen." We follow Lasson because his reading seems to agree with Hegel's thought on pp. 115–6 above.

thing in-itself. From the outset the exposition and the philosophizing are about man and are directed to man: "*We* find ourselves placed on earth, and it is there that *our* actions take place, so it is there that *our* cognition comes to be; as our moral character turns out, so does our insight in everything connected with it," etc.[70] Man is the perennial focus of meditation, his rational instinct is praised, and the tale of his sense and sensibility is told. Against this should be set the manforgetful maxim of Epictetus that Jacobi quotes, in the *Superfluous Pocketbook* (p. 22): "But since I am a rational being, it is my business to praise God" (and not man). "This is my vocation, I will fulfill it."[71]

*Herder's way of doing philosophy* is only a slight modification of this typical pattern. The Absolute cannot be tolerated in the form that it has for rational cognition, but only in a game with concepts of reflection, or in sporadic invocations which bring philosophy directly to an end, just as they seem to be about to begin it—even as Kant ends with the Idea in practical faith. Or else the rational can only be tolerated as beautiful feeling (*Empfindung*), as instinct, as individuality. But Herder's philosophizing has the advantage of being somewhat more objective. Jacobi calls Herder's philosophy Spinozistic froth, a preaching that confuses Reason and language alike.[72] But the froth and the sermonizing arise precisely from Herder's putting a reflective concept in the place of rational thought. This veils the rational, just as the expression of feeling, subjectivity of instinct, etc.—which Jacobi puts in the place of rational thinking—does. Herder says that "when unfolded" (he means folded up) "the concept of might as well as the concepts of matter and thought all coincide in the concept of a *basic force* (*Urkraft*) according to the Spinozistic system itself" (*God*; 2nd ed. p. 126);[73] "the eternal basic force, the force of all forces is solely one,"[74] etc., page 169. "The real concept, in which all forces are grounded, but which even in their totality they do not exhaust—this infinite excellence is *actuality, reality,*

70. *Ibid.*, IV, 1, 231–2.

71. *Ibid.*, III, 217.

72. *Ibid.*, IV, 1, 216–7 n. and IV, 2, 79.

73. Hegel owned both editions but he had only the second at hand (Gotha, 1800). The text is now in Herder, *Sämmtliche Werke* (ed. B. Suphan et al.), XVI, 479–80. The English reader can also find the quotation in its context in F. H. Burkhardt's translation (p. 198–9).

74. Herder, *Werke* (ed. Suphan) XVI, 502; Burkhardt, pp. 140 and 202. The following quotation is from the same passage.

active [363] existence; it is Spinoza's core concept."—Or on page 245: Nature is "a realm of *living* forces" and "innumerable *organizations,* each of which is not only wise, good and beautiful of its kind, but perfect, *that is to say,* an imprint of Wisdom, Goodness and Beauty themselves" etc. [75] "The hair that falls out, the nail that is cut off, enter once more a different region of the world-context where they again act or suffer in perfect accord with their present place in nature,"[76] etc.

Is not all this in line with what Jacobi calls "the greatest merit of the seeker, namely to reveal and manifest existence"?[77] Of course, it is not a revelation and manifestation appropriate for philosophical cognition any more than Jacobi's is. On the contrary, both authors share the effort to abolish the scientific form of rational cognition wherever it is present. Herder is fully conscious of what he is doing when he expounds the central thesis of the Spinozistic system as follows (*God;* 2nd ed., p. 77): "I do not know any *substantive word* under which the actual and operative activities, *thought* in the spiritual world, and *motion* in the corporeal world, could be comprehended with so little constraint as they are under the concept of *force, power, organ.* With the *word, 'organic force'* one signifies at the same time the inner and outer, the spiritual and the corporeal. But it is still only an *expression,* for we *do not understand* what force is, *nor* do we *claim* to have *explained* the *word* 'body' by it."[78] This is exactly Jacobi's concern: to replace philosophical Ideas with *expressions and words* which are not supposed to give knowledge or understanding. These words and expressions may well have a philosophical meaning; but Jacobi's polemic is directed precisely against the philosophies which take them seriously and make their philosophical meaning articulate. No one states better what it is all about than Koeppen in his final peroration for Jacobi's essay on critical philosophy (in Reinhold's *Contributions,* number 3): "free, immortal being, man, brother, full of solemn reverence, devotion, love, how can the letter of *your philosophizing Reason* teach you more effectively what *lives in the holy of holies of your soul when you have faith, hope, and knowlege;* the infinite holding sway above you, virtue coming forth from

---

75. *Ibid.,* p. 546; Burkhardt, p. 172–3.

76. *Loc. cit.*

77. Jacobi, *Werke,* IV, 1, 72.

78. Herder, *Werke* (ed. Suphan), XVI, 452; Burkhardt, p. 195 (Hegel's quotation marks).

freedom, and eternal life!" etc.[79] This is the sort of chilly and insipid emotional effusion that comes from the "Reason as instinct," to which Jacobi forever appeals; and this forsooth, is worth more than any proposition made by philosophizing Reason, which it proposes to dispense with.

We must here touch briefly on a *polemical* piece [by Jacobi] against Kant's philosophy, which rests on the same basis as the polemic against Spinoza. It is entitled: *On the Attempt of Criticism to reduce Reason to Understanding and to give a new Direction to Philosophy generally* (see Reinhold's *Contributions,* Number 3).[80] With his instinctive hostility to rational knowledge, Jacobi has, of course, fastened on the very point where Kant's philosophy is speculative. Kant's terminology is not in itself [364] very clear. Having been borrowed from reflective thinking it is useless for speculative Reason; and deriving as it does, from a culture that is dead and gone it hinders Kant's exposition, which loses itself on its speculative side in the product. Kant's terminology makes it all the easier for Jacobi to make fun of his philosophy, and to make nonsense of it by and for unspeculative reflection. The character and principles of the philosophy of reflection are decisively articulated in this polemic.

A proper critique of it would have to mention its empty shouting, how snappy and spiteful it is, and how it twists things to the point of sheer malice. Among these malicious twists we count a passage in the "Preamble" where Jacobi uses Kant's exposition of the forms of intuition as an example of a discord within the system, and of the mixture of empiricism and idealism in it.[81] To this end Jacobi first shows by way of *textual* evidence that [according to Kant] space and time are mere forms and are "never *able to become objects.*"[82] He refers us to *Critique of Pure Reason,* p. 347: "The mere form of

79. Jacobi, *Werke* III, 194–5.

80. *Ibid.,* III, 59–195. This is the essay which Koeppen completed, on the basis of Jacobi's notes (see *ibid.,* pp. 66–7). His part begins on p. 158. Hegel has touched on the essay several times already. (In translating the title we have bowed to established tradition by rendering *Verstand* as "Understanding.")

81. *Ibid.,* pp. 77–9.

82. *Ibid.,* III, 77. Jacobi emphasizes *Gegenstände* (not *werden können*). The reader should take note that Jacobi did not *quote* any of the passages on which he relies in the present context. Hegel has followed up the references given in Jacobi's footnotes, and is reporting what he has found. Hegel's own citations of Kant's text are by no means word perfect, as can be seen even from a comparison with the translation of N. Kemp Smith which we have cited (with minor adjustments) in the following notes.

intuition without substance is, in itself, no object—pure space and pure time, which, to be sure, *are* something, they are forms for intuiting, but *are* not themselves objects which are intuited."[83] There is not a single word here to the effect that they are not *able to become* objects (in what sense we shall see at once). "They cannot be intuited, or perceived," continues Jacobi, and he refers us now to page 207 of the *Critique*—where, in fact we find nothing at all about their not being intuitable. About perceptibility [Kant says] that they are not perceived *in themselves* because they are pure formal intuitions and not appearances (that is, identities of intuition and sensation), not objects of perception.[84] And *yet*, so Jacobi says, these very same, non-objective forms of intuition are also objects, according to other passages such as *Critique of Pure Reason*, p. 160, where it says (in the note, for there is nothing about 'objects' in the text): "Space regarded as *object* (italicized by Kant himself), as we are required to treat it in geometry, contains *more* than the bare form of intuition."[85]

---

83. *Critique of Pure Reason*, A 291, B 347; "The mere form of intuition, without substance, is in itself no object, but the merely formal condition of the object (as appearance) as pure space and pure time (*ens imaginarium*) which are, to be sure, something, as forms of intuiting (*als Formen anzuschauen*), but are not themselves objects which are intuited."

The crucial "als Formen anzuschauen" is grammatically quite awkward here as its primary meaning would be "to intuit as forms" or even "as forms to be intuited," whereas the context seems to demand "as forms of intuiting." ("als Formen des Anschauens" rather than Kant's "als Formen anzuschauen.") . . . It should be noted that this passage occurs in the context of a fourfold distinction of the concepts of something and nothing, as a correction of traditional ontology, and this correction is itself an appendix to the Appendix on "The Amphiboly of Concepts of Reflection" which concludes the whole Analytic (A 260–292; B 316–349).

84. *Critique of Pure Reason*, A 166; B 207: "Perception is empirical consciousness in which there is also sensation. Appearances, as objects of perception, are not pure (merely formal) intuitions, like space and time (for these, as such, cannot be perceived at all).

85. *Critique of Pure Reason*, B 160–1 note (not in A): "Space represented as *object* (as we are required to present it in geometry) contains more than the bare form of intuition. It contains *unification* of the manifold, of what is given according to the form of sensibility, in an *intuitive* representation so that the *form of intuition* gives only a manifold, whereas the *formal* intuition gives unity of representation. In the Aesthetic I had treated this unity as belonging merely to sensibility, simply in order to note that it precedes any concept although it presupposes in fact a synthesis which does not belong to the senses but through which all concepts of space and time first become possible. For by its means (in that the understanding determines the sensibility) space and time

Here, however, Kant distinguishes between formal intuition as unity of the intuitive representation, and the form of intuition which appears as mere manifold relative to the concept of the intellect, though it [the intuitively formed manifold] has unity in itself. As he remarks expressly in § 24, the understanding as transcendental synthesis of imagination is itself the unity of space and time and first makes this unity possible.[86] This is one of the very best points in what Kant says about sensibility and *a priority*. Now where is the contradiction in this: the form of intuition, as [365] a purely abstract form opposed to the concept of the understanding, *is* not an object, but it can be made an object, as in geometry, because of space's inner unity, which is *a priori*, though the unity does not *emerge* as such in space as a bare form of intuition?—Finally, together with the preceding contradiction, there is supposed to be a contradiction involved in the fact that space and time are not mere forms of intuition, but are themselves intuitions and as such they are single representations at that.[87] "Single, individual representations" (as opposed to the concept) mean the same in Kant as intuition, and this can only be described as excellent and as one of his purest and most profound concepts. —Anyway, quite apart from its truth or falsity, where is there any contradiction between the above and what Jacobi brings forward as inconsistent with it, except the one that Jacobi introduces by giving false references?

On the following page Jacobi says: "*Fichte to whom it seemed incomprehensible how the Ego borrows its reality and substantiality from matter*," etc. [88] Is not this a magnificent exposition of the

---

are first *given* as intuitions; hence the unity of this *a priori* intuition belongs to space and time and not to the concept of the understanding (cf. § 24)."

While it is true that on B 160 Kant speaks explicitly of space as object only in this footnote, Jacobi may have had in mind the passage in the text of B 160 which reads "But space and time are represented *a priori* not merely as *forms* of sensible intuition, but as themselves *intuitions* which contain a manifold. . . ."

86. In the first part of § 24 (B 150–152) Kant develops the concept of the transcendental synthesis of imagination as mediating between the pure concepts of the understanding and the pure manifold of sensible intuition. Following Fichte and Schelling, Hegel sees in Kant's transcendental synthesis of imagination an anticipation of the basic principle of speculative philosophy. See pp. 72–3, 78 ff. above.

87. See *Critique of Pure Reason*, B 136 n. (Jacobi gives the reference, but Hegel does not repeat it here.) Compare also A 25, B 39 and A 31/2, B 47.

88. Jacobi, *Werke* III, 79.

Kantian system? And Jacobi makes it *en passant*, just as he disposes of Fichte *en passant*. In support of the view that [in Kant] *the Ego borrows its reality and substantiality from matter*, Jacobi refers us to pages [B] 277–8 of the *Critique of Pure Reason*. The passage actually begins on [B] 276 and continues on [B] 277: "But in the above proof" (Kant's refutation of idealism) "it has been shown that outer experience is really immediate,[89] and that only by means of it is inner experience—*not indeed the consciousness of our own existence*, but *the determination of it in time*—possible. Certainly, the representation 'I am,' which expresses the consciousness that can accompany all thought, *immediately* includes in itself *the existence* of a subject; but it does not so include *any cognition of that subject*, and also therefore *no empirical cognition*, that is, no experience of it. For this we require, in addition to the thought of something existing, also intuition [and] in this case inner intuition [. . . which] is itself possible only mediately, and only through outer experience.[90] Note 2. With this thesis, too,[91] all employment of our cognitive faculty in experience, in the determination of time, entirely agrees. Not only are we unable to undertake[92] any determination of time save through change[93] in outer relations [. . .][94] relatively to the permanent in space (for instance, the motion of the sun [. . .])[95] we have nothing permanent on which, as intuition, we can base the concept of a substance, save only *matter*; and even this permanence is *not* obtained from *outer* experience, but is *presupposed a priori as* a *necessary* condition of all determination of time, and therefore also as a determination of inner sense, with respect to our own existence, through the existence of outer [366] things. The consciousness of myself in the presentation 'I' is not an intuition, but a merely intellectual presentation of the spontaneity of a thinking subject. This 'I' has not, therefore, the least predicate of intuition, which, as permanent, might

---

89. Kant adds here an important footnote.

90. Thus far the quotation is from "Note 1" of the three Notes which Kant attached to the proof of the thesis that "the mere, but empirically determined, consciousness of my own existence proves the existence of objects in space outside me" (B 275).

91. Hegel wrote *auch* where Kant has *nun*.

92. The original text, which Hegel follows, has *vornehmen*. Many modern editors have accepted the emendation *wahrnehmen*.

93. Hegel omitted the article here.

94. Hegel omitted "(die Bewegung)."

95. Hegel omitted "relatively to objects on the earth."

serve as correlate for the determination of time in inner sense—
in the manner in which, for instance, impenetrability serves in our
empirical intuition of matter."[96] We have copied the whole passage
so that direct inspection may reveal what a malicious fake Jacobi's
entirely unwarranted interpretation is, according to which *the Ego
borrows its reality and substantiality from matter.* Kant requires for
experience something which, as enduring, allows the determination
of the lapse (*Wechsel*) of time. This something which endures is
matter, namely as something *a priori*. Substantiality, [in turn] is this
durability in time, durability determined with respect to experience.
Kant explicitly excludes from these *predicamenta* the "I am" and
even the existence of the subject. Hence, what Kant says is *toto cælo*
different from what one finds in Jacobi where there is no explanation
of reality, substantiality and matter. Kant gives to reality, substantiality, and matter, as well as to the Ego, a quite different significance
from that which they have when Jacobi vacuously says that the Ego
*borrows* its substantiality from matter. Surely it is treating Kant
worse than a dead dog to quote and mishandle him like this?[97]

Kant rightly represents the three moments of experience, sensation
as well as intuition and category, as merely productive of appearance:
they do not give any cognition of the In-itself and the eternal. Jacobi
interprets this as meaning that "all claims to the cognition of *truth*
are razed to the ground and what is left is a faith more blind and
utterly devoid of cognition than anyone ever imputed to man before."[98] This altogether spiteful way of treating Kant's position is
comprehensible in the light of Jacobi's principle, which was brought
out earlier, that the finite and appearance are absolute. Jacobi's philosophy thus debases the expressions 'truth' and 'faith' to the plane
of the most common and vulgar empirical facts. But in philosophical
intercourse 'truth' deserves to be used, not of empirical fact, but
solely of the certainty of the eternal [actuality], and 'faith' has indeed

96. N. Kemp Smith's translation has been very slightly adapted. ('Cognition'
replaces 'knowledge' and one interpretive insertion has been eliminated.) Hegel's
omissions and his copying mistakes have been pointed out in the footnotes.
(The emphases are Hegel's and rarely coincide with Kant's.)

97. Lessing had remarked (in his conversations with Jacobi) that Spinoza's
critics treated him like a dead dog (Jacobi, *Werke* IV, 1, 68).

98. Hegel is here quoting from a footnote in Jacobi's essay on the Critical
Philosophy which was not reprinted in his *Werke* (vol. III) in 1816. But this
part of the note is very nearly a *verbatim* quotation from a passage in the
essay on Hume which Hegel cited earlier (Jacobi, *Werke* II, 217).

been generally so used. Jacobi becomes as abusive about the nullification of this empirical [367] truth and of faith in sense-cognition as if it were an act of sacrilege or a temple robbery.

A third ingredient of Jacobi's polemical exposition that must be added to false references and violent invectives, is a sort of burlesque verbal juggling (*Galimathisieren*). The trick is very simple: reflection gets hold of the rational and translates it into the language of the intellect, so that it becomes in and for itself an absurdity. We have already seen, for instance, how time was juggled into Spinoza's eternity and infinity. So when Kant calls synthesis an action and then later, speaking of its connection with imagination, says that it is an *effect* of imagination, Jacobi extracts from this the question, "how can this *faculty* be an effect?" His industrious disciple loyally repeats this question, and supports Kant in calling synthesis the mere effect of blind imagination (p. 85).[99] But let us pass over perversions of this sort and not go into the details of this or that example; for the entire essay proceeds like a burlesque display and delights itself in the cooking up of absurdities. Let us turn rather to the main point, which is Jacobi's conception of the relation between the so-called faculties. In our exposition of Kant's philosophy we showed[100] how, in this sphere, Kant brilliantly posits the *a priori* [ground] of sensibility in the original identity of unity and the manifold, which at the level where unity is completely immersed in the manifold, is transcendental imagination; and he posits the intellect in the raising of the *a priori* synthetic unity of sensibility into universality, so that this identity faces sensibility in a relative antithesis. Reason, in turn, becomes the higher level of the preceding relative antithesis, though only in such a way that this universality and infinity is pure formal infinity, and as such fixated. This is an authentically rational construction in which the misleading 'faculties' persist only in name; the truth is that Kant posits all of them in *one* identity. Jacobi transforms this rational construction into the view that the faculties *rest* upon one another. "You [Kant] let Reason *rest on* the intellect, the intellect *on* imagination, and imagination *on* sensibility; the sensibility in turn rests *on* imagination again as a faculty of *a priori* intuitions; and this imagination finally rests—on what? Plainly on nothing. Here then is the true turtle, the absolute ground, that which

99. Jacobi raises the question, *Werke* III, 129; Koeppen recurs to it, *ibid.*, pp. 162–3. (For the objectionable proposition in Kant, see A 78, B 103).

100. See pp. 69–70 above.

gives being to all beings (*das Wesende in allen Wesen*). From itself alone, it produces itself[101] and being itself the possibility of everything possible [. . .] it produces not only what is possible but also —perhaps!—the impossible."[102] What a beautiful bond Jacobi establishes between the faculties! The idea that there is something which rests on itself—though certainly it is not the imagination in so far as it is isolated from the totality—seems to Jacobi to be as unphilosophical as the [368] image that those foolish Indians invented, who let the world be carried by a being that rests on itself; and not only is it unphilosophical, it is also sacrilegious. Everyone knows from his early years and from psychology, that imagination, after all, is a faculty for making things up, so Jacobi would have it that philosophy seeks to convince us through an imagination of this sort that the whole of human life is actually nothing but a fabric without beginning and end, a fabric made of mere delusion and deception, of phantoms and dreams; and that men have invented and fabricated for themselves religion and language, etc. He scolds and orates interminably on this theme in the *Pocketbook*.[103] In brief, Jacobi takes [the transcendental] imagination and self-originating Reason to be something arbitrary and subjective, and he takes sensuous experience as eternal truth.

On behalf of his burlesquing of the Kantian construction of the cognitive spirit Jacobi bears witness for himself on p. 52 "so that it may be seen that he has grasped your [the Kantian] cause well enough;" and he is so magnanimous as "not to accuse you [Kant] of conscious deception."[104] The editor, Reinhold, annotates this "*truthful*" exposition [of Kant] as follows: "If the Kantian philosophy wishes to preserve *at least the semblance of consistency*, it will have to acknowledge that the functions here described are the *tacitly* presupposed principles of its theory of the cognitive faculty. Fichte's philosophy, *on the contrary*, lays down the *said* functions in an *explicit* way and *does so with* an intuiting thinking and willing of all of them."[105]

101. Hegel omits Jacobi's "*a priori*." Jacobi's text would have to be translated: "It produces itself from itself in a pure *a priori* way." For the origin of the metaphor of the "true turtle" and for Hegel's use of it, see D. Henrich, "Die Wahrhafte Schildkröte," *Hegel-Studien* II, 1963, 281–91.

102. *Werke* III, 115–6 (Hegel's quotes).

103. See especially "On a Prophecy of Lichtenberg's," Jacobi, *Werke* III, 218–9, 229–30; and in his "Criticism" essay, *ibid.*, pp. 95–102.

104. *Ibid.*, III, 121.

105. Reinhold, *Contributions*, number 3 (Hegel's quotation marks).

The main question asked by Jacobi is this: How does the Kantian philosophy arrive *a priori* at a judgment? How does it get the Absolute to give birth to finitude, pure time to give birth to times, space to spaces?[106] This is the eternal dilemma of reflection: if philosophy recognizes a transition from the eternal to the temporal, it can be easily shown that philosophy posits the temporal in the eternal itself and therefore makes the eternal temporal. On the other hand, if philosophy does not recognize this transition, if it posits that for intuitive cognition totality is an absolute *simul*, an absolute together, so that the different [i.e., the manifold of differentiated particulars] does not exist in the form of [spatial] parts and temporality, then philosophy is deficient, for it is supposed to have the temporal, the determinate, and the single before it and explain that also. It is in this second platitude of reflection that Jacobi believes he has the monkey-wrench that will break up even the Kantian philosophy. He conveniently misinterprets—it was just bound to happen!—the totality of intellectual intuition, *the a priori* synthesis which includes the difference in itself, without residue, as an abstract unity. In this way, he has the parts, not in the whole, but *side by side with* the abstract unity which he has turned the whole into. So he takes it to be necessary that, "if a synthesis a priori is to be *explained*(!) a pure antithesis[107] will have to be *explained* at the same time; but, we do not find the slightest hint of such [369] a need [in Kant]. . . . The manifold to be synthesized is presupposed by Kant as empirical; yet it is supposed to remain if one abstracts from everything empirical."[108] As if the original synthesis were not an identity of the different—though, to be sure, the different is not contained in it as some-

---

106. Jacobi, *Werke* III, 112–158. As a token of Jacobi's style we translate a passage which begins *ibid.*, p. 112. "For eighteen years now I have been trying to understand—and with every year I have understood less—how you [Kant] can conceive a manifold to which the unity, and a unity to which the manifold merely *supervenes*; how you can think this *pure event* in any way at all. If you cannot do so, but if both manifold and unity presuppose or condition one another in such a way that they can only be thought one in the other and at the same time, as *forma substantialis* of all thought and being: what use is then your whole *a priori* web?"

107. Jacobi's "*Antithesis*" (which occurs also on pp. 128 and 130 n. 120 below) is not unlike Hegel's *Gegensatz* (which is what "antithesis" usually stands for in this translation). But it is typically narrower in its reference: it refers to Kant's manifold over and against the unifying unity (Jacobi's "*Synthesis*") of transcendental apperception.

108. *Ibid.*, III, 79–80.

thing purely finite and antithetical as Jacobi wants to have it. Original synthesizing would be, in Jacobi's terms, an original determining, and original determining would be creation out of nothing.[109] We have pointed out earlier[110] that for reflection the nothing begins where there is no absolute, isolated finitude, no finitude in abstraction from the absolute substance; and that what is reality for reflection, the something as opposed to the nothing of reflection, is just simply this absolute opposition and absolute finitude. That synthesis is pure unity and therefore has not difference within it, is the one and only thought behind an endless battering and yelling that works itself up into absurdities and gives itself the wildest airs. Jacobi draws his idea of synthesis and of the whole Kantian philosophy out of isolated passages. If Kant happens to say among other things that synthesis is "the action of putting *distinct* representations together, and grasping their manifoldness in one cognition,"[111] what could be clearer than that he already presupposes the antithesis to his identity? Jacobi makes a proper muddle of everything that is organic in Kant's construction. He makes time, space, transcendental imagination clear and pure as he pleases, turning them all into pure, solid units that have nothing to do with one another. He turns himself into the absolute solidity of infinite space and now asks: How will you be able to break into my solidity and originate just one distinct point in it?[112] How will time, space and unity of consciousness break one into one another? He forgets that the purity of time, space and transcendental imagination are just as fictional as the pretence that *he*, Jacobi, is the intuition without squabbles or clouds, of the infinite solidity of space. He is somewhat happier with time; for he finds it to be a bridge between the realt (*Reale*) and the idealt (*Ideale*), the conceptual (*Intellektuale*) and the material, and he can take it for a sense: for it is bi-polar, and in some sort of mid-position, and what characterizes sense in general is its bi-polarity, and its standing in the middle between object and subject. But still, even if imagination gives birth to a time that has in it beginning, middle and end, it would not know, according to Jacobi, how to indicate whether these

109. *Loc. cit.*

110. See pp. 107–9 above.

111. *Critique of Pure Reason*, A 77; B 103. Compare Jacobi, *Werke* III, 128 ff.

112. Jacobi, *Werke* III, 146–56. Nothing here is exactly quoted and some of it is improvisation. But the theme is Jacobi's.

eggs that it lays are big or little ones.[113] It must determine this by way of space, into which Jacobi now passes.[114] He posits himself as its infinitude, pure, unpolluted identity and continuity; firmly placed in this unity, he maintains that a pure and empty imagination, if it were alone with space, could not, in all eternity, generate a point. If [370] finitization in pure space is to be conceived, as Jacobi narrates very nicely, then that which posits finitization (or better, reality) must be "something which is raised above pure intuition as it is above pure concept, above pure concept as it is above pure intuition, and above both in the same way."[115] It must be something which falls neither under a (sensuous) intuition nor under a concept. For Jacobi, this leads to a partly true and partly distorted description of this something: it does not itself intuit and does not itself conceive concepts, but is the "utterly pure activity of both [intuiting and conceiving] equally. As such it is called *synthetic unity of transcendental apperception*."[116]

With these words Jacobi arrives at the point where for the first time the argument might perhaps get at the heart of the matter (*die Sache selbst*). Instead, this is the point where his own labour of interpretation comes to an end.[117] So far he had talked about nothing but empty unities and had burlesqued intellect, imagination and Reason; but at the point where the previous senseless grumbling and yelling might acquire some interest, he breaks off—and he explains this with the bulletin about his health in the "Preamble." Any hope that he might himself have produced something better later on is completely removed by his saying that he "does not see any more truly dangerous passages ahead, but only a short stretch that is rather difficult to travel, but still with the roads *more than half made already*" (Preamble, p. 5).[118] If this is not understandable enough from the preceding pages it will become more understandable from what Jacobi says [to the Kantians] on page 61 especially:[119] in vain

113. *Ibid.*, pp. 142–5.
114. *Ibid.*, p. 146.
115. *Ibid.*, p. 157.
116. *Ibid.*, p. 158.
117. Hegel speaks of "die eigentliche *Ausarbeitung* Jacobis" here because Jacobi's text ends (*Werke* III, 158) with the note "Here begins the *Ausarbeitung* (the working up of my notes) by my friend Koeppen."
118. *Ibid.*, III, 65. The "bulletin about his health" follows directly after this.
119. *Ibid.*, 132–134 (paraphrased).

do you [Kant] try to introduce a distinction within your pure qualitative unities and continuities by *naming* one of them *synthetic* (as
if it were a matter of names). I [Jacobi] tell you that the one is no
more able to divide and add than the [two] other[s].[120] Synthesis
does not come about through it [the transcendental unity of apper-
ception] for then it would also have to contain the ground for the
antithesis [the sensuous manifold] within itself. *Hoc opus, hic labor*
[this is the task, here is the work]. But it is not possible that either
empty space or empty time or consciousness should contain the origin of the antithesis.—In short, the matter stands as follows: the
absolute synthetic unity, totality includes all parts and difference
within itself; but I, Jacobi, say that it is only a name. I say that the
absolute synthetic unity is an abstract unity, an empty unity. How,
then, could it be itself the ground of divisibility and antithesis?

The concept of identity and of transcendental unity becomes quite
understandable thanks to the cordial aid of his executive [Koeppen].
To him, too, the terrain of the transcendental unity appears to have
no perils and the roads to be more than half made. Jacobi conceived
of space etc. as pure unity, and pure unity is no manifold. Koeppen
thinks that after 81 pages of this monotony (not counting the Preamble) the thought that pure unity is no manifold may *still* perhaps
be in need of some explanation. The grumbling and brawling of
Jacobi's river grows faint in Koeppen's flatlands. Jacobi broke off at
the *a priori* synthesis; about this we find [in Koeppen] the following:
"Suppose there were a pure [371] manifold, what would then make
an integration possible? Clearly what would make it possible would be
that it *took place in a third.*" This clear idea Koeppen clarifies in the
following way: "Suppose *we have* a differentiated manifold (*ein
Verschiedenes*) in space, *its integration* consists precisely in its being
*situated* in space." Even clearer: "Suppose *we have* a differentiated
manifold in consciousness, its integration consists in its being *present*
in consciousness." Even greater clarity: "Now, *what integrates* the
two spatial objects? *Space. What integrates* the manifold of consciousness? *Consciousness.* The whole synthesis reveals nothing more to
us than *an identity.*" All this is rendered still more comprehensible

120. The "pure qualitative unities" which Jacobi discovers in the *Critique of
Pure Reason* are space, time and transcendental apperception. "These three unities are your [Kant's] *theses,* your principles. In the third thesis, the transcendental apperception, the synthesis is supposed to be already contained, but—
without antithesis [the manifold]. In the two others [space and time] antithesis
without synthesis is supposed to be present." *Ibid.*, 122.

by the following comment: "*Insofar* as two objects are *situated* in space they are, *qua spatial*, completely identical (*gleich*); *insofar* as they are *situated* in consciousness, they are, *qua present in consciousness*, completely the same (*dieselben*). *Where is the need* here for *an additional particular action* of integration? Is not *the whole synthesis* already *complete* through space and consciousness, as *passive receptivities*? . . . So the intellect does nothing but posit identities and in order for this to be possible the *finding* of identities and nonidentities is *presupposed*. . . . Any judgment is the expression of a *found* identity of this sort. . . . Apart from what is not to be distinguished in a judgment [i.e., this identity] anything else that may be in it belongs to its *matter* (*das Materiale*) and hence it does not have its origin in the intellect. And this business of the intellect, this attending to and comprehending of a *given* (*vorhanden*) identity [for whose sake imagination must destroy all particularity and suspend all difference], this is what *synthesis* means?? Nay, rather, all synthesis is suspended by it."[121]

Thus Koeppen on the transcendental [i.e., synthetic] unity of transcendental apperception or of productive imagination. He expresses Jacobi's conception of knowledge in an easily intelligible way: we human beings receive the things as matters of fact through sense and through the supernatural revelation[122] of seeing, perceiving and feeling. (Men, who have superior organization and sense, have an experience superior to that of inferior organization and sense.) Yet what is taken from experience is *always already synthesized* and does *not* need to be *first* synthesized by us, nor indeed can it be synthesized; for our activity as directed upon this synthetically given is the reverse of synthesizing, it is the analysing of the given and this analytic unity, which we *find* in the object, is so little a synthesis, a linking up of the manifold that, on the contrary, the manifold, the material [of experience] is shredded by the analytic unity. Space, consciousness, etc., objective world, nature can be conceived by us only according to analytic unities, we can only dissect them, and

---

121. *Ibid.*, 161–2. Hegel does not indicate the ellipses but the quotation is *verbatim* except for the clause in square brackets at the end—in which Hegel summarizes one of the ellipses. Nor did Koeppen print his final rhetorical question with two question marks in 1816 (this may be—as Lasson surmises—a misprint in the *Critical Journal*—but it may also be another of Hegel's ironical asides).

122. Compare p. 138 below.

(*Letters on Spinoza*, p. 424):[123] "this opens an *immense* field for our investigations"—a field without end or totality—"that we are forced to work on anyway, simply for the sake of our physical [372] conservation. [. . .] The things [. . .] whose mechanism we have discovered are the things we can produce if the means are *in our hands*. What we are thus able to construct, *at least in idea*, that we comprehend, and what we cannot construct, we do not comprehend either." The cognitive activity of the intellect is "a ceaseless positing of identities which we call linking; it is nothing but a continual reduction and simplification of the manifold which would, if this were possible, go on until the manifold was entirely discarded and brought to nothing" (*Pocketbook*, p. 32).[124]

rational cognition is something quite different from Jacobi's conception.[125] It does not analyse nature, it does not tear something given apart into an analytic unity and a manifold. But rather, being itself an organic, living totality, it creates the Idea of totality and constructs it as absolute and original identity of the universal and particular. This is the identity that Kant calls synthetic, not as if a mani-

We declare, on the contrary, that transcendental imagination or fold lay before it, but because it is in itself differentiated, bi-polar so that unity and manifold do not supervene each to the other in it, rather they detach themselves from one another within it, and are held together forcefully, as Plato says, by the middle.[126] As for sense Jacobi readily concedes that it is bi-polar. Yet there seems [to him] to be no room for argument about its having to do with a *given* object, and being mere passivity and receptivity, in spite of its own bi-

123. *Ibid.*, IV, 2, 153.

124. *Ibid.*, III, 227.

125. Hegel wrote, "transcendental imagination and rational cognition is . . . ." He frequently uses sentences of the ungrammatical form, "A and B is . . . ." It is often difficult to say whether this is a matter of carelessness in the use of the conjunction or carelessness about the singular form of the verb. The translator must opt between changing "A and B" to "A or B" (= A, i.e., B) or changing the singular form of the verb to the plural form. In the present case— transcendental imagination and rational knowledge—the options are wide open. We prefer changing A and B to A or B (A, i.e., B) in order to stress that Hegel and Schelling believed that the core of what Kant meant by transcendental imagination was "really" the same as what they meant by rational and speculative knowledge. Méry, on the other hand, opts for changing the singular to the plural, no doubt for the good reason that, notwithstanding their supposed identical core, there remain enough differences between the two concepts to keep them from being one.

126. *Timæus*, 35a.

polarity, —as if the poles were not already contained in its being bi-polar and middle.

In the superfluous[127] *Pocketbook* of 1802 Jacobi cooks up the rumbling and squabbling of the essay in the *Contributions* for an unphilosophical public and for the palate of philosophical dilettantes. For this purpose he mixes his bitters with shots of Jean-Paul's[128] sentimentalism; but he also uses some of Lichtenberg's[129] serio-comic sallies to hang his own bitter-sweet pronouncements on. This is not to their advantage; for the contrast with Lichtenberg's profound and witty good humour directly heightens the impression they give of a shallow and bitter ill humour. These defamatory outcries against the Critical Philosophy serve no instructive purpose; they can only be effective as a good old fire and brimstone sermon, to fill the unphilosophical mass of the people with terrified horror and loathing at such a spectre as the Kantian philosophy. How far they are well designed for that is something for a critic of another kind to decide. We can also leave to him the problem of whether such aphorisms and sentimental sayings as the following are uncommonly witty and edifying or not: "*The drive* of any living being is the *light* of this being, its right and its force. Only *in this* light can it dwell, only with this force can it act. —No finite being has its life in itself and therefore not from itself—the *flame* of its light, the *might* of its heart."—[373] "The gift of life takes many forms, and the awakening to it is manifold; manifold are its conduct and use. Like unto the beast man, too, awakens first as a sensuous creature through the merely sensuous nature."—"Behold him then smiling, and beginning to babble, etc."[130]

Like Jacobi's philosophical essay in Reinhold's *Contributions*, his popular essay in the *Pocketbook* contains passages that look to the naive outsider as if they might have philosophical meaning. For example the footnote on p. 40 (the emphasis here is that of the *Pocket-*

---

127. See p. 115, n. 65 above.

128. Jean-Paul, pseudonym of J. P. Friedrich Richter, 1763–1825, poet, novelist, etc.

129. Georg Christoph Lichtenberg, 1742–1799, professor of physics at the University of Göttingen. His *Aphorisms* appeared posthumously, Göttingen, 1800–1806. Schleiermacher's review of Vols. I and II appeared in 1801 in the *Erlanger Literatur Zeitung*, to which Hegel also contributed.

130. Jacobi, *Werke*, 203–4 (the added quotation marks indicate the breaks). The final remark about the human baby, which makes little sense as an apothegm in isolation is, no doubt, chosen because it expresses Hegel's opinion of Jacobi's own performance very aptly.

*book*): "Sensation,—memory and imagination presuppose something first and original in consciousness and activity, a *principle* of life and knowledge, a *being*-in-*itself* (*in sich Seiendes*) which, as such, be neither *quality* nor *effect* nor *anything that originated* in some way and fashion *in time*. It [must] be *self-being, self-cause*"—(yet according to the *Letters on Spinoza*, p. 416[131] the *causa sui* has its origin in the ignoring the essential difference between the principle of sufficient reason and causality)—"something *extra-temporal*, and with this property it must also be in possession of a consciousness that is *extra-temporal*, a merely *inward* consciousness. This extra-temporal, merely inward consciousness is most clearly distinguished from an *outward* and *temporal* consciousness. It is the consciousness of the *person* who *enters* time, of course, but does not *originate* in time as a *merely temporal* being. The *intellect* pertains to the *temporal* being; and Reason pertains to the *extra-temporal* one."[132]

One might suspect that Jacobi is now ready to consider the principle of sufficient reason and the *principium compositionis* of the older metaphysics rather more satisfactory for Reason[133] [than he had thought previously]; for in this passage he himself excludes from Reason, conceived as extra-temporal, the very succession of whose absence he complained earlier. One might further suspect that Kant's *blind* imagination is also contained, in principle, in this Reason which is an *in*dwelling and *extra-temporal* consciousness clearly distinguished from the temporal and *out*going consciousness; for what is called seeing is solely in the outgoing and temporal consciousness. Jacobi continues: "the intellect *isolates*, it is materialistic and non-rational; it denies Spirit and God. Reason *isolates*, it is idealistic and non-intellectual; it denies nature and makes itself God. The whole and undivided, true and actual man is both Reason and intellect simultaneously" (which cannot mean side by side or else they would be two pieces or parts); "he has an undivided faith and an identical kind of trust in *God*, in *nature* and in *his own spirit*."[134] So we must comprehend [374] the undivided faith as identity of Reason and intellect, that is, as a *simul*, of the denial of God and of self-deification, of the identity of the temporal and extra-temporal, i.e., of an eternal

---

131. *Ibid.*, IV, 2, 146 note 2.

132. This note (which actually begins on page 39 of the *Pocketbook* for 1802) was not reprinted in the *Werke* of 1816. In spite of his comment about preserving Jacobi's emphases, Hegel has omitted several and added one.

133. Compare pp. 98 ff above and Jacobi, *Werke*, II, 193.

134. *Pocketbook*, 1802, pp. 40–1 n. (not reprinted in Jacobi's *Werke*).

time etc.; and we can do so without in the least burlesquing Jacobi's philosophy as he burlesqued Spinoza and Kant by carrying into the undivided what is characteristic of the isolated *qua* isolated.* Yet on the other hand this *undivided* faith must be conceived as an undivided pure, pure, pure waveless Unit, as Uni-Form-Ity[136] without beginning, middle or end, without any gender, he she or it," etc. (Compare his essay in Reinhold's *Contributions*, number 3; *passim*).[137]

Anyone who could take pleasure in twaddling along on the trail of nonsense and bombast would find the best possible occasion for it in these essays, when Jacobi discusses the undividedness of the extra-temporal and the temporal, or of being-in-itself (*Selbstwesenheit*) and experience, etc. For the meaning of Jacobi's composites [i.e., syntheses] is not that the temporal sinks to its ground in the extra-temporal, or the empirical consciousness perishes in rational intuition, that all finitude is engulfed in the infinite and that just *one* totality

---

* Jacobi concludes this footnote as follows: "This trinitarian and universally unphilosophical faith must be able to become a *philosophical* faith in the strictest sense, a faith confirmed in reflection." (But, if confirmation in reflection makes any sense at all, the form of faith will disappear as a result of it.) "And I make so bold as to say that I know faith can become philosophical and that I see the way by which a *reflection* (*ein Nachdenken*) gone astray can return and arrive at such a faith. Then only will it produce a true philosophy, a knowledge and wisdom that illuminates the *whole* man." Reinhold had called himself a reflector (*Nachdenker*).[135] Jacobi thinks, then, that Reinhold in this present period has gone astray and he believes there will be a second metamorphosis, in which Reinhold will be hatched out into the sylphide of an immortal philosophy whose principle combines denial of God and self-deification, intellect and Reason, while leaving man wholly as he is. This notice to the philosophical dilettante regarding the coming of the true philosophy may be ignored by the philosophical public until the metamorphosis comes to pass.

---

135. We try in this way to give an inkling of the play on "*nachdenken*," which has here not only the usual sense of "reflecting" and "meditating," but also of "thinking after . . ." (where "*nach*" has the sense as in "*nachgehen*" and "*nachforschen*" $=$ in pursuit of") and "thinking through." Cf. *Difference between Fichte's and Schelling's Systems*, p. 179, where Reinhold is quoted as saying that he *nachdachte* Bardili, i.e., that he thought in pursuit of Bardili's thoughts and thought through them.

136. Jacobi's word was *Einfachheit* (*simplicity*) but he divided the syllables for emphasis: *Ein-Fach-Heit*. "Uniformity" is probably the only English word in which the parallel with *Ein-heit* can be preserved.

137. There is a fairly close parallel to the last lines of this quote in Jacobi, *Werke* III, 114.

should be recognized as the In-itself which is neither isolated intellect nor isolated Reason. For in that case the consequences would be too horrible [for Jacobi]: the finite being of things would come to nothing and the finite things would turn into appearances and ghosts. If Reason recognizes that the finite is not absolute or eternal, then man (*Pocketbook*, p. 36) "can only have existence through fancy, and through Reason he can only come to nothing. Yet to be robbed of Reason is the hardest thing for man to bear, and the fate that loss of Reason opens for us is a fate of the utmost horror and despair."[138] But no, according to this most strident of all syncretisms, Reason as cognition of the extra-temporal and of that which exists in itself (*das Selbstwesen*) must concede the rights of the intellect, [375] that is, of the temporal and nonessential (*das Unwesentliche*) [i.e., appearance]. And when Reason builds a temple to the Godhead, it must be humane enough to let the devil have his chapel there too.

From what we have seen so far of both the positive and polemical aspects of knowledge in Jacobi's philosophy, the character of knowledge as he conceives it emerges: Reason may analyse matters of fact, separate the universal from the particular and proceed by way of empty identities. If any philosophy establishes an absolute identity of universal and particular, this identity will at once be turned back into a universality cut off from the particular, and Jacobi will demonstrate the necessity that particulars have first to be added to the universal, or that universality only supervenes to the *given* particulars. Where Jacobi himself acknowledges a bi-polarity, a subject-objectivity, it must have the form of a sense, a thing, something experienced which is not allowed to lose the character of a datum, of being immovably opposite to the subject that thinks it. It must not be expressed as free Idea of Reason or as having the universal validity that belongs to scientific knowledge, but only as something subjectively inspired. Thinking and being, the universal which remains formal identity, and the particular which remains a given, inspired subjectivity and the objectivity of knowledge do not flow together in cognition. The given matter of fact and the subjectivity thinking it are, both alike, absolute.

We must now deal with the question of how absolute identity relates to absolute subjectivity; for the absolute identity [according to Jacobi] cannot be in cognition, although at the same time it absolutely must have existence for the subjectivity that posits itself as

138. Jacobi, *Werke* III, 231.

absolute. Now, this relation of an absolute finitude to the truly absolute is *faith*.[139] In faith, the subjectivity does acknowledge itself to be finite and nothing before the eternal, yet it manages this acknowledgment in such a way that it saves and maintains itself as having its own intrinsic being outside of the Absolute. But Jacobi extends faith [belief] also to the non-conceptual (*ausser dem Begriff*) knowledge of the particular, i.e., the immediate empirical representation of ordinary objects. For the universal, if separated from the particular, is not only opposed to the absolute identity of universal and particular, but to the particular as well. He took over this idea [of empirical belief as faith] from those radical arch-empiricists, Hume and Locke. More than anyone else, these two have immersed philosophy in all this finitude and subjectivity, and have put the search for the grounds of cognition and the critique of the powers of the human mind in the place of cognition itself, they have posited the particular as such as the Absolute. Through the analysis of sensuous experience they have driven out metaphysics, and their reflective approach, spun out more extensively and systematically upon German soil, is now called German philosophy, that is, the philosophy of Kant, Jacobi and Fichte. Quite apart from the connection between faith and philosophy, Mendelssohn and others[140] did not [376] dream that Jacobi extended the name of faith to cover the certainty of what is objective in the ordinary sense—for there was still a tradition as to what the *object* of philosophical cognition is. They did not dream that by this means Jacobi had for his part endowed the certainty of ordinary objectivity with the same importance which Hume, Kant and Fichte had given it in a different fashion. Jacobi affirmed this certainty, Hume, Kant and Fichte denied it, but both parties gave equally absolute status to limitedness and finitude, and so the important point is one and the same for both; for it does not matter at all whether finitude is something objective (in the vulgar sense) or something subjective, as long as it is absolute. When Jacobi said (*Letters on Spinoza*, p. 92): "my religion knows no duty to remove doubts of this kind except by appeal to rational grounds; it commands *no faith in eternal truths*,"[141] Mendelssohn took Jacobi's faith to be, not the

---

139. [Or belief].
140. The reference is mainly to the participants in the *Pantheismusstreit* between Jacobi and Mendelssohn—which began with Jacobi's *Letters on Spinoza* and was concerned with the nature of Lessing's "Spinozism."
141. Jacobi, *Werke* IV, 1, 116.

certainty of temporal things, but the certainty of ordinary consciousness without rational cognition concerning the *eternal* and *extratemporal*. In speaking of eternal truths as the object of philosophy, Mendelssohn had the idea that philosophy does not occupy itself with the certainty of empirical fact (*Wirklichkeit*) and that Jacobi did not mean Hume's belief in sensuous perception by his "faith" either.

Jacobi, on the contrary, did not have eternal truths in mind at all, but the ordinary truth of fact, and it is to this that Jacobi's first declaration against Mendelssohn is directed at once (*Letters on Spinoza*, p. 215): "Dear Mendelssohn, we all are born in faith and must remain in faith [. . .] Through faith we know that we have a *body* and that there exist other bodies and other thinking beings outside us. A genuine, miraculous revelation! For we only *sense* our *body*, in this or that state or with this or that quality and in so sensing its state we become aware *not only* of its changes, *but also* of *something* quite different that is neither mere sensation nor thought, we become aware of *other existing things*" (underlined by Jacobi himself) "and we do so with the same certainty with which we are aware of ourselves: for without the *Thou* the *I* is impossible. [So it is only *through qualities we accept* that we obtain all the ideas that we have, and there is no other way to real cognition; for the objects (*Gegenstände*) to which Reason gives birth, are *phantoms*.] We have, then, a revelation of nature which not only commands but compels each and every man to believe and to accept eternal verities upon faith." Here Jacobi does not just include ordinary knowledge of fact, the realm of sense perception, within faith; [377] he limits faith and the eternal verities to this realm completely. Jacobi continues: "the religion of the Christians teaches but does not command a different sort of faith: a faith, whose object is not eternal verities, but the finite contingent nature of man."[142] —As if Jacobi's eternal verities about having a body, about other bodies, and about the existence of other bodies and existing things outside us did not concern the contingent, finite nature of man. And what a wretched sort of nature must our nature be, if it is finite and contingent even in relation to [and comparison with] that first nature, and what sort of religion is the Christian re-

---

142. Hegel marks this quotation from the second edition (Breslau, 1789). The text in the *Werke* of 1816 is somewhat different (IV 1, 210–2). The sentence in square brackets is not in the *Werke* and its "durch Beschaffenheiten, die wir annehmen" allows of several renderings, none of which seems to be entirely satisfactory.

ligion if it has this lower nature as its object, this nature that is more finite and contingent [than the first, i.e., the realm of external existence].

In this declaration—which has even more weight because the particular circumstances that occasioned it guarantee that it was made quite deliberately—Jacobi explicitly restricts faith and eternal verities to what is temporal and corporeal. He is therefore quite consistent in his abhorrence of Kant's and Fichte's philosophies, because these philosophies aim to show that there is no truth in the finite and the temporal and are especially great on their negative side: they show what is finite and appearance and nothing. Since the Kantian and Fichtean philosophies maintain a fixed antithesis between cognition and faith, they posit opposition directly and absolutely, and hence posit finitude itself absolutely, *qua* finitude. But they are distinguished [from Jacobi] in this: their finitude is an empty finitude, it is nothing but the pure, infinite concept of finitude, so that it becomes the same (*gleich*) as infinity; for any content or filling that is given and must be given to this finitude by itself, *ought* to count as nothing. Jacobi, on the contrary, desires these nothings in their whole length and breadth and screams blue murder over the bringing of this nothingness to nothing. Furthermore the philosophies of Kant and Fichte definitely affirm the immediate certainty of the supersensuous as faith. On this point not the slightest misunderstanding is possibile, notwithstanding the fact that Kant denies all reality to the Ideas with respect to theoretical Reason; for, on his view, theoretical cognition is determination through the categories which have their reality solely in the sensuous world and experience, or [in other words] it is only intellectual cognition that they make possible, not rational cognition. There cannot be any misunderstanding about this either. Kant denies all reality to the concepts of Reason [i.e., the Ideas], in the sense, namely, that they cannot be given in sensuous perception and in an experience mediated through the concepts of the intellect [i.e., the categories]: in the field of experience they are merely regulative principles[143] for the employment of the intellect. Jacobi sees here the nullification of the Ideas themselves, because a temporal and corporeal existence for them is thus denied [378]. And in Reinhold's third issue (p. 36) Jacobi asks *"every honest man upon his conscience* if he could ever for any cause whatsoever return to

143. Compare *Critique of Pure Reason*, A 642 ff.; B 670 ff.

these Ideas as *objectively true* and real notions and place a sincere and heartfelt confidence in them, once he had clearly understood" that the Ideas have a merely problematic status for corporeal and temporal knowledge and experience, and for sensuous perception, and "have been proved once and for ever to be *objectively ground-less*" (N.B. in what sense)—"*I say* it is impossible!"[144]—One ought *rather to say* this: it is only possible to put trust in the Ideas when that kind of reality [i.e., empirical reality] has been brought to nothing; it is quite impossible to put trust in the Ideas as long as the dogmatism of absolute finitude and subjectivity is maintained, a dogmatism that puts the eternal verities in bodies and other matters of fact.

This blind hatred of the nullification of temporality, along with the holy zeal for the good cause of matters of fact, results in a high degree of malicious distortion. The way Jacobi cites Kant in this present instance is an example that we cannot pass by. (We do not mean to say that this quotation with the others presented above are the only ones of the kind; but they are the only ones that we have checked up on in Kant.) On pages 99–100 of Reinhold's third issue,[145] Jacobi or Koeppen says: "It would therefore be much more consistent if we did not think of any objectivity at all in respect of any *representation* of God and immortality and if we said with the author of the *Critique of Pure Reason: everything to do with religion and freedom is a mere* Idea of Reason, mere heuristic fiction and, apart from its usefulness as a guiding principle of the intellect, it is a mere thought-thing whose possibility cannot be proved."[146] As the source for this we are referred to *Critique of Pure Reason*, p. 799, which says: "the *concepts of Reason* are mere Ideas and have no object that can be met with in any experience. [. . .] they are thought only problematically, etc."[147] The discussion here concerns the concepts of Reason solely and exclusively in a theoretical connection [i.e., with respect to their cognitive employment only]. Jacobi or Koeppen extend what is said without any conditions or limitations to *everything to do with religion and freedom*: it is all mere fiction. What Kant said of the theo-

144. Jacobi, *Werke* III, 102–3 (Hegel himself put quotation marks around the concluding parts of this passage).

145. The *Critical Journal*, has "5. Heft," a misprint which Lasson failed to correct. The passage is in Koeppen's "working out" of Jacobi's notes—hence the doubt about who is responsible.

146. Jacobi, *Werke* III, 181.

147. *Critique of Pure Reason*, A 771; B 799.

retical reality of the concepts of Reason is now said of their reality in general.

Jacobi, then, has pulled faith down into the realm of fact and sensuous experience, and this is all that he means by "faith" in his polemic against Mendelssohn. But, besides this faith he has still another faith, a faith, not in finitude, but in the eternal. This faith, which has the eternal as absolute object, keeps cognition sundered from it and not united with it. It excludes rational cognition; for it acknowledges cognition only as something subjective and as formal knowledge. We must ask about this faith if it is not polluted *even as faith* by being transposed into the relation to reflection.[148] [379]

The faith of a man who has not lifted himself to the level of abstract reflection, is naive because it is not opposed to reflection. Such a faith lacks the reflective awareness that its connection with the eternal is confronted by rational cognition, even though they do not necessarily clash. The connection with the eternal in this simple faith is immediate certainty, that has not been made objective and given conceptual form by thinking. [Indeed] it has no connection with any opposition at all. It is a pure position without regard to anything else; it is not a negation either of another faith in something else, or even of another form for its own content. How the naiveté of this faith might be affected by a regard of this kind [to something opposed to it] is not relevant at this point; only the regard itself is relevant. For where faith as such is bound up with an awareness of itself and negates formal, finite knowledge [there the question arises] whether a faith that has this reflective attitude to finite knowledge is truly able to raise itself above subjectivity and finitude, since no rational knowledge is supposed to be achievable. This is the negative and conscious shape in which faith occurs in Kant, Jacobi and Fichte. In true faith [however] the whole sphere of finitude, of being-something-on-[one's]-own-account, the sphere of sensibility sinks into nothing before the thinking and intuiting of the eternal. The thinking here becomes one with the intuiting, and all the midges of subjectivity are burned to death in this consuming fire, and *the very consciousness* of this surrender and nullification is nullified. Similarly, among the religious acts in which faith is feeling and intuition, some are more and some less pure and objective: in song, for instance, consciousness and subjectivity melt to a greater degree into the uni-

---

148. The "pollution of faith by reflection" is another topic that recurs in the *Phenomenology*; see especially Baillie, pp. 570–80.

versal objective harmony, than when they suspend themselves in quiet prayer.[149]

When it is introduced into philosophy, however, faith completely loses this pure naiveté; for now it is Reason which flees from reflection into faith in order to nullify finitude and suspend subjectivity, —just for this reason, faith itself is affected by the occurrence of this opposition to reflection and subjectivity. Since it now acquires this negation as part of its meaning, faith preserves reflection on the *nullification* of reflection; it preserves the subjective consciousness of the nullification of subjectivity. Subjectivity has thus saved itself in its own nullification. In a consciousness that does not reflect on its faith, finite thinking and faith lie apart and because of this apartness, the consciousness is a non-philosophical one. Its finite doings and dealings and its sense perception on one side, alternate with divine worship on the other. To the religious man everything finite and objective presents itself at the same time under an eternal shape as well [as its ordinary one]; and his own conduct [380] expresses an eternal shape, too. But this shape of eternity is here something subjective; it is the ethical beauty of the individual which sets itself forth. This beauty achieves true objectivity and universality in art and philosophy, where the antithesis with respect to the Absolute of faith and reflection disappears.[150] Both the unconscious antithesis present in ordinary consciousness, and the conscious one present in the philosophies of reflection disappear. As far as the unconscious antithesis in ordinary consciousness is concerned, faith and what springs from faith is capable of being pure; for subjectivity and finitude are totally outside it, they do not touch it, they are not connected with it. But faith introduced into philosophy does not remain pure. For here it reflects and involves negation; and in this negating it is concerned with subjectivity, and thereby preserves it. Faith is [thus] infected by the antithesis itself, just as its content, as supersensuous, has a stubborn sensuousness set against it, [and] the infinite faces a stubborn finitude. And since both nullified subjectivity and saved subjec-

---

149. Compare *Phenomenology*, Baillie, p. 717. The "hymn" is thought expressed in music. Hegel has earlier compared Jacobi's piety to the music of the Idea without the thought (p. 115 above). In the *Phenomenology* medieval piety is similarly music without *logos* (Baillie, pp. 257, 263, 265).

150. The German text would seem to allow also this translation: ". . . where the antithesis of faith and reflection disappears in its connection with the Absolute."

tivity are present in this faith, subjectivity is justified, for it defends itself with its own nullification; whereas in ordinary unreflective faith subjectivity has truly disappeared, and is something unholy in its sight.

This pollution of faith and this hallowing of subjectivity must lead us briefly into the practical philosophy of Jacobi. Kant's practical reason, being the empty concept in its unmoved opposition to nature, can produce nothing but a system of tyranny [of the Law of Reason over human nature],[151] a rending of ethical integrity (*Sittlichkeit*) and beauty, or else like Kantian morality cleave to so-called duties of a formalistic kind that determine nothing. In their enumeration and exposition these duties lack scientific consistency because they yield to the consistency of nature. By admitting the possibility of casuistry, the system also admits its scientific nullity, yet it is this scientific consistency alone that allows the straining toward ethical Ideas to become visible [in Kant's "Doctrine of Virtue"].[152] But in the "Doctrine of Right"[153] definiteness is necessary and cannot be permitted to slide back into the indefinite; so this science [the Doctrine of Right] must, of necessity, besmirch ethical nature with the most shamefully evident disgraces. Jacobi, on the other hand, is hostile toward the concept in his philosophy, and this necessarily leads him to despise the concept in its objective ethical form and above all to despise the pure law, the formal principle of morality. Among other outstanding passages on this point, the following from the *Letter to Fichte* (p. 32) is beautiful and quite pure:

"Yea, I am the atheist, the godless one, the one who, in defiance of the will that wills nothing, wills to lie as dying Desdemona lied, or to lie and deceive as Pylades did in feigning to be Orestes; to murder like Timoleon, to break law and oath like Epaminondas, or John de Witt; who wills suicide like Otho, or temple-robbery like David —yes, I even will to pluck the ears of wheat [381] on the Sabbath for no other reason save that I am hungry, and because the law is made for man and not man for the law. . . .For I know, I know with the most holy certitude within me—that the *privilegium aggratiandi*,

---

151. For the "tyranny" here referred to, see especially "The Spirit of Christianity" (1798/9) in *Early Theological Writings*, ed. Knox and Kroner, pp. 209–15.

152. See the *Metaphysical Principles of the Doctrine of Virtue*. This is the second part of the *Metaphysik der Sitten* (1797).

153. See the first part of the *Metaphysik der Sitten*.

for crimes of this sort against the pure letter of the absolutely universal law of Reason, is man's authentic right of majesty, the seal of his dignity, of his divine nature."[154]

Jacobi is speaking in the first person: *I am* and *I will*. But this cannot jeopardize the objectivity of the passage. The expression that the law is made for man and not man for the law—without regard to the meaning it has where Jacobi took it from—certainly acquires in this context a more universal meaning, but it also retains its true meaning. [155] This is why we have called this passage quite pure. —Ethical beauty must not lack either of the two sides. It must have the vitality of the individual who refuses to obey the dead concept. It must have the form of concept and law, of universality and objectivity, —the side which Kant abstracted in an absolute fashion as the *only* one, utterly subjecting individual vitality to it, and killing it. Our quotation deals with the other side, the side of the vitality and freedom of the ethical life (*Sittlichkeit*), and although it does not exclude objectivity, it does not express it. Regarding the necessity and objectivity of the ethical life we shall have to look for other data [in Jacobi].

154. Jacobi, *Werke* III, 37–8. Jacobi is thinking of Kant's discussion of the sovereign prerogative of mercy and pardon ("Rechtslehre," Section 49, *ad fin.* *Akad.* VI, 337), Kant says: "The right to pardon a criminal (*jus aggratiandi*), either by mitigating or by entirely remitting the punishment is certainly the most slippery of all the rights of the sovereign. By exercising it he can demonstrate the splendor of his majesty and yet thereby wreak injustice to a high degree. . . . he can make use of this right of pardon only in connection with an injury committed against himself (*crimen læsæ majestatis*). But, even in these cases, he cannot allow crime to go unpunished if the safety of the people might be endangered thereby. The right to pardon is the only one that deserves the name of a right of majesty." (Ladd, pp. 107–8).

It seems that "right of majesty" is a Kantian coinage, for Roman lawyers did not refer to the *right*, but only to the *injury* of "majesty." The *crimen læsæ majestatis* was originally an offence against the sovereignty of the Roman People; see Ulpian, *Digest*, 48, 4, 1. This, rather than the later sense of "lèse majesté," is clearly what Kant had in mind.

We have not been able to trace any earlier technical use either of Kant's *jus aggratiandi* or of Jacobi's *privilegium aggratiandi*. For reasons of etymology the expression cannot be very old: the "Latin" aggratiare derives from modern Italian.

(The Kant reference was pointed out to us by Prof. Klaus Hartmann; the etymology of *aggratiare* by Prof. Peter Preuss. We also wish to thank several other correspondents who have endeavored to help us in this connection).

155. Jacobi took it from Matthew 12 and/or Luke 6; Hegel had discussed the "true meaning" in his unpublished essay on the "Spirit of Christianity." See *Early Theological Writings*, trans. T. M. Knox, p. 208.

Jacobi seeks to clarify his Idea of ethical life by appealing to examples of ethical characters. What he stresses in his examples shows up at once his neglect of the lawful and objective side. With the Spartans Spertias and Bulis (*Letters on Spinoza*, p. 240) it is their *experience* which determines their ethos. As Jacobi remarks, they do not tell Hydarnes who wanted to persuade them to become friends of the king: "you are a fool. [. . .] They rather confess that *by his own standard* he is wise, has insight and is good. Neither did they try to impart *their* truth, [. . .] they did not invoke their own understanding, or their refined judgment; they appealed only to *things* and to their liking for these things. Nor did they take pride in their virtue, and they had no philosophy to offer [. . . .] They merely confessed the way of their hearts, *the way they felt*. Nor were they any more *explicit* with Xerxes" than with Hydarnes to whom they mentioned *their experience*. "For to Xerxes they said: 'How could we live here, how could we abandon *our country, our laws, and such men* that for their sake we voluntarily undertook so great a journey to die for them?"[156] Could the ethical really be made more explicit? Is it only subjectivity of experience, subjectivity of sense, of inclination that is visible here [as Jacobi has it? On the contrary] the two Spartans showed their contempt for the satrap plainly, when they spoke to him of *his* and *their experience* and *inclination*. Under the form of another subjectivity they confronted his subjectivity with their essential being. To the majesty of the monarch, however, they showed their respect in that they made themselves *perfectly explicit* before him: [382] they named what was most objective, and what was as holy for him as it was for them, country, people, and laws. But Jacobi calls country, people and laws things; he turns what is most alive into something one has got used to as one does get used to things. He comprehends them, not as holy things, but as everyday things.[157] Toward the holy there is no such relation as getting used

---

156. Jacobi, *Werke* IV, 1, 232–4. Hegel has changed the sequence of some of Jacobi's sentences. We have indicated his omissions. He marked as a quotation only the speech of the two Spartans to the King of Persia in Herodotus from whom the story comes. (Jacobi supplies the reference: Herodotus, *Histories* VII, 129; but in the Oxford classical text, Spertias is Sperchias, and the correct reference is VII, 134–6.)

157. *Dinge*. Hegel's preference for the word *Sache*—even sometimes when he is dealing with Kant's *Ding-an-sich*—is probably connected with the pejorative connotations that *Ding* acquired in the warfare of Enlightenment against superstition (compare p. 57 n. 6 above).

to it, and being dependent on it. What Jacobi conceives as contingency and dependence is the supreme necessity and the supreme energy of ethical freedom: living in accordance with the laws of a people and of the Spartan people at that. What is rational above all else he conceives as something vulgarly empirical. Moreover, no one would expect Spertias and Bulis to fall into the petty subjectivity of invoking their refined judgment and understanding or glorying in their own virtues, and the mere absence of such pettiness is something too trivial to be signalized as a virtue in them.—There is even less reason to regard the story of Kleomenes in *Woldemar*[158] as emphasizing objectivity; for the Spartan is introduced there not in his relations with his country and in the strength of his true virtue, but in his downfall as an individual. And for whose edification is this? for emptyheaded or affected females and for sentimental bourgeois.

Since Jacobi is very hostile to objectivity and the concept in the interest of ethical beauty, we cannot do anything else but hold fast to the models (*Gestalten*) in which he meant to make his Idea of ethical beauty clear. And the key-note of these models is this conscious lack of objectivity, this subjectivity holding fast to itself; not the constancy of tranquil self-possession (*Besonnenheit*), but of reflection on one's personality, an eternally returning introspective concern for the subject which puts extreme meticulousness, nostalgic egoism and ethical sickliness in the place of ethical freedom. This preoccupation with self produces the same transformation in the beautiful individuality that came over faith.[159] That is to say, through this consciousness of individual beauty one gives oneself the consciousness of subjectivity suspended and egoism brought to nothing; whereas one has thereby set up, and simultaneously justified, the most extreme subjectivity and inner idolatry.[160] In the poets who can tell what is eternal and what is finite and damned, we find Hell and damnation expressly identified as being bound forever to one's subjective deed, being alone with what is most peculiarly one's own; it is a deathless consideration of this possession. Think of Dante among

158. Jacobi, *Werke* V, 393–417, especially pp. 401–14. Jacobi follows Plutarch's account of the attempt by King Kleomenes to revive in Sparta the traditional *Sittlichkeit* of the Lycurgan constitution.

159. Compare p. 141 ff. above.

160. It is worth while to compare here the way "the law of the heart" develops into the "frenzy of self-conceit" in the *Phenomenology* (Baillie, pp. 395–9).

the earlier poets,[161] or of Goethe's Orestes who surrenders to Hell
for a period while still alive.[162] In Jacobi we can observe this very
same torment of eternal self-contemplation in the heroes Allwill and
Woldemar;[163] but they do not even contemplate themselves in a deed,
they contemplate themselves in the even greater boredom and
impotence of their empty [383] being. This spiritual debauch with
themselves is presented as the ground of the catastrophe in their not-
very-novelworthy histories, but we also see that in the final denoue-
ment this principle is not suspended, and even the virtue of all the
surrounding characters who are not brought to catastrophe by it, is
in a greater or lesser degree marred by the stain of that hell.

Thus, in Jacobi Protestant subjectivity seems to return out of the
Kantian conceptual form to its true shape, to a subjective beauty of
feeling (*Empfindung*) and to a lyrical yearning for heaven. But faith
and individual beauty now have an essential ingredient of reflection
and of consciousness of this subjective beauty, and are thus cast out
of that state of innocence and unreflectedness which alone makes
them capable of being beautiful, devout and religious.

From what has been said it emerges that, within the sphere common to both, Kant's philosophy is the opposite of Jacobi's. Kant's
philosophy posits absolute subjectivity and finitude in pure abstraction and thus acquires the objectivity and infinity of the concept.
Jacobi's philosophy does not take up finitude itself into the concept;
it makes a principle out of finitude in its finiteness, out of finitude
as empirical contingency and consciousness of this subjectivity. The
sphere common to both philosophies is the absoluteness of the antithesis between, on one side, finitude, the natural, knowledge—which
in this antithesis is bound to be merely formal knowledge—and, on
the other, the supernatural, supersensuousness and infinity. For both
of them what is truly Absolute is an absolute Beyond in faith and in
feeling; for cognitive Reason it is nothing. In both philosophies the

161. The clearest, as well as the most celebrated example, of what Hegel
means, is probably Francesca in Canto V of the *Inferno*.

162. The Hades to which Orestes descends in a swoon (in Goethe's *Iphigenie
auf Tauris*, Act III, Scene 2) can hardly be what Hegel means here unless his
"tenacious memory" has failed him badly. For Orestes there encounters the
whole house of Atreus, murderers and victims alike, *their deeds forgotten*.
Hegel must be thinking more of the way Orestes is pursued by the Furies for
the murder of his mother Clytæmnestra.

163. The philosophical novels *Allwills Briefsammlung* and *Woldemar* are in
*Werke* I and V.

speculative Idea comes to the fore. In Kant, it occurs in pure [i.e., uncorrupted] form in the deduction of the categories, only to become at once a pure [i.e., abstract] identity, a unity of the intellect; in other places it occurs as a merely possible thought which cannot acquire any reality in thinking because reflection is to be dominant without qualification. In Jacobi likewise the speculative Idea occurs in subjective form as something personal (*partikuläres*), as a spirited sally; it can no more be allowed entry into universality than Reason can be allowed to rise from instinct and subjective individuality to intuition, and so neither is allowed to become something for thinking [i.e., to function as it should in speculative thought].

Once philosophy moves in the direction of the reflective form, the prevalence of the subjective and finite aspect is inevitable. In Jacobi's philosophy the subjective and finite prevail. To be sure, the same emphasis is also evident in other philosophical efforts, but in some it is more feeble and in others less ambitious. In the form which Jacobi gave to philosophy theoretical and practical subjectivity and the beyond of faith are more clearly articulated than anywhere else. This is why we have chosen to expound it as the exemplary representative of its species. It should also be noted, however, that the side of the subjective and finite can be apprehended in a higher and nobler shape [to which we now turn].

On the one hand, as we have already [384] noted,[164] Jacobi's way of doing philosophy comes close in its principle to the subjective beauty of Protestantism. For it exalts the individual and the particular above the concept and emphasizes subjective vitality. Protestantism does not admit a communion (*Umgang*) with God and a consciousness of the divine that consists in the saturating objectivity of a cult and in which *this* nature and *this* universe are enjoyed in the present and seen in a sight that is in itself clear. Instead it makes communion with God and consciousness of the divine into something inward that maintains its fixed form of inwardness; it makes them into a yearning for a beyond and a future. Although this nostalgia cannot be united with its eternal object, it has its beauty and its infinite joy in this: its object is in truth what is eternal, and it does not try to trap it in order to get something back for itself. But on the other hand, Jacobi's principle tarnishes the beauty of individuality and its form of feeling and love and faith. For insofar as its object is the eternal, his faith has a polemical aspect, and therefore it inevita-

164. See p. 146 above.

bly reflects subjectivity. Furthermore, as absolute certitude, it extends over the temporal and the actual so that the testimony of the senses is accepted as a manifestation of truth, and feeling and instinct are assumed to contain the rule of ethical conduct. Beauty and faith are also tarnished through reflection on personality, that is, through the reflection that man in general and the particular person is the subject that has sensations and love of this beautiful sort—for this reflection turns man's yearning into basking in his subjectivity, in his beautiful thoughts and sensations. But neither the truth that is in nature—the truth in the form of actuality and temporality, nor the consciousness [in man] of his absolute personality—can assuage the grief of religious nostalgia, and call it back from its beyond. For nature taken as something temporal and the individual taken as absolute in his singularity, are not nature as universe, in the intuition of which his yearning could find its peace; for it is the intuition [not of a beyond] but of a presence. Nor is the absoluteness of the subject in his personal singularity and his abiding opposition to the eternal, a Reason that sees, a love that is pure, or a faith that is alive. On the contrary, the beauty of subjective nature, its faith and its love and its feeling in general, can only be defiled in a reconciliation in which the yearning finds truth and certainty in the temporal, the subjective and the empirical.

Jacobi's principle, then, allows the grief and yearning of Protestantism to proceed to a reconciliation. But the reconciliation is of the general eudæmonist type, i.e., it is by way of the finite. Here the finite is from the outset the reflective consciousness of feeling and of yearning, and this reflective consciousness [385] turns the subject of it, *qua* subject into something. When yearning proceeds to pollute itself, and to take ordinary actuality and temporality as a revelation [it abandons the beyond for the things of this world and] finds this world in itself. So yearning thus reflected in itself could find a higher level (*Potenz*) than Jacobi expounds. For its deification of the subject could be made into a more elevated object.[165] The sense as well as the intuition of oneself and of the world could be grasped in a more ideal (*idealisch*) way. Viewed from the other side, this amounts to turning the highest intuition itself into something subjective, something that remains private and personal. When this world (*das Dies-*

---

165. The grammar of the German sentence that ends here is a Gordian knot which we have had to cut with some unavoidable disloyalty to the text.

*seits*) that has truth is the Universe instead of [temporal] actuality, and the reconciliation with nature is identity with the Universe, then Jacobi's principle will have reached the highest level of which it is capable, and Protestantism in its quest for reconciliation in the here and now, will have driven itself to the highest form [it can reach] without stepping out of its character of subjectivity. As feeling, this identity with the Universe is infinite love, while as intuition, it is religion. But this identity must remain something strictly subjective and particular whether in the passive form of apprehension and inner copying or in that of [active] virtuosity. The outward manifestation of the identity must not be stabilized, its living force must not be entrusted to objectivity. The [reconciled] Identity must maintain the reflection of [unreconciled] yearning upon the subject as before.

Jacobi's principle has in fact attained this highest level in [Schleiermacher's] *Speeches on Religion.*[166] In Jacobi's philosophy Reason is conceived only as instinct and feeling; ethical conduct occurs only in a context of empirical contingency, and as dependence on things given by experience and inclination and the way of the heart; and knowledge is nothing but an awareness of particularities and peculiarities, whether external or internal. In [Schleiermacher's] *Speeches*, by contrast, nature, as a collection of finite facts, is extinguished and acknowledged as the Universe. Because of this, the yearning is brought back from its escape out of actuality into an eternal beyond, the partition between the cognitive subject and the absolutely unattainable object is torn down, grief is assuaged in joy, and the endless striving is satisfied in intuition.

But even when the individual casts away his subjectivity, and the dogmatism of yearning dissolves its antithesis in idealism,[167] still this Subject-Objectivity in the intuition of the Universe has to remain something particular and subjective. The virtuosity of the religious artist[168] has to be allowed to mingle its subjectivity into the tragic

166. [Friedrich Schleiermacher]: *On Religion: Speeches to its Cultured Despisers*, Berlin, 1799. The abridged English translation by John Oman has now been reprinted (New York, Ungar, 1955). Friedrich Ernst Daniel Schleiermacher (1768–1834) was a Lutheran minister and professor in Berlin.

167. The dogmatic antithesis is the opposition between the Beyond and this world. The object of yearning is this-worldly as revealed in experience, and idealism here stands for the double-headed identity: the identity of the Beyond and this world, an identity which Hegel calls on these pages the universe, and the identity of the Subject with the Object, that is, Subject-Objectivity.

168. In the second edition of his *Speeches* (1806) Schleiermacher abandoned the term "religious artist" altogether.

earnestness of religion. His individuality must not be veiled and embodied in an objective representation of great figures and their mutual motion which is, in turn, a veil for the motion of the Universe in them—as it was in [the] epics and tragedies which artistic genius built for the church triumphant of Nature.[169] Nor are lyrical expressions to be deprived of their subjectivity [386] by their simultaneous presence in the memory [of the "folk"] and their entrance into everyone's discourse. Instead, this subjective element is supposed to constitute the essential vitality and truth both in the exposition of one's own intuition of the Universe and in its [re]production in others; art is supposed to be forever without works of art; and the freedom of the highest intuition is supposed to consist in singularity and the possession of personal originality (in dem für sich etwas Besonderes Haben). —What is a priest but a tool and a servant whom the congregation offers as sacrifice, and who offers himself for its sake and for his own, in order to enact what is the bounding and the objective [moment] of religious intuition? All his might and strength before the mature congregation can belong to him only as a representative. But [in Schleiermacher] the congregation takes the role of immaturity on itself and is supposed to have the aim and intent of letting the priest, as a virtuoso of edification and enthusiasm, produce in it the inwardness of intuition. Instead of extinguishing or at least not acknowledging a subjective privacy of intuition—a man is called an idiot insofar as his life is private[170]—one is to give in to it so far that this particularity forms the principle of a private congregation. So it is that the little congregations and peculiarities assert themselves and multiply ad infinitum; they float apart and gather together by happenstance; every moment the groupings alter like the patterns in a sea of sand given over to the play of the winds. Yet at the same time —as is only fair—every group regards the private and distinctive peculiarity of its view as something so otiose and even unremarkable that it does not mind whether it is acknowledged or not, and gives up all claims to objectivity. All these little groups can stay peacefully

169. This is an echo of a theme from Hegel's earliest manuscripts. See especially the "Tübingen Fragment" of 1793 (translated in Harris, Toward the Sunlight, Oxford, 1972, pp. 481–507; compare p. 507) and the following passages from subsequent essays, translated by T. M. Knox in Hegel, Early Theological Writings (Chicago, 1948), pp. 82, 143, 147–8, 154–5, 184–5, 193, 197–8, 288 ff., 252. Compare also Richard Kroner's Introduction to that book.

170. Hegel here plays on the fact that idiotes is the normal Greek word for a citizen in his private capacity. The word here translated as privacy, private, is Eigenheit.

side by side in a pervasive atomism; and certainly the enlightened separation of church and state fits in here very nicely. In this Idea of pervasive atomism an intuition of the Universe cannot be an intuition of it as spirit; for that which is spirit is not present in the Universe in the atomic state; and altogether the catholicity of religion consists [here] only in negativity and in the universality of singular being. So, although the subjectivity of yearning has raised itself to the objectivity of intuition, and reconciliation is effected, not with actuality, but with that which lives, not with singularity, but with the Universe, still even this intuition of the universe is itself transformed back into subjectivity. For on the one hand this intuition is virtuosity—or in other words it is not even the yearning, but only the search for the yearning; and on the other hand the intuition is not to constitute itself organically, nor is the authentic virtuosity to express itself properly in laws, and achieve its objectivity and reality in the body of a people and of a universal church. Instead outward expression is to have a strictly inward significance, it must be an immediate outburst or emulation of some singular and particular enthusiasm. The genuine externalization, the work of art, must not be present.

# C. Fichtean Philosophy

In Kant's philosophy, thought, the infinite, the form of the objective is what comes first. The absolute antithesis between thought [on the one hand,] and being, the particular, the finite [on the other,] is within the cognitive subject, but not consciously: the antithesis is not objective for the subject. Or alternatively we might say that the absolute identity in which the antithesis is suspended, is purely objective, it is just a thought. It comes to the same thing either way, for this form of absolute objectivity, the identity as something beyond cognition, never converges with the subjective [side, i.e., with] cognition, to which the absolute antithesis is transported. In the philosophy of Jacobi it is the consciousness of the antithesis that comes first; and in order that it may be represented as resolved, the antithesis that is within cognition flees into its counterpart, i.e., into a realm beyond cognition, just as in Kant. There is, indeed, still a middle between this transition to absolute opposites, but this middle is itself something subjective: it is a yearning and a grief. In Fichte's philosophy, this yearning is synthesized with the Kantian objectivity, though not in such a way that the two opposite forms are extinguished in a true identity and indifference and the absolute middle emerges. Rather, Jacobi's subjective unification within the living experience of the individual is itself taken over in a merely objective form. In Kant's philosophy there is not the least sign of worry about the contradiction between empty universality and living particularity. In the theoretical sphere the contradiction is absolutely affirmed; and in the practical sphere, whose concept implies the suspension of the contradiction, a formalism of legal theory and morality emerges which is without vitality and truth. Jacobi's philosophy secures the identity of the universal and the particular in individuality, but the individuality is subjective. Hence a union of this kind can be nothing but worry and yearning, and particularity must become something permanent, something hallowed and absolute. In Fichte, this subjectivity of yearning is itself turned into the infinite, it is something thought; it is an absolute requirement, and as such it is the climax of the system: the Ego *ought* to be equal to the non-Ego. But no point of indifference can be recognized in it.

We have pointed out already[1] how the system rises toward the negative side of the Absolute, toward infinity, toward the Ego as absolute thinking. In this respect it is pure [388] idealism. But since this negative side is itself set up as what is absolutely positive, the idealism becomes something formal† and is confronted by a realism. It is able to establish the identity of the antithetic opposites [i.e., to achieve intellectual intuition] only in the infinite; or in other words it turns the abstractive thinking, the pure activity that is opposed to being, into the Absolute. So it does not truly nullify the antitheses. Like the idealism [of his system] Fichte's intellectual intuition is merely a formal† affair. Thought is confronted by reality, the identity of the intellectual intuition is confronted by the antitheses. The only identity here is the relative identity of the causal nexus in the [mutual] determination of one opposite by the other.

The task of philosophy as it was determined by the tradition (*Kultur*) of Locke and Hume is to compute and explain the world from the standpoint of the subject. The very opposition that holds between the world and the subject is transferred into the world that is to be explained. It splits [in Kant] into an ideal side and a real side in such a way that the ideal side in its relative antithesis to the real becomes the pure identity that abstracts from reality, i.e., the pure concept on the one hand; while on the other hand it is also the identity that is connected with reality, it is time, space, categories, the ideality of the real. In this cleavage of the world the objective, universal aspect of the real now consists solely in what belongs to the ideal side. Hence this idealism, which aims to explain the objective world, derives objectivity directly from the principle of the ideal side, i.e., from the Ego, the universal which in its overall opposition to the world is the subject. For this critical idealism has recognized objectivity as the ideal factor, and has thereby suspended the being in and for itself of the objective.

Fichte has highlighted this critical idealism which is quite evidently concerned with the form [of objectivity] only, in sharper outline. The universal aspect of the world that is opposed to the subject, is posited as Ego because it is posited as universal, as ideal, as thought. But the particular is necessarily left behind, so that if we accept the popular conception of philosophy and make explanation our business, the most interesting side of the objective world, the side of its reality, remains unexplained. To Kant, the real as given to sensation is some-

1. See pp. 61–65 above.

thing merely empirical which can be dismissed right away as unworthy of consideration. This is as unsatisfactory as Fichte's demonstration that sensation is something merely subjective, that the color red, [for example,] is first spread over a plane by the subject's hand, and thereby acquires objectivity.[2] For the problem is not at all about ideality, but about reality, and it does not matter whether the reality concerned is an infinite mass of sensations or of thing-qualities. In the practical part of the *Science of Knowledge* to be sure, it did [389] look as if the reality that is absolute for the ideal side, the things as they are in themselves were supposed to be constructed on the basis of how we ought to make them. But there is nothing deduced there except an analysis of the concept of striving and drive in a rational being and some reflective concepts about *feeling*, such as that feelings must be *different*. As for the task of constructing the system of things as they *ought* to be, only the formal† concept of *ought* is analysed; apart from this formal essence there is not the slightest trace of the construction of feeling itself as a real system or of the construction of the totality of the ought. For the ought admits, in and for itself, of no totality at all. On the contrary, the manifoldness of reality appears as an incomprehensible primitive fact (*Bestimmtheit*), an empirical necessity. Particularity and difference as such are [accepted as] something absolute. The relevant standpoint for

2. This is Hegel's summary of the following Fichte text:

"And this red is something positive, a simple sensation, a determinate state of yourself?"

"I understand."

"You should, therefore, see the red strictly as something simple, as a mathematical point, and you do see it only as such, do you not? In *you* at least, as your affection, it seems to be a simple determinate state, without any complexity, something that should be visualized as mathematical point. Or do you find it otherwise?"

"I have to admit you are right."

"But now you spread this simple red over a broad plane which you undoubtedly *do not see*, since you see *strictly speaking* only *the red*. How do you manage to arrive at this plane?"

"Strange indeed. —Yet I think I have found the explanation. To be sure, I do not see the plane, but I *feel* it when I pass my hand over it. My sensation through sight continues to remain the same during this [process of] feeling and this is why I extend the red color over the whole plane which I *feel* while I always *see the same red*." (Fichte, *The Vocation of Man*, in *Werke* II, 199–212; also Roderick M. Chisholm's translation, pp. 35–47, especially p. 41. Wherever Hegel refers directly to *The Vocation of Man* he does so to its first edition, Berlin, 1800.)

this reality [of the particular] is the empirical standpoint of any singular individual. For every such individual his reality is the incomprehensible sphere of common actuality in which he happens to be enclosed. We do not have to remind the reader that the formal idealism which proves that the empirical reality in its entirety is only a subjective thing, a feeling, is quite irrelevant to the absoluteness of the empirical reality. For this form does not alter the common and incomprehensible necessity of empirical existence in the slightest. Whether reality appears to us as the qualities of things or as our sensation, we cannot think for a moment that we have here a genuine idealization (*Idealität*) of actuality and of the real side [of experience].

We have brought out the formalism of this so-called idealistic [philosophical] knowledge in our discussion of Jacobi's philosophy[3] which had the most definite and candid awareness of it. So we do not need to clarify it further with respect to Fichte's philosophy. Fichte shares it with the others, because of the principle of subjectivity and because the absolute identity exists only for faith and not for cognition and knowledge. What this formalism comes down to basically is that either the pure concept, the empty thought, supervenes incomprehensibly upon a content, a determination of the concept, or vice versa: the determination supervenes incomprehensibly upon the indeterminateness [of the pure concept]. In Jacobi's dogmatism the objective, the given, is called the first upon which the concept supervenes later. Fichte, on the contrary, makes the empty knowing, the Ego into the first, which is essentially one and the same as the empty intellect of the analysing philosophy (*Wissen*); or, in other words, Fichte's Ego is an identity upon which determination supervenes subsequently as something alien, something which is incomprehensible since it does not originate in the Ego. But this contrast between Jacobi and Fichte makes not the slightest difference to the matter at issue.

According to Fichte's idealism the Ego does not sense and intuit things; it intuits only its sensing and its intuiting and knows only of its [390] knowing. Thus, the one and only primordial certainty [in his view] is pure and empty activity, action pure and free; there is strictly nothing but pure knowing, and pure intuiting, and sensing: Ego=Ego. We shall see later how the whole world of sense that is

3. Compare pp. 142–6 above.

thus nullified gets its reality anyway, through the absolute act of will. But what is incomprehensible is the knowledge of this reality, the relation of the absolute emptiness and indeterminateness of the knowledge to determinateness and to this reality. The particular and the universal are alien one to the other just as Jacobi's empirically given determinateness is alien to the indeterminateness, that is, to the concept employed by the analysing intellect. But Fichte's way of knowing only the knowing, his way of knowing only the bare identity prepares through its own formalism a road to the particular. Fichte acknowledges that the sole truth and certainty, that is, pure self-consciousness and pure knowing, are incomplete, are conditioned by something else; or in other words, that the Absolute of the system is not absolute, and that for this very reason we must go on to something else. This acknowledged incompleteness of the absolute principle and the acknowledged necessity of going on to something else in consequence form the principle of the deduction of the world of sense. Because of its absolute deficiency the completely empty principle [Ego=Ego] from which [Fichte] begins has the advantage of carrying the immediate necessity of self-fulfilment immanently within itself. It must go on to something other [than itself] and from that to something else in an infinite objective world. The necessity rests upon the principle's being nothing but a part and upon its infinite poverty being the infinite possibility of wealth.[4] In this way it plays a double role. In one role it is absolute, in the other strictly finite; and in the latter quality it can serve as the point of departure for the entire empirical infinity. Now, how could any principle have a higher degree of *apriority* than this one which immediately entails the necessity of the whole?

Looking at it on its own account, moreover, the formalism of this principle has the great advantage that it can easily be made comprehensible. The difficult requirement of intellectual intuition has aroused general complaint, and we have sometimes heard tell of people who went mad in their efforts to produce the pure act of will and the intellectual intuition.[5] Both the complaint and the madness were no doubt occasioned by the name of the thing, not by the thing itself,

---

4. See pp. 181 ff. below.

5. Fichte's writings on *Wissenschaftslehre* (1794–97) had elicited a host of critical and satirical responses. The best known "complaint" was perhaps that of Friedrich Nicolai; and it was Jean-Paul (Richter) who told the story of the man driven mad. Hegel singles out Reinhold's response in the *Difference* essay.

which Fichte[6] describes as common and easy enough, the only difficulty being perhaps to convince oneself that it really is just this simple everyday thing. The intuition of anything at all as alien to pure
consciousness or Ego, is empirical intuition; though the Ego too is,
as Fichte puts it, equally given in common consciousness.[7] Abstracting from everything alien in consciousness on the other hand, and
thinking oneself, is intellectual [391] intuition. Abstracting from the
determinate content in any sort of knowledge and knowing only pure
knowing, knowing only what is purely formal† in knowing, this is
pure absolute knowledge. Now surely, this abstraction is easy enough
to make, and everyone knows something he could abstract from. Nor
need anyone be bothered about what has been abstracted from; for
it does not get lost, indeed it comes back again in its whole empirical
extension and breadth both for knowledge and for action; except
that philosophy makes this contingency of ordinary consciousness
methodical without diminishing its contingency and ordinariness in
the least.

The methodical aspect of this knowledge, or the philosophy about
ordinary consciousness consists in this: first that the point of departure is something absolutely true and certain, namely the Ego, the
knowing in all knowledge, pure consciousness. But then, since pure
consciousness shows itself immediately to be the principle of deduction only because it is strictly incomplete and finite, its truth and
certainty are of a kind that is rejected by philosophy. For philosophy
can only find truth and certainty in what is not incomplete, not an
abstraction, not conditioned.

The emptiness of philosophical knowledge becomes the principle
of advance; for it is something radically deficient, and hence immedi-

6. Hegel is referring to the discussion of *Anschauung* in Book II of *The Vocation of Man*. Fichte does not say that it is "common and easy," but he does
speak of the critics of his position in ways which suggest that they are failing
to comprehend it because it is too obvious. "Do not let yourself be silenced by
sophists and half-philosophers: things do not appear to you through any representation . . . everything that you perceive outside yourself is always you yourself. This consciousness has been very aptly called 'intuition.' " (Fichte, *Werke*
II, 228; Chisholm, p. 64). "In intuition you can indeed become lost to yourself
. . . it is even natural and necessary that you become lost to yourself. This is
the observation to which those who defend a supposed consciousness of things
existing in themselves outside us appeal" (*ibid.*, p. 231; Chisholm, p. 67).

7. "Even in that same consciousness where you become lost to yourself in
the object [i.e., Hegel's "common consciousness"] there is always something
which is only possible through an unnoticed thinking of yourself and a close
observation of your own state" (*ibid.*, 232; Chisholm, p. 67).

ately in need of something other than itself, which becomes the point of attachment for the other that is its condition. The objective world supervenes upon pure knowledge as something alien that completes it. It does this by way of an inference from there being something missing in the point of attachment to the necessity of what is missing, an inference from the incompleteness of the Absolute, which is itself just one part, to the other part that completes it. But the insight that there is a deficiency in what is posited as Absolute, that the Absolute is just a part, is only possible through the Idea of totality or in general, through the awareness that for the sake of the so-called intellectual intuition, for the sake of thinking oneself and of pure knowing, we have abstracted from the alien other which is afterwards taken back again. Why does not this idea of the totality itself, the measure against which pure knowing shows itself to be incomplete, step forth as the Absolute? Why is the Absolute [in Fichte] something that is recognized as being only a part and as deficient? No reason can be found for it except that this part has empirical certainty and truth; of course everyone knows that he knows. Empirical truth of this sort is given preference over the absolute truth of the totality! The inference from one part to the other parts is nothing but a picking up again of what was abstracted from. This is to say: deduction is nothing but a transformation of signs, of the *minus* sign into *plus* sign; for the result of the abstraction [i.e., pure knowing] is directly but negatively connected with what it was abstracted from, and the latter is present in a negative form in the former. [392] In pure knowing, the world of sense is posited as a *minus*, the world of sense has been abstracted from, it has been negated. The inference to it consists in positing it now as a *plus* and in positing this *plus* as condition of pure self-consciousness. In the freedom of the rational being the objective sphere toward which its freedom is directed, is posited as a *minus*, so that the deduction of this sphere for freedom consists in giving the objective sphere the *plus* sign, or, in other words, positing it as being. An empty money-bag is a bag with respect to which money is already posited, to be sure, though with the *minus* sign; money can immediately be deduced from it because, as lacking, money is immediately posited.

In and for itself cognition by way of a deduction of this sort is not genuine cognition at all; for cognition that is genuine begins with the Absolute, and the Absolute is neither a part nor incomplete. Its truth and certainty are not just for experience, nor are they [reached] through abstraction, but through genuine intellectual intuition.

Fichte's cognition which proceeds from deficiency rests ultimately on the givenness of objects for the analysing thinking, the same givenness which Jacobi, Koeppen and others attribute to the manifold and its coherence when they happen upon it in the revealed facts of consciousness that they believe in—but what Jacobi and Koeppen happen upon has a positive sign, whereas in Fichte it has a negative sign. Jacobi and Koeppen *find* the very same thing present, that Fichte *finds* absent. Hence, this idealism is the true inversion of formal knowledge; but it is not, as Jacobi has claimed,[8] the inversion of the cube of Spinozism, for Spinoza's cube cannot be turned over; it floats in free ether and there is no above and below for it. Much less is there any ball or turtle on which it is grounded.[9] Rather, it has its balance and its ground within itself, it is its own ball and turtle. The irregular polyhedron of formal knowledge, on the other hand, rests on an earth that is alien to it, an earth in which it is rooted and which bears it. So there is an above and below for it. The ordinary sort of formalt knowledge has the manifold of experience as its ground but it draws up many a peak of concepts from the ground into the ideal atmosphere. Fichte's formalt knowledge reverses [the pattern of] this ordinary knowledge. It begins in the atmosphere where the very same thing [i.e, the manifold of experience] is encountered but only negatively and ideally; and being aware of this ideality, it lets down its negatively present content with a plus sign as reality.

What, now, can be said of the product of a cognition of this sort, which begins with the part that is certain and proceeds step by step from part to part wishing to express its deficiency as a totality posited for knowledge? It would seem as if the product not only can, but must be the totality. For it is only through the Idea of totality that we can recognize that our absolutely certain First [pure knowing] is only a part; so the Idea does seem to be our presupposition. [393]

8. "Strange that the thought never occurred to him [Spinoza] of turning his philosophical cube over; of making the upper side, the side of thought which he calls the *objective* side, into the lower side which he called the subjective, *formal [formell]* side. So he never investigated whether his cube would remain the same and preserve the sole true philosophical shape of the matter. Unfailingly such an experiment would have changed everything for him. What had been substance for him, the cubic, the *one* matter of two totally different beings would have disappeared before his eyes. Instead of it, a pure flame would have flared up, a flame burning solely out of itself, a flame in need of no *place* and of no *nourishing fuel*: Transcendental Idealism." Jacobi, *Werke* III, 11–2.

9. Compare p. 125–6 above.

And since it is thus what is truly First it would seem that the course of the development [both of the argument and of experience] must set it forth. But precisely because something recognized as a part and as deficient is supposed to have absolute truth and certainty, it is impossible that the entire progression should be totality. Pure experience, which knows nothing of a part and has not fixed the part in reflection as something which has being (*Wesen*) in the strict sense, can, of course, begin with a part and describe and set forth the whole circle by advancing from part to part; for experience, because it is experience, is not caught in the shackles of reflection which turns the part into an in-itself, and so makes it impossible to reach the whole. But a totality produced by, or rather found in experience does not exist for cognition, even if it is given as totality in presentational awareness (*Vorstellung*). For in cognition the parts must be absolutely determined by the whole; the whole must be the First of cognition. Fichte's formal cognition, transforming the negatively given into something positive, does not begin with the whole, but proceeds from the part to other parts; so it cannot transcend its partiality (*Teilwesen*) either in presentational awareness generally or in cognition. It seems that without the absolute Idea hovering before it, [Fichte's] empty [i.e., formal] knowledge would not recognize itself as something incomplete; but the Idea itself signifies here nothing but the negativity of something else that is needed, and this something else is only a finite being again, a part, an other thing, and so on *ad infinitum*. The absolute Idea shows itself to be strictly something formal,† because [Fichte makes] the part which is the finite linking point [between form and content or the ideal and the real], a being in itself, something absolute. This completely destroys any true Idea of totality. So what the deduction produces, with its sleight of hand by which negative is transformed into positive, is, of necessity, just the mass of common empirical reality, a nature that is finite throughout, a sense world. The abstraction from what is alien to the Ego was not a speculative abstraction, that is to say, the alien was not nullified. On the contrary, the very same formula in the very same context of ordinary actuality was posited again, but with a negative sign, in the form of a deficiency. As in the ordinary conception of experience (*gemeine Empirismus*), the mirror receives the sense-world and posits it ideally within itself, only to give it back afterwards just as it received it. And this giving back, this naming of what is lacking in the lack is called an immanent transcendental deduction.

The starting point is absolute, yet finite. Its finitude makes it impossible for the birth of cognition to be [the construction of] a genuine whole; for a genuine whole is only possible where no part exists in itself. So, a true Ideal in which the finitude of empirical reality would disappear and [subjective] affections would become Nature, is strictly impossible. No other wealth of representations [or ideas] is possible here, save a wealth of finite ones; and nature is nothing but the world of the senses. Ordinary empiricism suffers this [one] change: it gets deduced. [394] In other words, the system or rather —since a system is here unthinkable—the conglomerate of ideas necessary for ordinary consciousness appears first posited as a pure lack, and then linked up with the subject that lacks it, i.e., with the Ego. And it does not matter whether we wish to reflect on the subject's pure lack or on the mass of what is lacking. It is all the same whether we think always and only pure knowledge, emptiness, the Nothing, or the whole content of this Nothing as a mass of subjective affections that are no more than that. The alternatives are inseparable, the pure *minus* and what the Ego lacks in order to be a lacking. For the abstraction only is what it is in virtue of its connection with that which was abstracted from, or in other words because the latter is posited with a negative sign. Fichte's theoretical philosophy consists in the cognition of the lack and of the manifold which is lacking; but the latter only achieves authentic reality, the true *plus*, through the pure act of will. Still, the one never is without the other, the emptiness never is without what has been emptied out of it, whether this content is posited as ideal or as real, as subjective or as objective.

In the second act of *The Vocation of Man*[10] (the exposition [of Fichte's system]which we would like for the present to concentrate on) the character "I" allows himself to be set free by a Spirit. When, at last, he believes that he has actually been set free, he does not

10. By "the second act" Hegel means what Fichte calls "Book II: Knowledge." Hegel uses dramatic parlance here because Fichte makes a dramatic conversation out of the central argument. *Dramatis personæ* are "I" and "the Spirit." The Spirit is the guide who leads "I" from naive realism and empiricism towards the Fichtean version of critical idealism.

It should be noted that *"Bestimmung"* in *Die Bestimmung des Menschen* has very strong overtones of both "determination" and "definition" which are absent in the English word "vocation." Thus, the very title of Fichte's book involves the problem of freedom and necessity: is man "determined" by nature, as "Book I: Doubt" avers, or does he "determine" nature and himself, as "Book II: Knowledge" argues? Also, the very title indicates what one may call Fichte's moral existentialism: the definition of what man is must be found in what he is called upon to be, i.e., in his vocation.

think at all of his complete bondage in the chains of empirical necessity nor of the incomprehensible sphere of his ordinary reality [given] in feeling. When the Spirit asks him (p. 88): "You don't just have general feelings [. . .]?" the answer comes quite casually: "I: Not at all. Every sensation is determinate. There are never mere seeings or touchings or hearings, but always something definite that is seen, touched, heard—the red, green, blue color, the cold and the warm, the smooth and the rough, the sound of the violin, the human voice and *the like*. Let *that be counted as settled between us*."[11] (This "and the like" surely embraces the rest of nature, the most exquisite things in it having supposedly been mentioned by name: the green, the red, the sound of the violin. But examples of definite forms would be more interesting and more to the purpose than these examples of what is formless.) The character "I" believes himself to have been freed without more ado from all these determinates and from the determinateness of his empirical existence generally, because he is convinced that they are within himself, and are only his own affections; so that the knowledge of them is an immediate knowledge of his own state and the whole chain of ordinary necessity is only one-sided [i.e., in the subject]. Thus he is free because the subject is, in his conception of himself, through his affections and not through things, an absolutely [395] empirical being *(Wesen)*—a contradiction which must be counted among the most striking. On the basis of the conviction that the consciousness of *any* thing outside *us* is absolutely nothing more than the product of our own representative faculty, the Spirit declares "I" to be free and delivered for ever from the fear that humiliated and tortured him, free from a necessity which exists only in his thought and from the reality of things existing outside him. As if he were not in one and the same prison of his own condition, subject to the same necessity as before. To be sure, the necessity is no longer present in the form of his thinking of it as an external object. But it continues to exist with the very same factuality *(Wirklichkeit)*, arbitrariness and contingency in the series of affections and states.

Fichte's "I," then, is still endowed with the same wealth of realities as before, but in the form of sensations. So it is incomprehensible how "I" can get to fretting over the mode of thinghood which his system of affections has lost, and complain that "nothing now exists, nothing but representations, that is, determinations of a conscious-

---

11. Fichte, *Werke* II, 206; Chisholm, pp. 41–2 (Hegel's quotation marks).

ness as mere consciousness."[12] He should have lamented, not about his loss, for that mere mode of objectivity and corporeality of the sweet and bitter is not worth a tear—but about that wealth he still possesses. He should lament about the undamaged necessity in its whole length and breadth of sweet sensations and bitter ones, red ones and so on; and about the brute fact of intuition (p. 169).[13] The thing which is all that he has lost is first added to this sensation and intuition by thought. It is not for what it took away, but for the whole range of finitude which it left him that Fichte's "I" could fairly call the Spirit profligate.[14]

The immediate product of this formal idealism as we have seen it arise, has, then, the following shape. A realm of experience without unity, a purely contingent manifold, on one side, is confronted by an empty thought on the other. If the empty thought is posited as a real, active force, then like everything else that is objective, it must be recognized as something ideal. Or, in order to put the antithesis of the thought and the manifold realm of empirical necessity in its pure form, the thought must not be posited as a real active force— i.e., in the context of reality—but purely for itself, as empty unity, as universality completely set apart from particularity. Kant's pure Reason is this same empty thought, and reality is similarly opposed to that empty identity, and it is precisely the lack of concordance between them that makes faith in the beyond necessary. But in Kant's philosophy the reality [that can be known and] that necessarily lacks identity with [the reality postulated by] practical Reason is not merely dealt with in the wholly and simply empirical context (*Beziehung*) where it is present as the sensation of the empirical subject. This is the only way in which reality can occur in Fichte's idealism, [396] but Kant recognizes it also [in the *Critique of Judgment*] as a higher reality, namely as an organic system and beautiful nature. Kant's idealism loses with respect to the purity of abstraction; for abstraction completely detaches the identity from the difference and posits it, as one component of the antithesis, in opposition to the difference, the other being a merely empirical necessity and a manifold

12. *Ibid.*, p. 241; Chisholm, p. 76.
13. *Ibid.*, p. 243; Chisholm, p. 78–9. The demonstration that "the thing . . . is first added to this sensation and intuition by thought" is actually given earlier (*ibid.*, p. 230–40; Chisholm, p. 66–76.)
14. *Ibid.*, p. 245; Chisholm, p. 81.

lacking all identity. But Kant wins in another way as against this formalism, because he allows the speculative Idea to emerge at one more point of his system.[15]

Thus the system of knowledge, in Fichte's idealism, is a knowledge of a completely empty knowing that is absolutely opposed by empirical reality, a knowledge of a unity that is absolutely opposed by the manifold, and of a relative identity of the opposed terms. For a formal knowledge of this sort which cannot get beyond relative identity, and for the absolute antithesis within it, an antithesis which has, in Kant, the popular and less abstract form of a conflict between happiness and morality—for such a formalism the true identity must stand over against it as an absolute Beyond. Rational cognition and the speculative Idea are directly suspended and impossible, because thought and knowledge are simply and solely formal, mere antithetic opposites [of empirical reality], merely relative. The supreme effort of this formal thought is the acknowledgement of its own Nothing and that of the Ought.[16] Yet, because formal thought does not ever truly give itself up, the Ought is perennial: it is an enduring will which can only achieve a break-through to infinity and the Nothing; it remains incapable of breaking through infinity and the Nothing to positive rational cognition.

Fichte's whole system in all of his expositions of it, beginning with *The Science of Knowledge*,[17] expounds this triadic form: (1) position, thought, infinity; and then (2) being, opposition, finitude; and because these two sides [the triads (1) and (2)] remain radically distinct, there is (3) an interconnection of both for knowledge which is itself two-sided: a) there is an incomplete connection, the positive one for knowledge,[18] and b) there is the absolute identity of both which is outside the range of this science and cognition.

The two first parts [i.e., subtriads (1) and (2)] which make up the antithesis are contained in the first two basic principles of *The Sci-*

---

15. See pp. 85 ff. above.

16. Fichte's beginning point has been shown to be "the Nothing." This is the Ego that thinks. On the other side of the equation is the Ego that *ought* to be equal to the non-Ego.

17. The full title is *Foundation of the Entire Science of Knowledge*. Hegel uses the first edition (1794). See now *Werke* I, 83–328; and the English translation by Peter Heath and John Lachs (N. Y.: Appleton, 1970).

18. I.e., the causal relation whether *necessary* (as in theoretical philosophy) or *free* (as in practical philosophy).

*ence of Knowledge.* The first principle is Ego=Ego.[19] It requires a second principle not derivable (*erkennbar*) from "Ego=Ego," but absolute with respect to it. The second principle is necessary, but external and posterior to the first. And for this reason the first principle contains nothing but formal identity, nothing but infinity confronted by finitude. The second action is supposed to be conditioned as to its content: it is an acting relative to another acting.[20] Still, the condition (*Science of Knowledge,* p. 18) under which the counterpart of Ego=Ego was posited "cannot possibly result from Ego=Ego, since the form of opposing is not contained in the form of positing. On the contrary, the form of opposing is itself opposed to the form of positing."[21] [397] Let us suppose that the positing and the opposing are both an act of the Ego itself. The identity here would be the same as that which formerly belonged to the subject, namely the soul as a simple substance, the sustainer *common* to many opposite activities. This is no help, for it is the most formal† identity of all, and the very thing that this philosophy must despise more than anything else. One thing about Fichte's beginning with the antithesis [of positing and opposing] is that it is a preliminary, problematic way of doing philosophy, one that plays around with things that are nothing, with empty abstractions, and first procures reality for them in the synthesis that comes afterwards. Fichte himself acknowledges that if this pure Ego and pure Non-Ego are considered apart from and prior to the productive imagination, they subsist for thought only through an illusion of the imagination.[22] Another thing is that this problematic style of philosophizing simply does not resolve into a genuine identity: it sets the infinite and thought over against opposing and material stuff, simply postulating the manifold stuff or the opposing as an extra, picked up from experience on the ground that an opposing of this kind is to be found in anyone's consciousness.

19. The "strictly unconditioned principle" of the *Science of Knowledge* is the action (*Tathandlung*) in which "the Ego originally posits its own being" (*ibid.,* p. 98; Heath-Lachs, p. 99). But Fichte gets it from "A=A" via "Ich=Ich" (*Ibid.,* pp. 92, 94; Heath-Lachs, pp. 93–6).

20. The second principle "conditioned as to content" is not initially formulated as an action by Fichte (to show that it is an action of the Ego is the problem of his idealism). He says "a non-Ego is strictly opposed to the Ego" (*Ibid.,* p. 104; Heath-Lachs, p. 104).

21. Fichte here used "A=A," not "Ego=Ego." *Werke* I, 102; Heath-Lachs, p. 103.

22. *Werke* I, 224–5; Heath-Lachs, p. 200.

The third basic principle establishes the connection of the first two in the double respect mentioned above.[23] On one side [it is the relation typical] of formal knowledge, or the finite connecting [of subject and object] through the causal nexus. This remains entirely within the difference and the division [of Ego and Non-Ego]. On the other side, for faith the connection is the absolute identity that is beyond cognition. The two aspects of the connection, the form as knowledge and the matter of faith are quite radically incapable of becoming one. The emphasizing of one term of the antithesis, namely infinity, [and] a unilateral reflection upon the first principle, are what constitutes Fichte's idealism. But it is no more of an idealism than the most ordinary abstraction, which negates particularity and posits formal identity.

On account of this formal triplicity knowledge remains [for Fichte] in the difference [between Ego and non-Ego] while what is without difference is either [mere] infinity, formal identity or else it is beyond cognition. Thus Fichte's system does not go beyond the bounds of the principle of common human intellect. However, the verdict was that Fichte's system was a speculative system and not a system of common intellect and as this false prejudicial verdict spread, he has naturally exerted every effort in his more recent expositions of the system to uproot this prejudice.[24] Nothing could be plainer than the fact that Jacobi has misunderstood this system, when he says in his "Letter to Fichte," that he believes that the Fichtean way produced "a philosophy which is *all of one* piece, a genuine system of Reason, and indeed that the Fichtean way is the only way it can be done."[25] He opposes Fichte's philosophy on the grounds that "what I [Jacobi] understand by the true is something that is *prior to* and *outside* of knowledge."[26] But on this point Fichte's philosophy is in full agreement with Jacobi's. The Absolute exists for it in faith alone, not in cognition. Fichte is very far from sinning, as Jacobi claims (in the

23. Cf. p. 165 above. The third "formally conditioned" principle is: "The Ego posits in the Ego a divisible non-Ego opposed to the divisible Ego" (*Werke* I, 110; Heath-Lachs, p. 110). This third principle is supposed to reconcile the first two principles and to turn the second into the one about the Ego's action.

24. Hegel is probably thinking mainly of the *Vocation of Man* which is obviously designed for the ordinary reader. Compare *Werke* II, 258–63; Chisholm, pp. 93–9 (speculation and the voice of conscience are there contrasted, very much to the latter's advantage).

25. See Jacobi, *Werke* III, 19.

26. *Ibid.*, p. 32.

Preface to his "Letter," p. viii), [398] against "the majesty of the place" where the true resides outside the range of knowledge, nor does he want to "include it within the sphere of science."[27] On the contrary, absolute identity is, for him, quite outside of the sphere of knowledge, and knowledge is only formal†, just as Jacobi would have it, and within the difference [of Ego and non-Ego]. Fichte's Ego cannot be identical with the Ego [as it *ought* to be], his Absolute cannot be thought. Only the subject *and* the object can be thought, one *after* the other, one *determining* the other, both only within the causal nexus. About the supposed impossibility of thinking the identity of thought and being Spinoza says: "There are some who deny that they have any idea of God," i.e., they have no idea of God as Spinoza defines him; of the being whose existence is necessarily contained in his idea, or whose idea and whose existence are one—"Yet, as they say themselves, they love and worship Him. And even if you put the definition of God and the attributes of God before their eyes, you will still achieve nothing: no more, indeed, than if you endeavored to teach a man blind from birth the differences between colors as we see them. But unless we want to treat these people as a new kind of animal, midway between men and brutes, we ought to pay little attention to their words." (*Principles of the Cartesian Philosophy*, Part I, Prop. VI, Scholium.)[28]

We have already shown why Jacobi so violently abhors the nihilism he finds in Fichte's philosophy.[29] As far as Fichte's system itself is concerned, nihilism is certainly implicit in pure thought as a task [to be accomplished]. But this pure thought [of Fichte's] cannot reach it because it stays strictly on the one side [i.e., the side of the Ego] so that this infinite possibility has an infinite actuality over against it and at the same time with it. So the Ego is for ever and ever affected by a Non-Ego. This has to be the case because infinity, or thought, which is only one *relatum* in the antithesis, is to be posited as being *in itself*. And for this reason the *correlatum* cannot be absolutely nullified. With inexhaustible elasticity the *correlatum* springs back; for almighty fate has forged the pair of them together with

---

27. *Ibid.*, p. 6.

28. Hegel quotes the Latin text, probably from Volume I of the Paulus edition, which appeared in 1802. See now Gebhardt, Vol. I, 160; or the translation by F. A. Hayes in B. Spinoza, *Early Philosophical Writings* (Indianapolis: Library of Liberal Arts, 1963), p. 33.

29. See pp. 138–9 above.

fetters of adamant. The first step in philosophy is to recognize the
absolute nothing. Fichte's philosophy does not achieve this, however
much Jacobi may despise it for having done so. On the contrary,
both of them dwell in the nothing that is the opposite of philosophy.
Appearance, the finite, has absolute reality for both of them. Both
agree that the Absolute and eternal is the nothing for cognition. Jacobi reproaches the Kantian system for being a mishmash of idealism
and empiricism. Of these two ingredients, however, it is not the
empiricism, but the idealistic side, the side of infinity, which incurs
his reproach. Although the side of infinity cannot win through to the
perfection of the true nothing, still Jacobi cannot bear it because it
endangers the absoluteness of the empirical, and because the demand
for the [399] nullification of the antithesis is implicit in it.

Jacobi says: "*Either* God exists and exists *outside* me, a living being subsisting apart; *or else* I am God. *There is no third way.*"[30] Philosophy, on the contrary, says *there is a third way*, and it is [authen-
tic] philosophy only because there is one. For philosophy predicates
of God not only being but also thought, that is, Ego, and recognizes
him as the absolute identity of being and thought. Philosophy recognizes that there is no *outside* for God, and hence that God is not
an entity that subsists apart, one that is determined by something
outside it, or in other words, not something apart from which other
things have standing. Outside of God nothing has standing at all,
there is nothing. Hence the *Either-Or*, which is a principle of all formal logic and of the intellect that has renounced Reason, is abolished
without trace in the absolute middle [which the Either-Or excludes].
Jacobi's philosophy is completely summed up in this basic thought
[that either God is outside of me or I am God, and there is no third
way]. But we could show that he contradicts it, not only on the very
page that precedes its first utterance—where he says, "I affirm that
man finds God because he can only find himself in God"[31]—but in
a hundred other places where he calls Reason divine, etc. But we have
already said enough elsewhere to show that these *first sparks* of philosophical thought should simply be taken as spirited *aperçus* and
not as philosophy. Wherever Jacobi finds that these *aperçus* of his

---

30. Jacobi, *Werke* III, 49.

31. What Jacobi actually says is this: "I affirm that man finds God because
he can find himself only *zugleich mit Gott*, at the same time that he finds God."
Jacobi continues: "And man is unfathomable to himself because the nature
(*Wesen*) of God is necessarily unfathomable to man." *Werke* III, 48.

have been taken up philosophically by others, and seriously set forth as truths for [philosophical] knowledge, he does not merely scent atheism etc., but dogmatically accuses the culprits of it. And wherever he himself goes beyond having bright ideas, and begins thinking thoughts he remains within the confines of an absolute dualism. In any case, Jacobi's basic principle is just as much Fichte's. In Fichte too, the moral world order that exists in the context of faith (*welche im Glauben ist*) is strictly *outside* the Ego. Only through an infinite progress does it acquire reality for the Ego, only so does the Ego enter into it or vice versa. Things simply cannot become for the Ego what they ought to be, precisely because, if they did, the non-Ego would cease to be and become Ego. The Ego=Ego, as truly absolute identity, would be without a second principle. The Ego would suspend something it had itself posited and would itself cease to be Ego. Thus Fichte's system of knowledge is as little able to transcend dualism as Jacobi could possibly want. The reality that is not dualistic exists for Fichte only in faith, and the Third that is truly the First and the Only One[32] is not to be found in his system; nor can the negativity which is not dualistic, infinity, the nothing, be pure in it. It ought to be pure, but it does not become pure. Rather, it get itself fixed again, so that it becomes absolute subjectivity. Jacobi, who focused his reflection on the one side of the antithesis, on infinity, on formal identity, felt that this nihilism of the transcendental philosophy would tear the heart out of his breast. But he only needed to reflect on the other side of the antithesis which is present with the same absoluteness. [400] There he could find, fore and aft, all of our affections and states of mind, and everything empirical, which was [for him] a matter of revelation and of faith.

What this idealism calls *Theoretical Science* is nothing but bringing forth the antithesis of infinity and finitude: on one side the abstraction "pure knowing and thinking *qua* knowing and thinking" and on the other side the abstraction "the non-knowing and non-thinking," or "the non-Ego." Both sides are posited only in and for knowledge, and each side is an abstraction and an emptiness like the other. The empirical side in this theoretical realm is generally speaking the abstract manifold, it is a non-Ego. Since the real itself is here posited in an entirely formal† or ideal way,[33] the whole apparatus of

32. *Das Erste und Einzige*. Compare *Difference*, pp. 123–6.

33. I.e., as a *Tathandlung* of the Ego reconstructed in the pure thought of the philosopher.

this theoretical idealism is nothing but the construction of logical forms,[34] in abstraction from all content. The scientific route which this formalistic or logical idealism takes in its transition to reality (which it calls a "deduction" of reality) has already been characterized above.[35] Its own proper content is the [sequence of] relative identities that link empty thinking with the abstraction "manifoldness." All three members [the two opposites and the relative identity between them][36] themselves fall entirely within the region of empty knowledge. Our task at present is to consider the content with which this emptiness is integrated. In the theoretical idealism [i.e., the "theoretical" part of the Science of Knowledge] the empirical is an abstraction. In the practical idealism [i.e., the "practical" part of the Science of Knowledge], however, it comes forth as true, empirical reality, visible and tangible. Nature, which in theory was just a non-Ego, something merely negative, defined as the opposite in general, now steps forth out of the abstraction of knowledge into the wealth of its reality and the glory of its full vitality—namely as something sour or sweet or bitter, something blue or red.

This integration is directly present in Jacobi's philosophy because it is empiricism right from the outset and because the particularity of the subject has not been removed by abstraction. In Kant's philosophy, too, the particulars which the universality of Reason needs —Reason insofar as it has this need is called practical Reason—are accepted empirically without a second thought. The presence of the particular, of inclinations and passions, of the pathological in general that is to be combated by reason, all this is presupposed as given. In a word, what is presupposed as given is nature, for Reason to work on, and to subject to its purpose; for Reason's purpose is not yet realized in nature, and as to its content, the *summum bonum*—happiness according to desert, and hence universal happiness since everyone ought to deserve it—what that happiness consists in is likewise empirically presupposed. Fichte's integration of ideality and reality happens *a priori*, namely, through faith, which is the general principle of the transition from lack to fulfilment, or the pure form of the [401] transformation of *minus* into *plus* and of the linking of both in their reciprocal [causal] influence upon each other. But it is only the form. For the matter itself, which was abstracted from in the

---

34. *Ie.*, Ego/non-Ego, positing/opposing, infinity/finitude, thinking/being, etc.
35. See pp. 157–8 above.
36. See pp. 165–6 above.

minus of ideality is, as it necessarily has to be, just as empirical and without totality as in the preceding systems [of Kant and Jacobi].

The ideal is to be integrated through[37] the real, empty thought or Reason is to coalesce with its opposite, the sense world (which is how nature appears in these systems). The all controlling basic principle of this integration consists in this: the one side is absolutely not what the other is, and no genuine identity emerges from any linkage between them. Just as for knowledge true identity and eternity are in a Beyond that is faith, so in the practical [i.e., moral] sphere, the sphere of reality, they are in a Beyond that is the infinite progress. And just as, in the theoretical sphere, empty thought is absolute and pure knowledge, i.e., as theoretical Reason, so it is absolute in the practical sphere as pure will, i.e., as practical Reason. And the opposite of empty thought, the empirical world of sense is absolute likewise. The relative identities of practice which Kant did not go very far in elaborating will now follow in their different branches.

The first and the most important step in the integration must be to re-introduce reality into both members of the antithesis each against the other, that is to say, to suspend the theoretical abstraction, to establish faith in terms of its product. The theoretical sphere consists in the ideality, i.e., in the reflection on infinity; and this infinity is infinity as such, empty knowing, pure thinking [or Ego] as well as absolute opposition [or non-Ego]. $0 = + 1 - 1$[38] and each of the two [Ego and non-Ego] is defined as not being what the other is. The one is only insofar as the other occurs; and as the other occurs, the first is not. The reality of infinity or empty thinking consists in the $+ 1 - 1$, and the standing of this antithesis provides the content of this idealism, that is, the logical forms.[39] But at the same time these opposites are ideal ($=0$) and their true truth is in the infinity, or in other words, in their being nothing.

Now, in the practical sphere this ideality is to be suspended. $+ 1$ and $- 1$ shall not equal $0$. The reality that they receive is this: infinity, empty thought, $0$, which is the middle between $+ 1$ and $- 1$ wherein $+ 1$ and $- 1$ vanish, steps out of the middle onto the side and, over against it, the world of the senses stands forth, the realm

37. We have decided to translate the *durch* literally here, because it seems quite probable that Hegel means something more than would be expressed by the normal English "with."

38. The zero is ideality, the empty thinking of infinity; $+1$ is the self positing of the Ego; $-1$ is the oppositing of the non-Ego.

39. See note 34 above.

of finite existence. Thus both are constituted as realities, and this constitutive act is called *the pure act of will.* This is the act that decrees that the nothing—the nothing of $+ 1$ and $- 1$—is to be an absolute something. This is where all the popular doctrines originate; you exist in order to act; your action determines your worth;[40] practical Reason is absolute, the absolute freedom etc.

However, after these nothings that stand in absolute opposition have simply been decreed to be realities, everything that follows depends *formaliter* on faith, [402] which is the expression of the required identity of both nothings [i.e., of the world of sense, and the world of (misconceived) Reason]. But with respect to the cognition and construction of the practical, faith is something wholly formal,† for it expresses nothing but this requirement, the pure line of a thread which cannot have any filling at all, any length, breadth, or depth at all, and only permits relative identities which will always be pushed further by the requirement [that Ego ought to be equal to Ego].[41] Subjectivity, Ego, pure will is opposed to objectivity and this antithesis is absolute. The task of constructing identity and integration simply cannot be performed.

Pure will is to become real through acting. The reality which originates for it through acting is to come from the pure will, it must be its own. Hence, the reality must at first be present as an idea in pure will, that is, as an intention and end of the subject. The Ego is to produce the concept in strict freedom out of its own absolutely self-sufficient power as intelligence. And the will is not to be affected by any other reality that it accepts as given from elsewhere and makes into its own end, for as pure will it must have only the end that is its own free project. When man determines himself to action there arises for him the concept of what will happen in the future as a consequence of his action, and this is the formal† side of the concept of end. But [these Fichtean conceptions do not work; for] the will is pure identity without any content and is only pure insofar as it is something thoroughly formal and without content. It is in itself im-

40. Echoes from *The Vocation of Man*, Book III: Faith (Fichte, *Werke* II, 249; Chisholm, p. 84).

41. Hegel always maintains that Fichte cannot get back to his initial Ego= Ego once he has left it. He could only regain it by advancing to Schelling's position. Instead he arrives at an Ego which is *eternal striving.* This Ego is never equal to its real self theoretically, or to its ideal self practically. This *ought* is what Hegel refers to as the *partial connection for knowledge.* The absolute identity is *beyond,* in the realm of faith.

possible that the will's concept of end should get its content from the will itself. So, nothing at all remains but this formal idealism of faith which posits the empty subjectivity of the end as an equally empty objectivity without the will being at all able or permitted to give any inner reality or content to the end; for if it did, the will would no longer be determining [but determined]. So there is nothing left but the hollow pronunciamento that the law must be obeyed for law's sake, duty done for duty's sake; and declamations about how the Ego raises itself above the sensuous and supersensuous, how it soars above the wreckage of the world, etc.[42]

This sublime hollowness and this uniquely consistent emptiness must then so far yield as to take account of reality. If the content is to be established for the purpose of science as a system of duties and laws, then either idealt reality—that is, the content of the laws, duties and virtues—is picked up empirically, as Kant is specially wont to pick it up, or else they are deduced in Fichte's fashion from a finite point of departure in a running chain of finitudes, beginning arbitrarily with *one* rational being, and one which has no body, etc. But reality cannot be anything but a manifold while it remains in opposition to ideality. Therefore no matter how the system is established, there arises a mass, indeed an infinite plurality, of duties, laws and virtues which cannot constitute a totality or even achieve the external completeness of a system. Moreover, the duties, laws and virtues must necessarily contradict one another in their definiteness; [403] and no mutual limitation or pattern of precedence and subordination is possible because each is posited in its ideal form, and hence comes forward with the pretension of absoluteness. The moral sciences of Kant and Fichte provide the empirical evidence for this.[43]

On one side, then, stands pure Reason, integrated. If it maintains and affirms itself as pure will, this affirmation is hollow rhetoric; while if it gives itself a content it must get it empirically—and once it has given this content the form of practical ideality, i.e., made it into law and duty, an absolute clash is posited in this content, a clash that suspends all science and makes totality impossible.

42. This final declamation is an echo of Fichte's *Appeal to the Public* (1800); see *Werke* V, 237. The bulk of the paragraph contains echoes from the *Vocation of Man*, Book III (*Werke* II, 250 ff.; Chisholm, pp. 85 ff.).

43. "The moral sciences of Kant and Fichte" placed together by Hegel are: Kant, *Die Metaphysik der Sitten* (1797); Fichte, *Grundlage des Naturrechts* (1796) and *System der Sittenlehre* (1798).

On the other side stands nature turned into empirical reality and made absolute by the act of pure will. Because the idealistic side decrees itself to be absolute, what it nullifies must re-emerge as absolute. If empirical reality, the sense-world did not have the whole strength of its being the opposite, Ego would not be Ego; it could not act, its high vocation would be gone. The supersensuous world is only the flight from the sensuous world. When there is nothing left to flee from, flight and freedom and supersensuous world are no longer posited. This empirical world is, then, as much *in itself* as the Ego. At the same time the relation [to the Ego] which the sensuous world receives in the act of will determines the way it has to be. For the essence of the Ego consists in acting: the absolute, empty thinking shall posit itself; but it *is* not posited, no being pertains to it. Yet the objective world is the being of the Ego [the absolute thinking] which can only attain to its true essence by nullifying this being. Thus nature is determined as a mere sense-world, as something to be nullified, and it must be recognized as such. On the other hand, if the Ego recognizes that it has being as well as the objective [world], then it recognizes itself as strictly dependent on the world and as trapped in an absolute necessity. The Ego must only recognize itself as the negation of the sense-world and it must therefore regard the sense-world as something to be negated, that is, as something absolutely bad.

The initial cognition of the world as something real† prior to the act of pure will, the act in which it acquires absolute reality once more, but a reality that has to be nullified or, in other words, the worst reality imaginable—this is what is presented in the first act of *The Vocation of Man*.[44] Here the character "I" recognizes himself as "a manifestation, determined by the universe, of a force of nature that determines itself. And he recognizes that it is nature which acts in him, that he is subject to the eternal laws of nature, to a strict necessity; that the best way to peace of mind would consist in subjugating his desires to it [Nature], since his being is wholly [404] subject to it." But this rational thought "conflicts with his desires. Why should he conceal from himself the sadness, the loathing, the

---

44. Book I of *The Vocation of Man* is entitled Doubt. It has the form of a monologue in which "I" presents himself as split between his knowledge that he is merely part of "the system of nature," and his desire which attests to his being part of "the system of freedom."

horror [. . .] which seized upon his inmost heart at such a conclusion."[45]

The monstrous arrogance, the conceited frenzy[46] of this self who is horrified, filled with loathing and sadness, at the thought that he is one with the universe, that eternal nature acts in him—to be filled with loathing, be horrified and sad over the resolve to subjugate oneself to the eternal laws of nature and to its hallowed and strict necessity, to be in despair because one is not free, free from the eternal laws of nature and its strict necessity, to believe that one makes oneself indescribably miserable by this obedience—all this presupposes an utterly vulgar view of nature and of the relation of the singular person (*Einzelheit*) to nature. This view is one which is denuded of all Reason, for the absolute identity of subject and object is entirely alien to it, and its principle is their absolute non-identity. So it can only comprehend nature in the form of the absolute opposite, and hence as a pure object with respect to which it is only possible either to be dependent on it, or to make it dependent upon oneself. For the whole view is situated in the context of the causal nexus; it is the view of nature as a thing in which (*Vocation of Man*, p. 106) the differences between "green, sweet; red, smooth; bitter, fragrant; rough, sound of violin; stink, sound of trumpet,"[47] have their place. What can the laws of nature be [on Fichte's view] apart from qualities such as these? We shall see later[48] what other, teleological qualities Fichte admits in nature. So often we hear it said of the laws of nature that "No created spirit can penetrate into their inwardness"[49]—as if the laws of nature were something quite different from rational laws! As if they were laws which a moral self would be ashamed to submit

45. Hegel prints the whole passage as one continuous quotation. But in fact it is a summary that contains some direct quotation. To mention one of several changes, Hegel heightens "Inneres" to "Innerstes." See *Werke* II, 189–90 (compare Chisholm, pp. 24–5).

46. *Wahnsinn des Dünkels*: the "frenzy of self-conceit" in the *Phenomenology* (Hoffmeister, pp. 271–4; Baillie, pp. 397–9) is *Wahnsinn des Eigendünkels*. But the two states of mind are not at all the same and there is no suggestion here that Fichte's philosophy leads to the "frenzy of self-conceit." The "conceited frenzy" here is directed against being part of *Nature* as a whole. The "frenzy of self-conceit" is directed against being part of an *ethical* whole.

47. *Ibid.*, p. 214 (Chisholm, p. 50). The semicolons were added by Hegel.

48. Actually in the very next paragraph.

49. This is an echo both of the *Vocation of Man* (*Werke* II, 189; Chisholm, p. 25) and of Albrecht von Haller's poem "Human Virtues": "*Ins Innre der Natur dringt kein erschaffner Geist.*" Compare further, *Difference*, p. 193.

to, and as if obedience and subjection to them would make him indescribably miserable and bring him to despair!

As we saw earlier,[50] in the second Act of his self-definition this "I"
thinks that the philosophical cognition of nature makes him lose the
nature that so horrified him.[51] But he is as disconsolate and desperate
about the loss of Nature as he was about its being. So [in the third
Act] he establishes it—as a nature that must be nullified—by determining his vocation as action, as the act of pure will.[52] This view
of nature as something which is nothing in itself, something that is
a pure appearing, so that it has neither truth nor beauty in itself,
becomes the basis for a teleology of nature and for a physico-theology
which is directly opposed to the older tradition in its content, but is
grounded in the same principles with respect to its form. For traditional teleology connected the singular items of nature to ends that
were external to them, [405] so that every item was posited only for
the sake of something else. But the whole of nature formed a system
which, though it had the source of its life outside itself, was yet a
resplendence of absolute beauty and of Reason; it bore within itself
the highest, most blissful truth, the perfect law of the supreme wisdom. Fichte's teleology similarly expounds that which appears as
nature as present for the sake of something else, namely to constitute a sphere and provide elbowroom for free beings and to be capable of falling into ruins above which the free beings can raise themselves and so fulfil their vocation.[53] That Nature is something
absolutely unhallowed and lifeless, that it is nothing in itself, and
exists only in connection with an Other—this is the vulgar, teleological principle which Fichte's philosophy shares with all teleology, and
particularly with Eudæmonism. But Fichte's teleology is directly op-

50. Cf. pp. 162 ff. above.

51. Aided by the ambiguity of *"Bestimmung"* (cf. p. 162 n. 10 above) Hegel
shifts his reference from the second Act of Fichte's *Vocation* to the second step
in the "I"'s definition of himself. (See Fichte, *Werke* II, 240–1, 245; Chisholm
pp. 76, 80.)

52. Hegel wrote: ". . . so stellt er sie sich durch seine Bestimmung, das
Handeln und den reinen Willensakt her . . . ." A literal rendering would be:
". . . so he established it through his determination, through acting and the
pure act of will . . . ." But see the preceding note.

53. A more distant echo of the "Appeal to the Public" (1800). Compare p. 174
n. 42 above; for the rest of this paragraph compare the *Vocation of Man*,
Book III, especially the last pages of Section I (*Werke* II, 261–3; Chisholm, pp.
96–9).

posed to the earlier teleology in its conception of what nature is through and for the other.

In physicotheology nature was the expression of eternal truth, whereas it is only something to be nullified in the moral theology of Kant and Fichte. The end of Reason is forever still to be realized in nature. Nature is devoid of truth, it bears the law of ugliness and irrationality within it. The most hackneyed litanies about the evils of the world break in here. Kant put the pessimism of these litanies in the place of the optimism [of the older tradition]. *Voltaire* [to be sure] had already set pessimism against the optimism which had been pulled down by a perverted religiosity into the ordinary experience of daily life; and since he adopted the standpoint of experience himself he was quite consistent in setting the two against one another in an *ad hominem* way. But Kant, and Fichte after him, gave this pessimism a philosophical form and proved it systematically. The consistency of Voltaire was completely lost as a result. The relative truth of one empirical theory as against another is treated as an absolute truth. Voltaire's procedure is an authentic example of sane common sense which Voltaire possessed in such high measure, while others babble about it all the time in order to pass off their insanities as sound sense. When a philosophical Idea is pulled down into the realm of appearance and bound up with the principles of experience, it immediately becomes one-sided. Truly sane common sense promptly confronts its with the other onesidedness which likewise has its place in the phenomenal realm, and thus shows the untruth and ridiculousness of the first view.⁵⁴ For phenomena and experience were appealed to on its behalf, whereas sane common sense discovers the opposite in the same realm of experience and phenomena. But the actual application of the second view, and its truth do not, of themselves, go beyond this, and sane common sense expects no more of it. It is the pedants of the schools who make fools of themselves again in the same way, vis-à-vis sane common sense [406] because they accept what it applied only in a relative, *ad hominem* way, as absolute and cast it into a philosophical form in all seriousness. This is the meritorious service that Kant and Fichte have rendered for Voltaire's argument. It is just what the Germans generally boast about: they take a French *aperçu* and develop it; then they return it improved, put in its proper light, thoroughly worked out and scientifically formulated. In other words, they rob the idea of the relative

---

54. For Hegel's views on this topic, see further *Difference*, pp. 98–103.

truth that it has by bestowing upon it a universally valid truth that it is incapable of.

Because of the absolute subjectivity of Reason and its being set against reality, the world is, then, absolutely opposed to Reason. Hence it is absolute finitude devoid of Reason, a sense-world lacking [internal] organization. It is supposed to become equal to Ego in the course of an infinite progress, or in other words it is absolute and remains so. Thus nature reveals its essential irrationality already at the physical level (*Vocation of Man*, p. 221 seq.): it grudges to provide sustenance for our species so that "*immortal spirits are compelled to bend all their thoughts and labours, their every effort to the soil that brings forth their nourishment. Even today* it frequently happens that [. . .] hostile weather destroys" what required the labor of years, and "the industrious and painstaking man against whom nothing can be charged" (through frequently he has debts enough!) "becomes the prey of hunger and misery [. . .] floods, hurricanes, volcanoes," earthquakes; even in the present year of grace "diseases *still* carry off men in the flower of their strength and children who pass from existence without fruit or trace"; then there are epidemics and so on. "*But it ought not to remain so forever.*"[55] All the same, there is more sense in the behavior of non-conscious nature than in the way the human race goes on. "Even today [. . .] hordes of savages wander through enormous wildernesses," and when they meet they *devour one another festively*; and armies kill each other on sight. "Armadas, *furnished forth with the mightiest inventions of the human intellect*, cut through the waves and tempests of the oceans"[56] to destroy one another. These perverted men, among whom one group holds another as slaves, are perpetually at war among themselves; but still, as soon as they catch sight of the good, which on its own account is ever the weaker part, they make alliance with one another against it. They do so quite needlessly; quite apart from the fact that the good is already the weaker part on its own account, the good men themselves do their thing (*Sache*) just as badly [as the bad

---

55. Hegel placed the whole passage in quotation marks although only parts of it are direct quotation and there are several omissions. We have indicated the direct quotations as well as the omissions. For the full context see Fichte, *Werke* II, 266–7; Chisholm, p. 112.

56. These two passages, which we have enclosed in quotation marks, come from Fichte, *Werke* II, 269 (Chisholm, p. 104). The rest is a free summary of Fichte's text down to the end of the same section of the *Vocation of Man* (*ibid.*, pp. 269–71; Chisholm, pp. 104–6).

men]. The goal of mankind lies in the active conduct of those who are good, and it is their conduct which is counted upon in the moral order of the world. Reason itself is the warrant that the end of Reason will be achieved without fail. Yet the good behave like pigheaded philistines in promoting it: [407] often they harbor a secret self-love, they censure and find fault with one another. Each of them thinks that the improvement he proposes is the most important and the best, and will accuse the others, for whom his concern is less important, of betraying the good cause (*Sache*). All this and more can be read in greater detail in *The Vocation of Man* itself. In brief, a moral sentimentalism, directed only toward the ugly and useless aspects— just as religious sentimentalism, on the other hand, used to be directed toward the good and useful aspects—has become the rational view of the world. Philosophy has taken up the ordinary standpoint of a subjectivity which, being itself a contingency and whim, that is, an evil, sees only evil, i.e., contingency and whim in the object. Philosophy has completely abandoned its own elevation [i.e., the higher level to which it belongs] even as it has abandoned the elevation of its view of the world from the view of an empirical necessity which is at one with contingency, to that of an eternal necessity which is at one with freedom, the necessity of the wisdom that exists in the course of the world.[57] And it no longer recognizes the truth of what Plato says about the world, that God's Reason gave birth to it as a blessed god.[58]

This view of the world in the philosophy of absolute subjectivity is not the religious view at all. The philosophy of absolute subjectivity conceives of the [physically] bad (*das Übel*) merely as contingency and whim in an already intrinsically finite nature. Religion expounds evil (*das Böse*) rather as a necessity of finite nature, as one with the concept of finite nature. But at the same time, it expounds an eternal redemption for this necessity, which is to say that it is a truly present and real redemption, not one that is put off into an infinite progress and hence never to be realized. Religion offers a possible reconciliation with nature viewed as finite and particular. The original possibility of this reconciliation lies in the original image of God on the subjective side; its actuality, the objective side lies in

57. *Weltlauf.* Since philosophy is here said to have fallen *below* the recognition that Wisdom exists as the *Weltlauf*, its situation is analogous to that of "Virtue" in the section of the *Phenomenology* called "Virtue and the course of the world" (Baillie, pp. 402–12).

58. *Timæus* 34b.

God's eternal Incarnation in man, and the identity of the possibility with the actuality through the spirit is the union of the subjective side with God made man.[59] Thus the world is *in itself* reconstructed and redeemed and hallowed in quite another way than the volcanoes, etc. which will not always remain as they now are because in the Ideal of the moral world order they will gradually burn themselves out, or the hurricanes which will become milder, the diseases less painful, the miasma of swamps and jungles will improve etc. In religion the world is hallowed in its essence. So it is only for limited cognition, empirical intuition and a selfish choice of ends that the world will be posited as unhallowed. Perfect intuition and eternal bliss will be explicitly placed *beyond* that realm of limitedness which is to be forever abiding and immanent in the moral world order [408] for the sake of which volcanoes are to burn out, earthquakes to become tamer etc., nations are no longer to war against one another, or plunder one another etc.[60] In this philosophy[61] the world is not original and divine nature, nor yet is it reconciled on its ethical side; it is something intrinsically bad (*schlecht*). For finitude, however, the evil is only something contingent and capricious; and if the physical and ethical world were in themselves more than the bad world of the senses, if the badness were not absolute, then the other Absolute would fall away, the realm of freedom, this pure will that needs a world in which Reason is still to be realized. Thus the whole worth of man would fall away because this freedom exists only by negating and it can only negate while what it negates exists.

Just as Fichte has not truly recognized the original fount as nature, or absolute Reason as having being in itself, and not first coming to be in the infinite progress, so too he has not grasped the differential relation [of subject and object etc.] in its truth. For he conceives the difference as an in-itself, and hence as something that cannot be

59. "So God created man in his own image" Genesis, I, 27. This "image" of God the Father exists as an ideal in our consciousness, even though that consciousness is "fallen," being now sundered and reflective. But *nature*, and especially human nature, is also the creative act of the *Logos*, the Son of God (John I). When the meaning of the Christian gospel is fully grasped the human religious community will both be and know God in spirit, the *union* of Father and Son. See further the note on p. 81 above.

60. Fichte, *Werke* II, 267–9; Chisholm, pp. 102–4.

61. We have passed over Hegel's *hingegen* here, because the contrast with traditional Christianity is evident enough, and any contrasting phrase introduced at this point would only confuse the reader.

suspended. The bad (*das Übel*) is supposed to be a contingent fact from the viewpoint of the differential relation, though [the truth is that] it is only the relation itself which is bad. But if there is to be something bad that characteristically pertains to the differential relation and the separation from the eternal, it cannot possibly be defined in any other way than as the opposite of this absolute separation. And the opposite of the separation[62] is nothing but being one with the eternal, so that this would have to be the bad, just as we saw earlier[63] that what is most horrifying and saddening for Fichte's "I" is being one with the universe, having the universe live and act in me, being obedient to the eternal laws of nature and to the hallowed necessity. Since difference, or the bad, is so incorrectly conceived, the reconstruction cannot be authentic either. For the infinite is posited as originally un-unified and un-unifiable with the finite, the Ideal (*das Ideelle*) cannot be united with the real or pure Reason with existence.

[To be authentic] this reconstruction would have to unveil the essence of the spirit and [first] expound how nature reflects itself in the free spirit. Nature takes itself back into itself and lifts its original, unborrowed, real beauty into the ideal realm, the realm of possibility. Thus nature rises as spirit. This is the moment which—when the identity, as the original fount, is compared with the totality—appears through the comparison alone as movement and disintegration of the identity and as its reconstruction. [Secondly the reconstruction would have to expound] how the essence of nature, in the form of possibility, i.e., as spirit, has enjoyment of itself as a living Ideal[†] in visible and active reality; and how it has its actuality as ethical nature in which the ethical infinite, that is, the concept, and the ethical finite, that is, the individual, are one without qualification.[64]

In Fichte's formalism, however, the spirit as indifference is absolutely fixed as opposed to the differentiated. Hence the ethical cannot have any true reality, there cannot be a true oneness of its concept and its [409] actuality. The practical Ideal[†] [in Fichte] is the concept of the end posited by the pure will, which is just that pure indifference and emptiness, whereas the content is the particularities of the individual

---

62. Here and in the preceding sentence "separation" represents *Absonderung* or *absondern* (not *Trennung* or *trennen*). The synonymy seems to be complete.

63. See p. 176 above.

64. Hegel attempted this "reconstruction" in his lectures on "the real spirit" in 1802 (see pp. 41–4 and the relevant notes above).

or the empirical conditions of his well being. Content and Ideal† are
incapable of union in an ethical totality. The absolute manifoldness
of this empirical content is taken up into the indifference, i.e., into
the concept, in a formalistic way. The result is a manifold of rights
in a formalistic totality, which becomes real in the legal constitution
(*Rechtsverfassung*) and the State. The principle of the system is that
the concept in this rigidified form of oppositeness is absolute. It follows that legal right and the construction of legal right as a State is
something that has an independent being and is absolutely opposed
to the sphere of life and individuality. It is not the living being itself
which posits itself at the same time in the law as universal and becomes truly objective in a people (*Volk*). Rather, the universal, fixed
apart, confronts life as rigorous law. Individuality finds itself under
absolute tyranny. Right shall prevail; not, however, as the inner freedom of the individuals, but as their external freedom, which is their
subsumption under a concept that is alien to them. The concept here
becomes something strictly objective and takes the shape of an absolute thing. To be dependent on this absolute thing is the nullification
of all freedom.

As for the other side [the *moral* as opposed to the legal theory in
Fichte's practical philosophy] it consists in the doctrine that the concept of the end that is produced by the pure will—if that concept
were actually capable of producing anything more than a mere for-
mality (*Formelles*)—is subjective and presents itself as the ethical
character (*Sittlichkeit*) of a single person, or in other words, as morality.[65] Here the content of the concept, the reality which has been
posited in the form of an idea as the end and intention, is anything
empirically given, and only the empty form is *a priori*. Still, it is not
the material part of the end, but its formal† side, the pure will that is
mine; the Ego is itself pure will. But here, too, we cannot think of a
true ethic (*Sittlichkeit*), that is to say, a true identity of the universal
and the particular, of matter and form.[66] The particular is something
strictly empirical precisely because the emptiness of the pure will and
the universal are what is truly *a priori*. So it would be contradictory

---

65. Compare *Difference*, pp. 149–54. For the opposition of *Sittlichkeit* and
*Morality*, see further the *Phenomenology* (Baillie, pp. 374–82) and H. A. Reyburn, *The Ethical Theory of Hegel* (Oxford, 1921), chapters VIII, and X.

66. This true identity of the universal and particular is the whole-part relation conveived organically; in theoretical philosophy it is nature (see above pp.
42–3); in practical philosophy it is *das Volk* (see preceding paragraph).

to determine what right and duty are in and for themselves, for the content at once suspends the pure will, duty for duty's sake, and turns the duty into something material. The emptiness of the pure sense of duty and the content continually get in one another's way. And since [according to Fichte] morality, in order to be pure, may not be posited in anything else but the empty form of consciousness —i.e., in my knowing that I am acting dutifully—it follows that an [individual's?] ethical way of life which is otherwise pure [410] must generate the content of its actions from its higher, truly ethical nature [i.e., the *Volk*];[67] whereas addition of this consciousness [that I am acting out of duty], which morality is supposed exclusively to consist in, serves no purpose except to taint and contaminate true ethical conduct. In a true ethic, subjectivity is suspended, whereas through moral consciousness of that kind the nullification of subjectivity is conscious, so that in its very nullification subjectivity is held on to and saved. Virtue, in transforming itself into morality, becomes necessarily the knowledge of one's own virtue, or in other words, it becomes pharisaism.

If we do not presuppose a genuine ethic, on the other hand, then since morality consists in the form [of universality], we are free to raise any moral contingency into the form of the concept, and thus to establish a justification and a good conscience for the unethical. As was shown earlier,[68] the duties and laws in this system [of formal morality] make up an infinite, dispersed manifold every element of which is equally absolute. So the manifold makes a choice necessary.

---

67. Ethical purity, so Hegel wants to say, consists, not in the consciousness of doing one's duty—let alone in doing one's duty for duty's sake—but in the higher, truly ethical nature of the *Volk* being the source of what the individual does. The individual *qua individual* has, in any given situation, various options to act; but the individual *qua organic part of the Volk* has no choice between different posible actions when the *Volk* needs him; and this is exactly what his authentic ethical freedom consists in. Paradoxically speaking, his ethical freedom consists in not having the freedom of choice. Thus for example, any native Vermonter, hearing the sound of the fire siren or seeing suspicious smoke, will at once interrupt whatever he is doing, fill his car with the proper utensils and rush to help "the neighbor" (which is a good word for what the parts of a *Volk* are to each other). The ethical character of his actions does not lie in his awareness of doing his duty; his freedom does not lie in his choosing between several equally open alternatives. His ethical character and his freedom, consist in his being one with the basic persuasions of his *Volk* concerning what to do in situations of this sort.

68. See p. 183 above.

This choice [between duties] is strictly a subjective matter, for the objective aspect, the form of universality, is what is common to all [duties equally]. Now, we cannot think up any actual case of an action that would not have several sides; for every intuition of an actual case is infinitely determinable through the concept. Some of these sides must constitute valid duties so that in obeying some duties, other duties will be violated and in violating some duties other duties will be obeyed. If the agent's own contingent bad (*schlecht*) sense determines this choice, then the sense is something unethical; but it justifies itself in its own sight and gives itself a good conscience through the awareness of that aspect of the action that makes it a duty. On the other hand, if the agent's disposition is decent enough to make him want to act objectively, he is confronted with the contingency of the duties, for there are so many of them and in the mass any singular one becomes contingent. So he is bound to fall into the state of sad indecision and weakness that arises from the following dilemma: there is nothing but contingency [in the options] open to the individual agent, and he cannot create any necessity by himself nor should he if he could. If he does decide for any one of the many duties, the possibility of the decision arises from his being unaware of the infinite mass of duties into which any actual situation for action can, and as a matter of duty must, be resolved; for such an actual situation, like anything that is actual, can be resolved into an infinity of qualities. The knowledge of these qualities which yield the duty concepts is impossible because the qualities themselves are empirically infinite. Yet, this knowledge is strictly required as a matter of duty. Since unawareness of the complete range of aspects relevant to the action, and [consequent] lack of the required insight are for this reason strictly inevitable, we are bound to have the awareness of the contingency of our actions, which is the same thing as being conscious of immorality. Thus, authentic ethical conduct is polluted by the addition of this kind of awareness of its dutifulness, and this morality makes ethical conduct as unethical as possible.[69] Unethical conduct [on the one hand] is provided with a justification for being unethical through the awareness [411] of some duty, an awareness which from the nature of the case cannot be lacking; and [on the other hand] men of good character straining [to do the right thing] are given the consciousness of being necessarily unethical, in that the contingency of insight [about what duty to perform] is the shape in

---

69. Hegel's *"womöglich"* could be rendered "so far as may be."

which the ethical appears here. This is exactly the shape which it ought not to have. This view of the ethical as morality transforms what is truly ethical into baseness, strength becomes weakness while baseness is justified as morality. This is why this image of it was able to pass over so easily from philosophy as science into general circulation, and achieve wide popularity.

The reality of the Ideal (*Ideale*), which we have been dealing with thus far, was the content which the empty idea (*Ideelle*) of pure willing received [in Fichte]. This is still something inward. There remains the external side of the concept of the end. This external side has a content too, and we have seen how it gets it.[70] This is the side of formal idealism in which what was thus far the supersensuous in the context of practical philosophy presents itself also as an appearance. Its appearance is the action as a whole. On the one hand, empirically intuited [as an event], the action is stretched out in time into change and effects. On the other hand, the reality of the supersensuous concept of the end is also supposed to be a fruitful continuation of the action in the super-sensuous world itself, i.e., the action is the principle of a series of spiritual effects.[71] This latter principle is nothing but experience and temporality projected onto the spiritual sphere, so that the spiritual sphere becomes a realm of spirits. For there is no series or sequence [of consequences] in what is truly spiritual, or in the Idea. We can only speak of spiritual consequences when we have first made the Idea into something finite. This is done by setting it up as the spiritual sphere in contrast to the sensuous sphere, and then splintering the spiritual sphere itself qualitatively into an infinite multitude of spiritual atoms, that is, subjectivities who are citizens of a thing called the realm of spirits. The speculative kernel here is that the Idea, which after all only occurs [in Fichte] empirically as the end of an action and as something affected by subjectivity, is the eternal aspect of what appears as a series of changes in the world of the senses. But this speculative kernel is needlessly and completely lost when it is expressed in the form of an absolute spiritual sphere, in which consequences follow [from actions] and which is antithetically opposed to a sensuous world that exists outside of it—as if the supersensuous world were not already sensu-

70. See pp. 182–3 above.
71. Fichte, *Vocation of Man*, Book III, sections 2, 3 (*Werke* II, 264–94; Chisholm, pp. 99–130.

ous enough. In the present context the ethical Idea is the End of Reason that is to be realized in the moral world order. But instead of holding on to the philosophical standpoint Fichte's construction of this Idea passes over into historical considerations of an empirical kind, and the eternity of the ethical Idea passes into an empirically infinite progress. There is no speculative element to be seen save the Idea of faith. Through faith the [412] identity of the subjective and objective, of the Ideal† and the real† is posited, but this Idea remains something strictly formal.† It only serves us to make the leap from the empty pure will to the empirical [content]. What is left at the foundation [of Fichte's philosophy] is the absolute finitude of subject and action, with a sense-world over against it that is devoid of Reason and must be nullified; and finally a super-sensuous world absolutely opposed to the sense-world and dispersed into an infinity of singularized rational beings.[72] Since all these finite entities are absolute, the genuine and fruitful identity [of this supersensuous world with the sensuous world] is beyond cognition; it has not emerged in any part of what we have seen [in Fichte] about the ethical. According to the system, the Ego as the Absolute acknowledges in its theoretical activity that it is affected by a non-Ego; whereas in the practical sphere it pretends to dissolve this temporality. Hence, the rational Idea of the identity of the subjective and objective is something purely formal† for [philosophic] science—it is a mere presumption. The only way we could prove this was by showing that this rational Idea does not get constructed in the practical part of the system. On the contrary, it is totally absent. Moreover, this practical part was shown to be dominated, not by a healthy intellect, but by one that has fallen away from health altogether, having ossified into reflective superstition and stuck in a formal† science which it calls its "deduction." We threw light earlier[73] on the subordinate sphere of this intellect, where speculation can be found, i.e., upon the Idea of the transcendental imagination in Kant's philosophy. Then we had to pursue the intellect into the reaches of what are for it the practical realities—the Ideals of the moral world order and of the End set by Reason—in order to show the absence of the Idea in them.

72. *Intellektuelle Einzelheiten* refers to the "atoms" into which the spiritual sphere is qualitatively splintered" above. Compare pp. 82–3 and note 36.

73. See p. 69 ff. above.

# [Conclusion]

In their totality, the philosophies we have considered have in this way recast the dogmatism of being into the dogmatism of thinking, the metaphysic of objectivity into the metaphysic of subjectivity Thus, through this whole philosophical revolution the old dogmatism and the metaphysic of reflection have at first glance merely taken on the hue of inwardness, of the latest cultural fashion. The soul as thing is transformed into the Ego, the soul as practical Reason into the absoluteness of the personality and singularity of the subject. The world as thing is transformed into the system of phenomena or of affections of the subject, and actualities believed in, whereas the Absolute as [proper] matter and absolute object of Reason is transformed into something that is absolutely beyond rational cognition. This metaphysic of subjectivity has run through the complete cycle of its forms in the philosophies of Kant, Jacobi, and Fichte—other forms that this metaphysic has assumed do not count, even in this subjective sphere. The metaphysic of subjectivity has, therefore, completely set forth [the intrinsic stages of] the formative process of culture[1]; for this formative process consists in establishing as absolute each of the [two] single dimensions [of being and thought, object and subject, etc.] of the totality and elaborating each of them into a system. The metaphysic of subjectivity has brought this cultural process to its end. Therewith the external possibility directly arises that the true philosophy should emerge out of this [completed] culture, nullify the absoluteness of its finitudes and present itself all at once as perfected appearance, with all its riches subjected to the totality. For just as the perfection of the fine arts is conditioned by the perfection of mechanical skills, so the appearance of philosophy in all richness is conditioned by the completeness of the formative process of culture, and this completeness has now been achieved.

There is a direct connection (*Zusammenhang*) between these distinct philosophical formations and [the one true] philosophy—though the linkage is most defective in the case of Jacobi. They have their positive, genuine though subordinate, position within true philosophy.

---

1. "Culture," "formative process" and "formative process of culture" all represent *Bildung* or *bilden* in this peroration.

[*Conclusion*]

This is clear from the results of [our discussion of] infinity in these philosophies. They make infinity into an absolute principle, so that it becomes infected by its opposition to finitude. For they recognize that thinking is infinity, the negative side of the Absolute. Infinity is the pure nullification of the antithesis or of finitude; but it is at the same time also the spring of eternal movement, the spring of that finitude which is infinite, because it eternally nullifies itself. Out of this nothing and pure night of infinity, as out of the secret abyss that is its birthplace, the truth lifts itself upward.

In [truly philosophical] cognition, infinity as this negative significance of the Absolute is conditioned by the positive Idea that being is strictly nothing outside of the infinite, or apart from the Ego and thought. Both being and thought are one. But, on the one hand, these philosophies of reflection cannot be prevented from fixating infinity, the Ego, and turning it into subjectivity instead of letting it directly somersault into the positivity of the absolute Idea. By this route infinity fell once more into the old antithesis, and into the whole finitude of reflection which it had itself previously nullified. But on the other hand, the philosophy of infinity is closer to the philosophy of the Absolute than the philosophy of the finite is; for although infinity or thought is rigidly conceived as Ego and subject, and must, in this perspective, share the same rank as the object or the finite which it holds over against itself, still there is the other perspective in which infinity is closer to the Absolute than the finite is, because the inner character of infinity is negation, or indifference.

But the pure concept or infinity as the abyss of nothingness in which all being is engulfed, must signify the infinite grief [of the finite] purely as a moment of the supreme Idea, and no more than a moment. Formerly, the infinite grief only existed historically in the formative process of culture. It existed as the feeling [414] that "God Himself is dead," upon which the religion of more recent times rests; the same feeling that Pascal expressed in so to speak sheerly empirical form: "la nature est telle qu'elle *marque* partout un Dieu *perdu* et dans l'homme et hors de l'homme." [Nature is such that it *signifies* everywhere a *lost* God both within and outside man.][2] By marking this feeling as a moment of the supreme Idea, the pure concept must give philosophical existence to what used to be either the moral precept that we must sacrifice the empirical being (*Wesen*), or the concept of formal† abstraction [e.g., the categorical imperative].

2. Pascal, *Pensees*, 441 (Brunschvicg).

Thereby it must re-establish for philosophy the Idea of absolute freedom and along with it the absolute Passion, the speculative Good Friday in place of the historic Good Friday. Good Friday must be speculatively re-established in the whole truth and harshness of its God-forsakenness.[3] Since the [more] serene, less well grounded, and more individual style of the dogmatic philosophies and of the natural religions must vanish, the highest totality can and must achieve its resurrection solely from this harsh consciousness of loss, encompassing everything, and ascending in all its earnestness and out of its deepest ground to the most serene freedom of its shape.

3. Compare jj. 39–41 above; compare also the "Golgotha of Absolute Spirit" in the last sentence of the *Phenomenology* (Baillie, p. 808).

# Bibliographic Index

All works referred to in Hegel's text or in the translators' introduction and notes are listed here (and identified as fully as possible) *except* classical and medieval authors (e.g., Herodotus, Horace, Aquinas, Dante), where the reference can be found in any good modern edition. (Where a specific edition has been cited—e.g., Cornford's translation of the *Timæus*—details are included.)

Baillie, Sir James Black, see Hegel, *Phenomenology of Mind.*

Bardili, Christoph Gottfried (1761–1808) *Grundriss der Ersten Logik.* Stuttgart: Löflund, 1800.

Chisholm, Roderick M., see Fichte, *The Vocation of Man.*

Croce, Benedetto (1866–1952), *Philosophy, Poetry, History,* an anthology of essays translated by Cecil Sprigge. London: Oxford University Press, 1966.

Fichte, Johann Gottlieb (1762–1814), *Briefwechsel,* edited by Hans Schulz. Hildesheim: Georg Olms Verlag, 1967 [originally published 1930].

———. *Sämmtliche Werke,* ed. I. H. Fichte, 8 vols. Berlin: Veit, 1845–46.

———. *Science of Knowledge* (*Wissenschaftslehre,* 1794, with the First and Second Introductions), edited and translated by Peter Heath and John Lachs. New York: Appleton-Century-Crofts, 1970.

———. *Appellation an das Publikum,* Jena Leipzig: Gabler (and Tübingen: Cotta), 1799, reprinted in *Werke* V.

———. *Die Bestimmung des Menschen,* Berlin: Vossische Buchhandlung, 1800; reprinted in *Werke* II.

———. *Grundlage der gesammten Wissenschaftslehre,* Leipzig: Gabler, 1794 (reprinted in *Werke* I).

———. *Grundlage des Naturrechts,* 2 vols. Jena and Leipzig: Gabler, 1796, 1797 (*The Science of Rights,* translated by A. E. Kroeger, Philadelphia, 1870; reprinted by Routledge and Kegan Paul, 1970.)

———. *System der Sittenlehre.* Jena and Leipzig: Gabler, 1798 (*System of Ethics,* translated by A. E. Kroeger, London: Trübner, 1884).

———. *The Vocation of Man* (translated by William Smith), edited by R. M. Chisholm. Indianapolis and New York: Bobbs-Merrill, The Library of Liberal Arts, 1956.

———. Unsigned review of Bardili's *Grundriss, Literatur-Zeitung,* Erlangen, II. nn. 214–5; reprinted in *Werke* II.

Fuhrmans, Horst, see Schelling, *Briefe.*

Goethe, Johann Wolfgang von (1749–1832), "Das Märchen," published in *Die Horen,* 1795; reprinted in *Werke,* Berlin edition, Aufbau Verlag, Volume 12 (1972), pp. 372–406.

———. "Iphigenie auf Tauris," in *Goethes Schriften,* vol. 3. Weimar: Göschen, 1787; reprinted in *Werke,* Berlin edition, Aufbau Verlag, Volume 7 (1972), pp. 639–708.

Hamann, Johann Georg (1730–1788), *Socratic Memorabilia* (text with translation and commentary by J. C. O'Flaherty). Baltimore: The Johns Hopkins University Press, 1967.

Harris, Henry Silton, *Hegel's Development I: Toward the Sunlight* (1770–1801). Oxford: Clarendon Press, 1972.

Heath, Peter and Lachs, John, see Fichte, *Science of Knowledge.*

Hegel, Georg Wilhelm Friedrich (1770–1831), *Briefe von und an Hegel,* ed. Johannes Hoffmeister and Rolf Flechsig, 4 vols. Hamburg: F. Meiner, 1961 (*Briefe*).

———. *Differenz des Fichte'schen und Schelling'schen Systems der Philosophie.* Jena: Seidler, 1801 (for current editions see Hegel, *Erste Druckschriften, Gesammelte Werke,* and *Sämtliche Werke*).

———. *Difference between the Systems of Fichte and Schelling,* translated by H. S. Harris and Walter Cerf. Albany: State University of New York Press, 1976 [D].

———. *Early Theological Writings,* translated by T. M. Knox with an introduction, and fragments translated by Richard Kroner. Chicago: University of Chicago Press, 1948.

———. *Erste Druckschriften,* edited by Georg Lasson. Leipzig: F. Meiner, 1928 (the texts of this edition of *Differenz des Fichte'schen und Schelling'schen Systems der Philosophie* and of *Glauben und Wissen* were each reprinted separately at Hamburg by Meiner in 1962).

———. *Gesammelte Werke,* Band 4, *Jenær Kritische Schriften,* edited by Hartmut Buchner and Otto Pöggeler. Hamburg: F. Meiner, 1968. (The present translation is based on the text of this edition, and the pagination of this edition is indicated herein). [N.K.A.]

———. *Glauben und Wissen* (*Kritisches Journal der Philosophie,* Band 2, n. 1). Tübingen: Cotta, 1802 (for current editions see HEGEL, *Erste Druckschriften and Gesammelte Werke*).

———. *Lectures on the History of Philosophy,* translated by E. S. Haldane and F. H. Simson, 3 vols. London: Routledge and Kegan Paul, 1892; reprinted 1955.

———. *Logic,* translated from the *Encyclopedia of the Philosophical Sciences* by William Wallace, second edition. Oxford: Clarendon Press, 1892.

———. *Phänomenologie des Geistes,* edited by Johannes Hoffmeister. Hamburg: F. Meiner, 1952.

———. *Phenomenology of Mind,* translated by J. B. Baillie. London: Allen and Unwin, 1931 (paper, New York: Harper and Row, 1967).

———. *Premières Publications,* translated by M. Mèry, 3rd edition. Paris: Ophrys, 1970. (French translation of *Difference* and *Faith and Knowledge* with analytical introductions and explanatory notes.)

———. *Sämtliche Werke,* "Jubilee" edition, edited by H. Glockner. Stuttgart: Frommann, 1927–30. (This edition is based on the *Werke* below; see Vol. I for *Glauben und Wissen.*)

———. *Theologische Jugendschriften,* edited by Hermann Nohl. Tübingen: Mohr, 1907; reprinted 1968.

———. *System der Sittlichkeit,* edited by Georg Lasson. Hamburg: Meiner, 1967 (reprinted from *Schriften zur Politik und Rechtsphilosophie,* second edition, 1923).

———. *Werke* (complete edition edited by a committee of his friends). Berlin:

Duncker und Humblot, 1832 ff. Vol. I: *Philosophische Abhandlungen,* edited by K. L. Michelet, 1832 (second edition, 1845).

*Hegel-Studien.* Bonn: Bouvier, 1961 ff.

Henrich, Dieter, "Die 'Wahrhafte Schildkröte. Zu einer Metapher in Hegels Schrift 'Glauben und Wissen,'" *Hegel-Studien* II (1963), 281–91.

Herder, Johann Gottfried (1744–1803), *Gott: Einige Gespräche,* first edition, 1787; second edition, revised, Gotha, 1800; both editions collated in *Werke* XVI (and in the translation below).

———. *God: Some Conversations,* translated by F. H. Burkhardt. Indianapolis: Bobbs-Merrill, 1940.

———. *Sämmtliche Werke,* ed. B. Suphan et al., 33 vols. Hildesheim: Olms, 1967.

Hoffmeister, Johannes, see Hegel, *Phänomenologie des Geistes.*

Hyppolite, Jean, *Genèse et Structure de la Phénomènologie de Hegel,* 2 vols. Paris: Aubier, 1946; translated by S. Cherniak and John Heckman, Evanston, Illinois: Northwestern University Press, 1974.

Jacobi, Friedrich Heinrich (1743–1819), *An Fichte.* Hamburg: Perthes, 1799; reprinted in *Werke* III.

———. *David Hume über den Glauben.* Breslau: Loewe, 1787; reprinted in *Werke* II, without the "Vorrede."

———. *Ueber die Lehre des Spinoza in Briefen an den Herrn Moses Mendelssohn.* Neue verm. Ausg. Breslau: Loewe, 1789; reprinted in *Werke* IV, i.

———. "Ueber das Unternehmen des Kriticismus, die Vernunft zu Verstande zu bringen" in REINHOLD'S *Beyträge* (q.v.): reprinted in *Werke* III, 59–195.

———. "Ueber eine Weissagung Lichtenbergs" in *Taschenbuch für das Jahr 1802,* edited by J. G. Jacobi, Hamburg; reprinted in *Werke* III, 197–243.

———. *Werke,* 6 vols. Leipzig: Fleischer, 1812–25; reprinted Darmstadt: Wissenschaftliche Buchgesellschaft, 1968.

Kant Immanuel (1724–1804), *Critik der reinen Vernunft.* Riga Hartknoch, 1781 [=A]; second edition improved throughout, 1787 [=B] (the two editions collated by R. Schmidt. Hamburg: Meiner, 1930).

———. *Critique of Pure Reason,* translated from R. Schmidt's collation of editions A and B by N. Kemp Smith. London: Macmillan, 1933 (the pagination of both A and B is indicated in the margin).

———. *Critik der praktischen Vernunft.* Riga: Hartknoch, 1788; reprinted in *Akad.* V.

———. *Critique of Practical Reason,* translated by L. W. Beck. Chicago: University of Chicago Press, 1949; paper, New York: Library of Liberal Arts, 1956 (the pagination of *Akad.* V is indicated in the margin).

———. *Critik der Urteilskraft.* Berlin and Libau: Lagarde and Friederich, 1790; second edition, 1793; reprinted in *Akad.* V.

———. *Critique of Aesthetic Judgement,* translated by J. C. Meredith. Oxford: Clarendon Press, 1911 (Preface, Introduction and sections 1–60 of the *Kritik der Urteilskraft,* 1793; the pagination of *Akad.* V. is given in the margin).

———. *Critique of Teleological Judgement,* translated by J. C. Meredith, Oxford:

Clarendon Press, 1928 (sections 61–91 of *Kritik der Urteilskraft*, 1792; the pagination of *Akad.* V. is indicated in the margin).

———. *The Doctrine of Virtue*, translated by M. J. Gregor. New York: Harper Torchbooks, 1964 (Part II of *Metaphysik der Sitten*; there is another translation, by James Ellington, in the Library of Liberal Arts series).

———. *Gesammelte Schriften*, edited by the Royal Prussian Academy of Sciences, 24 vols. Berlin: Reimer, 1902–38 *(Akad.)*.

———. *On History*, translated by L. W. Beck. New York: Liberal Arts Press, 1963.

———. *The Metaphysical Elements of Justice*, translated by John Ladd. Indianapolis: Bobbs-Merrill, Library of Liberal Arts, 1965 (abridged version of "Doctrine of Right" from *Metaphysik der Sitten*).

———. *Metaphysik der Sitten* (1797), reprinted in *Akad.* VI, 203–493.

———. *Prolegomena*, 1783, reprinted in *Akad.* IV, 253–383; translated by L. W. Beck, Indianapolis: Bobbs-Merrill, Library of Liberal Arts, 1950.

———. *Die Religion innerhalf der Grenzen der blossen Vernunft.* Königsberg, 1793; reprinted in *Akad.* VII.

———. *Religion Within the Bounds of Reason Alone*, translated by T. M. Green and H. H. Hudson (1934). New York: Harper Torchbooks, 1960.

Kierkegaard, Soren Aabye (1813–1855), *Either/Or*, translated by D. F. Swenson and W. Lowrie. 2 vols. Garden City, N.Y.: Doubleday, Anchor Books, 1959.

Kimmerle, Heinz, *Das Problem der Abgeschlossenheit des Denkens.* Bonn: Bouvier, 1970 *(Hegel-Studien*, Beiheft 8).

Knox, T. M. and Kroner, Richard, see Hegel, *Early Theological Writings.*

Koeppen, Friedrich (1775–1858), *Schellings Lehre oder das Ganze der Philosophie des Absoluten Nichts.* Hamburg, 1803.

Lichtenberg, Georg Christoph (1742–99), *Vermischte Schriften*, edited by L. C. Lichtenberg and F. C. Kries, 9 vols. Göttingen, 1801–6 (only the first two vols. were published when *Faith and Knowledge* was written); see now rather *Aphorismen*, edited by A. Leitzmann, 5 vols., Berlin, 1902–8.

Link, Heinrich Friedrich (1767–1851), *Ueber Naturphilosophie.* Leipzig, 1806.

Locke, John (1632–1704), *Versuch vom Menschlichen Verstande, aus dem Englischen übersetzt . . . von Heinrich Engelhard Poleyen.* Altenburg, 1757.

———. *Essay Concerning Humane Understanding*, edited by J. W. Yolton, 2 vols. London: Dent, Everyman's Library, 1961.

Mendelssohn, Moses, *Morgenstunden*, second edition, Berlin, 1786.

Mèry, Marcel, see Hegel, *Premières Publications.*

Nicolin, Günther, ed., *Hegel in Berichten seiner Zeitgenossen.* Hamburg: Meiner, 1970.

Nohl, Hermann, see Hegel, *Theologische Jugendschriften.*

O'Flaherty, James C., see Hamann, J. G.

Pascal, Blaise, Pensées, ed., León Brunschvicg. Paris: Hachette, 1897 (most modern editions show Brunschicg's numbering in a concordance).

Plato's *Cosmology* (The *Timæus*, translated by F. M. Cornford). New York: Liberal Arts Press, 1957.

Reinhold, Karl Leonhard (1758–1823), *Beyträge zur leichtern Uebersicht des Zustandes der Philosophie*, 6 vols. Hamburg: Perthes, 1801–3.

———. *Versuch einer neuen Theorie des menschlichen Vorstellungsvermögens.*

Prague and Jena: Widtmann und Mauke, 1789; reprinted Darmstadt: Wissenschaftliche Buchgesellschaft, 1963.

Reyburn, Hugh Adam, *The Ethical Theory of Hegel: A Study of the Philosophy of Right.* Oxford: Clarendon Press, 1921, 1967.

Rosenkranz, Karl (1850–1879), *Georg Wilhelm Friedrich Hegels Leben.* Berlin, 1844; reprinted Darmstadt: Wissenschaftliche Buchgesellschaft, 1963.

Schleiermacher, Friedrich Daniel Ernst (1768–1834), *Ueber die Religion: Reden an die Gebildeten unter ihren Verächtern.* Berlin, 1799 (abridged translation: *On Religion: Speeches to its Cultured Despisers,* edited by John Oman, New York: Ungar, 1955).

Schelling, Friedrich Wilhelm Joseph (1775–1854), *Sämtliche Werke,* edited by K.F.A. Schelling, 14 vols. Stuttgart and Augsburg: Cotta, 1856–1861 (the pagination of this edition is preserved in the reprinted *Ausgewählte Werke,* 8 vols., Darmstadt: Wissenschaftliche Buchgesellschaft, 1966–1968).

————. *Briefe und Dokumente,* edited by Horst Fuhrmans. Bonn: Bouvier, 1962 ff. (2 vols. published to date).

————. *System des Transzendentalen Idealismus.* Tübingen: Cotta, 1800; reprinted in *Werke* III (and in *Ausgewählte Werke,* 1799–1801).

————. "Ueber Mythen," *Memorabilien* V, Leipzig, 1795 (reprinted in *Werke* I).

Schulz, Hans, see Fichte, *Briefe.*

Schwarz, Hermann, *Immanuel Kant: Ein Lebensbild nach Darstellungen der Zeitgenossen Borowski, Jachmann, Wasianski.* Halle a. S.: Hugo Peter, 1907.

Spinoza, Benedictus de (1632–1677), *Early Philosophical Writings,* trans. by F. A. Hayes. Indianapolis: Library of Liberal Arts, 1963.

————. *Chief Works,* translated by R.H.M. Elwes, 2 vols. New York; Dover, 1951.

————. *Opera Omnia,* edited by H.E.G. Paulus, 2 vols. Jena: Akademische Buchhandlung, 1802–3.

————. *Opera,* edited by Karl Gerhardt, 4 vols. Heidelberg, n.d.

Wallace, William, see Hegel, *Logic.*

# Analytic Index

Absolute: XVI, 33, 46, 56, 61, 76, 94, 127, 137, 142, 147, 154, 157, 159, 168, 181, 189; cognition of 68, 167; and logic 10; and religion 58

antithesis (*Gegensatz*): absolute 62, 78, 93–94, 150; of Freedom and necessity 93, 94; in Kantian philosophy (*Antithesis*) 67, 87–88, 125; of natural and supernatural 110, 116

appearance (*Erscheinung*): 75, 77, 78, 82, 90, 91, 101, 106, 124, 139, 186; and beauty 57; *see also* phenomenon

Aquinas, Thomas (1225–1274): 56n

Aristotle (384/3–322 B.C.): 18

art: 23, 24, 41, 65, 142, 151; for Schelling XII

Bardili, Cristoph Gottfried (1761–1808): 2, 24, 45, 47

beauty: 119, 149; divine 12–13, 148–151; ethical 31, 142, 144, 146; for Kant 23, 86–88, 91; beautiful soul 31; subjective 57, 148–150; temporal and eternal 58

Bergson, Henri (1859–1941): élan vital, XIII

Böttinger, K. A.: 49

Catholicism: 41, 50, 152

causality: 75, 90, 93, 99–100, 104–105

Christianity: 32, 43, 138; *see also* Protestantism, Catholicism

civilization (*Kultur*): *see* culture

cognition (*Erkennen*): 9, 58, 72, 77, 85, 88–89, 102–103, 105, 116,137, 139, 159–161; a priori (*see also* Kant) 101, 103; of the esthetic 87; finite 66, 68, 91–92; formal 94; intuitive 99, 113; of nature 91; and Faith 141; rational 118–119, 132, 141, 165; *see also* knowledge

community (*Gemeinschaft*): 32; of things 101–102, 110

concept (*Begriff*): 47, 60–63, 117; absolute 112; infinite 15, 62, 64; for Jacobi 99, 101, 143, 147; for Kant 18, 62, 68, 70, 71, 87, 147; pure 63, 190

congregation (*Gemeinde*): 151–152

consciousness (*Bewusstsein*): 70, 100, 123, 128,130–131, 142; empirical 73, 74; for Fichte 36, 138; for Jacobi 100–101, 115–116, 134; reflective 149

*Critical Journal of Philosophy*: 1–3, 44

Croce, Benedetto: 47

culture (*Bildung*): 4, 60, 64–65, 189–190; civilization 55; philosophical 64–65, 98, 154

Dante Alighieri (1265–1321): 146